Vital Relations

CRITICAL INDIGENEITIES

J. Kēhaulani Kauanui (Kanaka Maoli) and
Jean M. O'Brien (White Earth Ojibwe), *editors*

Series Advisory Board
Chris Andersen
Emil' Keme
Kim TallBear
Irene Watson

Critical Indigeneities publishes pathbreaking scholarly books that center Indigeneity as a category of critical analysis, understand Indigenous sovereignty as ongoing and historically grounded, and attend to diverse forms of Indigenous cultural and political agency and expression. The series builds on the conceptual rigor, methodological innovation, and deep relevance that characterize the best work in the growing field of critical Indigenous studies.

A complete list of books published in Critical Indigeneities is available at https://uncpress.org/series/critical-indigeneities.

JEAN DENNISON

Vital Relations

How the Osage Nation Moves
Indigenous Nationhood into the Future

Illustrations by Weomepe Designs

The University of North Carolina Press *Chapel Hill*

This book was published with the assistance of the Anniversary Fund of the University of North Carolina Press.

Set in Arno Pro by Westchester Publishing Services
Manufactured in the United States of America

Library of Congress Cataloging-in-Publication Data
Names: Dennison, Jean, 1979– author.
Title: Vital relations : how the Osage Nation moves Indigenous nationhood into the future / Jean Dennison ; illustrations by Weomepe Designs.
Other titles: How the Osage Nation moves Indigenous nationhood into the future | Critical indigeneities.
Description: Chapel Hill : The University of North Carolina Press, [2024] | Series: Critical indigeneities | Includes bibliographical references and index.
Identifiers: LCCN 2024000332 | ISBN 9781469676968 (cloth ; alk. paper) | ISBN 9781469676975 (pbk ; alk. paper) | ISBN 9781469676982 (ebook) | ISBN 9798890887115 (pdf)
Subjects: LCSH: Nation-building—Oklahoma—Osage Reservation. | Settler colonialism—United States—History. | Relation (Philosophy) | Osage Nation—Politics and government—21st century. | BISAC: SOCIAL SCIENCE / Ethnic Studies / American / Native American Studies | SOCIAL SCIENCE / Indigenous Studies
Classification: LCC E99.O8 D39 2024 | DDC 976.6004/975254—dc23/eng/ 20240118
LC record available at https://lccn.loc.gov/2024000332

Cover art by Jessica Harjo.

To my fiercely creative daughter, Aelia.

May you always find ways to make a game out of life.

Contents

Acknowledgments

As this book has grown out of twenty years of research, it is hard to imagine doing justice to all the relations that have made it possible. To begin, I must start much further back, thanking all Osage leaders who have ensured our Nation had a future. Their constant and ongoing search for the best path forward is both the inspiration for my work and what I most hope this book passes forward. Building on this tradition, Jim Gray, the Thirty-First Osage Tribal Council, Leonard Maker, Hepsi Barnett, and the Osage Government Reform Commission did the essential work of moving the Osage Nation into the future through the creation of the 2006 constitution. They graciously offered me a front-row seat to this process, helping me understand the challenges and desires that motivated their hard work. I still miss the long chats I was fortunate enough to have with Maker during this period. His historical and philosophical understanding of the importance of Osage nationhood continues to serve as a guiding beacon for my work.

Many of the relationships that this book is built out of began during the government reform period. In pulling me in as a volunteer, consultant, and occasional contractor for the Language Department, Herman "Mogri" Lookout brought me into the vital yet deeply challenging work of learning and teaching a language with no fluent speakers. Over the past twenty years he has tirelessly offered me his unique perspectives, insights, and stories. His knowledge of the language and what will be lost if we don't continue to learn from it has motivated hundreds of students, including me, and inspired my focus on language as a core part of what Osage nation building entails. I am deeply indebted to him for all that he has shared with me, but especially for the weekly Zoom meetings he carved out with me as I was revising the manuscript. I hope this book honors our time together, but I am even more excited about our future work together sharing his many powerful life experiences and observations with others.

Many others I first met at the Language Department have offered me their time and insights over the past twenty years, including Debra Atterberry (formerly Littleton), Mary Bighorse, Vann Bighorse, Cherise Lookout, Tracey Moore, Veronica Pipestem, Cameron Pratt, Billy Proctor, and Jodie Revard. I want to thank Pipestem for her friendship and perspectives, as she has always been willing to geek out with me on all things Osage. As Atterberry and Revard moved through the many important Osage spaces their careers have taken them, I have always treasured our long chats and am deeply grateful for the detailed comments they offered to improve this book. Their insightful visions for the Osage Nation's future and dedicated commitment to bringing those vision into reality are my gold standard for Osage leadership.

More recent language employees, including Janis Carpenter, Christopher Cote, Dana Daylight, and Braxton Redeagle, have generously offered me their time, reflecting on their own motivations for and challenges in doing this work. Carpenter's insightful critiques of early drafts of the language chapter helped to shift my discussion in a more productive direction. Redeagle's commitment to both learning and sharing the language was always palpable in our engagements, both in our long discussions and when I was a student in his class. Even those language employees not directly quoted in this book have helped me to understand why the Osage language matters and what we must overcome to build relations with it again.

Following the passage of the 2006 constitution, I knew that things were going to change dramatically in the Nation, but it has been deeply impressive to see the immense transformation unfold. In the years following its passage, I listened in on congressional sessions and returned to Oklahoma at least twice a year, catching up with many Osage reform commissioners and leaders including Hepsi Barnett, Jim Gray, Priscilla Iba, Julia Lookout, Terry Mason Moore, Charles Red Corn, Mary Jo Webb, Kathryn Red Corn, and various Osage Congress members. These conversations offered me insight into how hard it was to, in Barnett's words, drive a car you were still building. The challenges of turning the tribal council into a three-part government were daunting, and something these leaders worked tirelessly to accomplish in the best ways they knew how. I am so thankful to those who shared their hopes and fears with me, as well as for the hard work these leaders put into expanding the Nation's infrastructure.

One of the entities we were all watching closely was the Osage Minerals Council, whose members had to reconcile being at once an independently elected group and a board within the Osage Nation. My conversations over the years with various members of the council, especially Susan Forman, Kathryn Red Corn, Talee Redcorn, Everett Waller, and Andrew Yates, all greatly shaped my understanding of how fraught a space the Osage Mineral Estate is. Before, during, and after she served on the minerals council, Kathryn Red Corn has been a good friend to me, offering important historical insights and perspectives on Osage nation building and culture. I am also thankful for Waller's wisdom, time, and leadership. In our many conversations it was always clear that his core motivation was a fierce devotion to creating a better future for Osage youth. I am also grateful to the leaders of the Osage Shareholders Association, who welcomed me into their meetings, deepening my understanding of the complexity of these problems. Finally, I appreciate Wilson Pipestem for our various conversations and his line edits. For Pipestem, working as the Osage Minerals Council's lawyer is clearly much more than a job and is part of a family legacy of advocating for the Osage shareholders. These individuals have all checked my naïve assumptions, helping me understand the myriad ways Osages have navigated colonialism historically and continue to do so today.

During one of these trips back to Oklahoma, I did a formal recorded interview with Geoffrey Standing Bear, who was at the time an Osage congressman. Standing Bear spoke at length about his hopes and dreams for the Osage Nation, foregrounding what would later become his successful Osage principal chief campaign platform. During that conversation and in the hundreds of hours I later spent with Chief Standing Bear during the research for this book, I was deeply moved by his vision, devotion, and passion. I would not have been able to write this book without the trust and access he offered me. He provided me a front-row seat to what the job of an American Indian chief entails. It quickly became clear that there are few harder jobs. Despite all the challenges he faced, Standing Bear not only welcomed me into these spaces but read a full draft of this book, clarifying and expanding on the material in each of the chapters. There are many books I could have written about these experiences, but I hope this book honors some of the larger projects Standing Bear's leadership has made possible for the Osage Nation.

I am also deeply grateful for the time and acceptance offered by all his staff and the many Osage employees who regularly populated Chief's many meetings. It is no small thing to accept a researcher in your daily workspace. During the height of my research, I would spend several hours multiple days per week with Chief Standing Bear's core staff at the time, including Sheryl Decker, Rebecca Fuhrman, Casey Johnson, Katie Yates, James Weigant, and Jason Zaun. Libby Gray, Jan Hayman, Scott Johnson, Patrick Martin, Melvina Prather, Holly Wells, and other key staff and program directors from across the Nation not only accepted my presence at their meetings but shared their unique insights and challenges with me. Many Osage employees were deeply generous with their time and willingness to help me understand the intricacies of their jobs. While most of these conversations are not directly featured in this book, they all helped me to understand the stakes and challenges of nation building.

Former Osage congressman and assistant principal chief Raymond Red Corn is perhaps the Osage leader I spent the most time with during the research for and writing of this book. Our many meetings, whether in his office, over lunch, or on the phone, provided essential insight into the debates happening within the Nation. Red Corn also read a full draft of the manuscript as it was being written, providing many additional perspectives I had not considered and pushed me to tell more complicated and nuanced stories. I am grateful for his trust, friendship, and perspectives.

One of the focal points of the book is the compacting of the Pawhuska Indian clinic from the Indian Health Service. Many Osage health leaders and employees welcomed me into their meetings and shared their perspectives, frustrations, and accomplishments with me. Michael Bristow, Candy Thomas, Manon Tillman, Laura Sawney, Paula Stabler, and Cecilia Tallchief all offered particularly important insights into the challenges of transition and accreditation processes. Stabler read an early draft of the health chapter, helping to strengthen the story I was able to tell. Tallchief was always willing to offer me the history and context of Osage health that so few knew.

Throughout my research, Osage Nation Congress members not only welcomed me to their meetings but were eager to share their experiences with me. They invited me into their working lunches, were always happy to answer my questions, and had many productive questions to ask of me and my research. In addition to some of the congressional leaders mentioned earlier, I want to thank Shannon Edwards, Alice Goodfox, Otto Hamilton, John Jech, Billy Keene, Brandy Lemon, James Norris, John Maker, Archie Mason, Eli Potts, Angela Pratt, Joe Tillman, Ron Shaw, William "Kugee" Supernaw, Maria Whitehorn, and R. J. Walker, for sharing their time and unique perspectives with me throughout my research. In addition to many long conversations, Goodfox read multiple chapters of this book, as well as a draft of the speech I gave at the 2022 Osage inauguration, offering helpful feedback. This book does not do enough to feature all the hard work these and other Osage congresspeople have done to move the Osage Nation into the future.

While I had long admired the work of Osage Nation Supreme Court chief justice Meredith Drent, it was not until I moved to Seattle in 2015 that we became friends and collaborators. Much of this book came out of our long conversations over meals, the presentations we gave at conferences, the article we coauthored, and our cotaught course Native Nation Governance at the University of Washington. Drent is the most impressive researcher I know, combining an astute ability to sort through and process vast information quickly with a deep knowledge of all things Osage. Our coauthored article in particular set the stage for this book's focus on moving, and I am deeply grateful for all the insights she has shared with me throughout my research and writing process.

When I went to write this book, I was initially surprised at how often I turned to the words of Eddy Red Eagle. While this elder of my clan was not directly involved in any of the stories that I was telling, he always seemed to be around when I, or others around me, was struggling to understand what was happening in the Nation. His deep knowledge of Osage origin stories and values meant that he knew just how to talk about the challenges the Nation was facing and what we needed to bring forward and seek out as we moved to a new country. In the final months of writing, I called Red Eagle many times and he always took my call, helping to broaden my understandings of Osage philosophies. I look forward to many more conversations with Red Eagle and all the brilliant Osage leaders I have gotten to know through this research.

As I wrote this book, I asked all the Osages quoted within it to review at least their quotes but also the larger chapter in which they appeared. Almost everyone responded, offering productive feedback and further enriching the book. I also asked some Osages not directly cited to review chapters, especially the introduction, including Jessica Harjo, Brian Hicks, Ruby Murray, and Moira RedCorn. RedCorn offered a very close and critical reading of the introduction, helping, among other things, to push the framing of the entire book from a focus on returning to moving. Harjo also offered important insights in her process of reviewing the book to design the cover and interior images.

This book was written in conversation with a large academic support community as well. I am deeply grateful for everyone who participated in our Indigenous studies writing group, which has been meeting weekly since I joined the University of Washington in 2015. Having this community of support was essential to my mental health but also made this book much stronger. In particular, I want to thank Sara Gonzalez, Sven Haakanson, Josh Reid, and Megan Ybarra for their close reads of and vital feedback on many chapter sections. I would also like to thank the Simpson Center for hosting my book project as part of their 2018–19 Society of Scholars. Kemi Adeyemi, Radhika Govindrajan, and Dian Million offered particularly useful insights that helped shift this book's focus. Govindrajan also read later drafts, offering important connections to other literature. Chad Allen provided important guidance on the title and other aspects of the book throughout my drafting process.

I am deeply grateful for the academic panels I have been part of and the talks I have been invited to give while researching and writing this book. The Native American and Indigenous Studies Association has been a particularly supportive venue for connecting me with many of the amazing scholars I cite and am influenced by. My research has especially benefited from my time on panels with Clint Carroll, Jessica Cattelino, Andrew Curley, Meredith Drent, Jill Doerfler, Alyosha Goldstein, Kēhaulani Kauanui, Courtney Lewis, Angela Parker, Dana Powell, Jami Powell, Alex Red Corn, Keith Richotte, Shannon Speed, Circe Sturm, and Robert Warrior.

I am grateful for the supportive publication process that the University of North Carolina Press has provided. Mark Simpson-Vos has been an excellent editor and gentle source of motivation since our first conversation. He not only read my entire dissertation and first book manuscript multiple times, but he secured me excellent reviewers and motivated me in all the right moments. He was always understanding of my needs and brings such care to all our conversations. Series editors Jean O'Brien and Kēhaulani Kauanui offered deeply influential feedback on the book proposal and helped to shepherd the book through the publication process. Clint Carroll and an anonymous reviewer for the University of North Carolina Press offered vital feedback that fundamentally reshaped this book. I spent a solid year working with the detailed feedback Carroll offered and cannot thank him enough for being such an amazing thought partner in this work.

I feel so fortunate to have a large community of dedicated scholars working in close relationship with Native nations who have helped me do this work in the best possible way. I am particularly grateful for my career-long mentor and friend Valerie Lambert. In addition to guiding my early career at Chapel Hill, she provided detailed and essential feedback on several of my chapters. Her commitment to sharing grounded stories of how Native people are navigating this world has fundamentally shaped my approach to storytelling. It is often her voice in my head that pulls me away from the easy tropes and stereotypes that too often plague Indigenous studies.

I also want to thank all my students who have helped to shape my thinking and given me a supportive environment in which to think through the tensions at work within the Osage Nation. I especially benefited from the work of and long conversations with of all of the graduate students I have worked with, especially my direct mentees Dianne Baumann, Jami Powell, and Brook Spotted Eagle. While all my classes have engaged with and pushed my research, I particularly want to thank my Winter 2023 Native Nation Governance students for being such productive readers of my entire book manuscript. Not only did assigning the manuscript push me to finish all my revisions in what was otherwise an impossibly busy quarter, but our conversations helped to clarify and fine-tune my writing. It is impossible to name all the influences on our thinking and writing, but too often we forget to name how much even unrelated conversations with students shape our thinking.

Finally, this project would not have been successful without my family. The generations that came before me made it possible for me to imagine myself as someone capable and worthy of telling stories, despite my many challenges learning to read and communicate effectively. My father never missed an opportunity to build me up, to tell me what was possible for me, and to offer me the tools I needed to navigate this world. While I was doing research, he was a daily thought partner. Especially when we disagreed, he helped me to understand the broader emotions and history at work. After his passing, his influence on this book only grew, as it was impossible to write it without acknowledging the direct influences he had.

My mom played the most active role in fostering my writing abilities, reading every draft paper while I was in high school, college, and graduate school and offering essential editing advice even on the notes I would leave her. She has continued to read all of my manuscripts, helping me to clarify my thinking and communicate more effectively. Over the last year she has talked with me daily about the writing process, offering vital editorial and emotional support. My husband has also played a similar role in not only fostering my writing career but strengthening this book by doing copyediting work on it and all my publications. This is the kind of familial support that almost no academics have, but it is what has made it possible for me to be an academic at all. There are so many reasons I know that I made the best possible choice in partners, and his editing prowess is just one.

Both my husband and daughter have offered me the kind of space and support that are required for any large undertaking. Writing this book required them to move with me to Oklahoma for months at a time, most often in the oppressive heat of the summer. They also offered me countless hours of uninterrupted writing time. They cheered me up when I was frustrated; cooked, cleaned, and crafted so that I could focus on work; and distracted me from various pressures so that it didn't become too overwhelming. I am so grateful for all that they bring to my life.

Vital Relations

Introduction

"Figuring Out What Is Going On with Her and Get Her Some Help"

Large clouds moved quickly across the vast open sky, offering classic prairie scenes along the country roads as my father and I set out for Pawhuska, Oklahoma, on a windy Thursday morning in early July 2015. During the meandering drive to the capital of the Osage Nation, we discussed my research plans. My husband, two-year-old daughter, and I had recently returned to live with my parents in Skiatook, Oklahoma. I was able to spend the better part of the next year there, conducting ethnographic research with Osage officials and employees to learn what the 2006 Osage Nation Constitution had made possible during its first ten years in effect.

In 2004 the Osage Tribal Council had convinced the US Congress to recognize our inherent sovereign right to determine our own form of government and citizenship after over one hundred years of operating within systems the US federal government had imposed on us.[1] The 2006 Osage Constitution turned the single minerals-focused council into a three-part government, with a robust board structure that managed businesses such as gaming. My father, always full of ideas, had many suggestions about what would be interesting to focus on, including things that were working in the Nation and things that we were still figuring out. He had suggested that I ride along with him that morning to the Osage Nation Court in Pawhuska, where he, an Osage citizen and lawyer in private practice, would be representing a young Osage woman who was navigating drug charges and addiction.

As we approached the building, we saw the grandmother of my father's client waiting for us in front of the round sandstone court building on the Hill, where the Osage have had our capitol for the past 141 years, after being forced to relocate from our Kansas lands. Finishing the round shape of the building was a buttressed awning, giving a sense that we were approaching an arbor. Arbors have special meaning to Osages, as we gather under them to build and heal our community, especially during our ᑎᘯᏬᏂ (dances held in each of our three districts, usually during June). The grandmother was pacing anxiously but froze when she saw us approaching. I went ahead into the courthouse while my father talked the grandmother through what was likely to happen at and following her granddaughter's initial hearing. As a small-town lawyer specializing in divorces, child custody, probates, and drug charges, he often acted as a counselor and mentor. He saw incarceration as a system of violence and oppression, and did everything he could to keep his clients not only out of jail but out of the court system. Mediation and compromise were his specialties, as were strong relationships with the judges and even prosecuting attorneys. He was hopeful that, as with many of his previous clients, he would be able to get her enrolled in a drug rehabilitation program and get her life back on track.[2]

The Osage Nation court chambers were marked with a small whiteboard at the front of the office announcing that court was held Thursdays at ten o'clock in the morning and custody cases every other Friday at the same time. After a few minutes, the solemn bailiff led everyone into the courtroom. While we waited for the judge to approach, my father talked with the prosecuting attorney for the Nation. He had worked with this attorney for years and had persuaded him that seeking incarceration was not the way to go, especially for those being prosecuted on drug charges. He began, "You know how I like to handle these."[3] The prosecutor nodded and discussed how they would release the client into the custody of the counseling center. My father then asked if the prosecutor had any information about the Osage Nation's Primary Residential Treatment (PRT) program, as the counselors he had worked with in the past were no longer there. One had passed away two weeks prior, and the other had just quit the day before.

The court reporter, who also acted as the bailiff when the court was short-staffed, then came into the room and began the court's proceedings. Everyone stood as chief trial court judge Marvin Stepson entered. The hearing was quick, with my father saying that he was there to represent the woman and that they were going to investigate treatment options. He suggested that they could have another hearing in a week if treatment hadn't been found. He concluded by saying, "The most important thing right now is figuring out what is going on with her and get her some help."[4] The judge and prosecutor agreed, and the hearing was adjourned.

After my father convinced the judge, we began searching the Nation for anyone who could support his client. The scavenger hunt that followed showcased not only the challenges of getting this woman the help she needed but also the soaring number of underfunded federal programs the Osage Nation was attempting to take over and run. As we attempted to navigate this maze of programs and services, it became very clear just how much work the Osage Nation had ahead of itself to create a system of care. This literal and figurative remapping is at the core of what Osage nation building has involved in the twenty-first century.[5]

We first drove to the building where my father had last worked with the counselors, but it now housed the prevention program. Stacked around the room were clear plastic bins filled with odds and ends. Some of these were art supplies, but most were materials that clearly needed to be archived or discarded. The overstuffed space was not a welcoming environment, but it was clearly a work in progress. A stack of yellowed flyers was the only recognizable aspect of a typical prevention program, but they looked to be from the 1980s. The woman working at the front desk explained that the Counseling Department's offices had moved, and she handed us a flyer showing where we needed to go. She explained that the woman next door had done some work for Counseling in the past and that we might also try there.[6]

We walked into the next-door office, where we were told that the woman we were looking for no longer rented the office space. This was now the office of the employment and training program for the Osage Nation. This space, too, needed a great deal of additional investment. At the time of our visit, there were a couple of ancient computers scattered about and dusty promotional posters lining the walls. Following the flyer we had been given by the woman in the prevention services office, we made our way to the new counseling office. Once we arrived, they sorrowfully explained that they could not help us either because the person seeking help was a woman and currently their PRT facility only served men. They also said they did not have anyone who could go to the jail and conduct her evaluation to find out what she was up against.[7] My father's frustration by this point was palpable. He had an Osage woman in serious need of help and no one in the Nation was available to support her. The labyrinth of underfunded and understaffed programs was a powerful example of the consequences of the disjointed federal grant structure. To make these programs successful, the Osage Nation was going to have to invest significant funds beyond the existing grants, as well as rethinking the larger approach and organizational structure. The many siloed services the Nation offered clearly needed to be unified.

We were next pointed in the direction of the Treatment Alternatives to Street Crime program, where there was supposedly a person who could do an evaluation. After we did not see the office where we were told to look, we were both about ready to give up. Giving it one last pass, we went down another street and I spotted the program office. We walked in and asked for the name we had been given, and after a short wait we were invited into a woman's office. The representative explained that the Nation's inpatient treatment had indeed been curtailed with the bulldozing of their building (to make room for the new Osage Nation services buildings) and only replaced with a trailer that did not have enough room for both men and women. She said she was overworked and overwhelmed by having to do various jobs in addition to her own, including that of the man who had quit the day before. She agreed to do an evaluation of my father's client but said she could not do a drug test, which is what my father said his client needed most. She also said she would try to find some recommendations of places the client could go.[8] As we left the office, my father and I observed that we could not imagine how someone with an addiction problem, or even concerned family members, could ever have navigated that day's labyrinth.

The challenge of turning this disjointed set of underfunded and poorly designed federal programs into a network of care that could support Osages exemplifies the motivations and challenges Osage officials and employees are currently facing as they engage in the ongoing work of Osage nation building. Specifically, this book looks closely at the Osage Nation's efforts to leverage technology, extractive industry, bureaucracy, and capitalism to increase usage of our language, foster self-governance, promote the health of our people, and buy our land back. Each of these projects has been deeply affected by a whole host of forces, historical and ongoing, many of which can be glossed as colonialism, but which were prompted by the actions of a whole host of actors, with deeply varied and at times conflicting goals. Osage leaders are attempting to use nation building to counteract these varied colonial limitations and enact our own desires for the future.

This book argues that Osages have always used nation building as a strategy to foster respectful, responsible, ordered, and layered relations. Relationality is a core principle of Indigenous studies, yet there is not enough discussion of what these relations look like in practice, especially in the messy context of Native nation governments' day-to-day operations. Focusing on the unique history and context of Osage nation-building efforts, *Vital Relations: How the Osage Nation Moves Indigenous Nationhood into the Future* provides a deeper vision of the struggles Native nations are currently facing, and our situated desires for the future. Throughout this book I understand nation building as an ongoing process that uses what appear to be the best tools available to try to meet our own unique needs as a people, a process I refer to as "moving the Osage Nation into the future." This introduction lays out some of the key frameworks that undergird the book, including Indigenous futurity, nation building, moving, and vital relations. It then turns to the methodologies this book deploys, which are centered on the vital relations of respect, responsibility, order, and layering. I then provide a summary of each of the chapters before describing developments within the Osage Nation PRT, a program designed to serve Osages like my father's client who are struggling with addiction.

"Enduring Indigeneity"

This book is about the ways Osage leaders imagine and work toward a future, despite ongoing colonial forces. By building on the important work of Black scholars envisioning Afrofuturisms, Indigenous scholars continue to produce important work about what is at stake in Indigenous efforts to create their futures.[9] This section discusses colonialism, its impacts, and some of the work Indigenous scholars have been doing to understand Indigenous futurity. This section, like this book, seeks to strike a delicate balance between understanding the challenges colonialism creates while also ensuring that such a focus does not further foreclose possibilities for an Osage future.

It is impossible to make sense of the challenges the Osage Nation currently faces without a robust understanding of the multifaceted aspects of colonialism. As Chicanx and Pascua Yaqui Tribe scholar Marisa Elena Duarte and Zuni Pueblo and Tlingit scholar Miranda Belarde-Lewis write, "Colonialism is both a socioeconomic policy and an expansionist ideology. . . . It is marked by generations of subjugation such that the profiting social group begins to build all social structures and institutions around themselves to support the belief in their superiority as well as their means of exploitative and violent profit-making."[10] The expansion and consolidation of capital is a core motivating force within most colonial practices, as stolen resources and land, expanding market opportunities, and the protection of white property privilege all work to support the growth of settler capital.[11] The Osage Nation resides within the confines of the American empire and has been subjected to extreme forms of colonialism over the last two hundred years, including the theft of vast territories, the abuses of extractive industries, repeated political meddling, outright murder, and subjection to colonial educational systems.

Colonialism, while never an agent in and of itself, does usefully name a broad spectrum of agents and actions. It takes the form of teachers who limited the use of the Osage language; federal agents who overthrew our government; US members of Congress who insisted on operating, but not adequately funding, the Indian Health Service; and settlers who stole our land. The varied, layered, and sometimes contradictory colonial forces described throughout this book have worked in tandem to limit the options available to Osages. It is vital to remember that no matter how cohesive colonialism seems, white missionaries, Indian agents, US presidents, Oklahoma state officials, federal judges, corporate executives, and other colonial actors have all been working toward their own ends.

I understand colonialism less as a comprehensive and totalizing system than as a shorthand for a wide set of actors and actions that work to limit Osage futures. Most commonly in the context of Indigenous peoples, this power structure is named *settler colonialism*. Settler colonialism, as Australian scholar Patrick Wolfe describes, is a persistent set of structures that attempt to eliminate Indigenous peoples, thus validating settler presence.[12] Building on the work of Indigenous scholars, particularly in Hawaii and Palestine, Wolfe's logic of elimination names the ongoing processes by which settlers attempt to justify the claiming of Native land through the denial of Indigenous histories, thus erasing their present existence and their futures.[13] Settler colonialism at once attempts to ensure a future for settlers and deny Indigenous futures.[14]

While settler colonialism is the dominant form colonialism takes in Native communities, colonialism targets more than just land. Resource colonialism extracts our natural resources, imperial colonialism expands the power of empires, and missionary colonialism spreads religious ideology.[15] Settlers tap into and further these myriad forms of colonialism, and their actions coalesce to create dangerous forms of oppression in the context of Indigenous communities. The Osage context provides a powerful example of the impacts that these colonial formations take. I find, similar to US scholar Brianna Theobald, that the more general term *colonialism* better "underscores the flexibility of colonial power" in Indigenous contexts.[16] In this book, I look closely at the role of a wide spectrum of colonial forms that have attempted to disrupt our everyday language usage, self-governance efforts, healthcare, and territorial base. I have chosen to use the wider concept of colonialism as a framework for naming this combined violence.

Additionally, there is nothing settled about colonialism. On the contrary, Native nations have long thwarted settler attempts at elimination and continue to find creative ways of ensuring Indigenous political futures.[17] Kanaka Maoli scholar J. Kēhaulani Kauanui argues that we must pay close attention to this enduring Indigeneity since "to exclusively focus on the settler colonial without any meaningful engagement with the indigenous . . . can (re)produce another form of 'elimination of the native.'"[18] This book demonstrates this enduring Indigeneity by showing the many ways in which, despite ongoing colonial systems and their lasting impacts, Osage Nation officials, employees, and citizens are striving to develop systems to ensure that the Osage people have a future.

Colonial and Indigenous actors are working toward fundamentally different futures. While settler futurity requires the erasure of Indigenous peoples, lands, and ways of knowing, Indigenous futurity requires the elimination not of existing settlers but instead of the structures that limit Indigenous possibilities.[19] As Kanaka Maoli scholar Noelani Goodyear-Ka'ōpua writes, "Indigenous futurities are enactments of radical relationalities that transcend settler geographies and maps, temporalities and calendars, and/or other settler measures of time and space."[20] Part of the relationality that Goodyear-Ka'ōpua is arguing for requires understanding the future as something that Indigenous peoples have always been envisioning, not as a rejection of or progression from the past. Instead, the future is in constant dialogue with both the past and the present. Rather than narrating the work of Indigenous peoples today as an attempt to return to something colonialism has destroyed, this book documents why and how Osage leaders are moving the Osage Nation into the future.

"Political Partners to Be Engaged with Rather Than as Social Problems to Be Ameliorated"

Nation is becoming a ubiquitous term to describe American Indian polities. Most commonly, nations are defined as a people who understand themselves as a polity and exercise sovereignty over their internal and external affairs; share, although not exclusively, multiple cultural traits (language, practices, beliefs, etc.); and can be traced back to a particular land base.[21] Importantly, with many American Indian polities, *nation* as a term is replacing the term *tribe*, which, while often utilized by Indigenous peoples strategically, has too often been used to diminish American Indian peoples' political status and rights to land.[22] *Nation* with a capital *N* usually follows the specific name of a Native polity, but this capital signals more than just a proper noun. Nations are entities with standing and authority. Nineteenth-century Mashantucket Pequot Tribe writer William Apes was an early advocate of Native peoples using the term *Nations* instead of *tribes*, as was later Standing Rock Sioux Tribe scholar Vine Deloria Jr.[23] Both argued that using *Nation* helped outsiders recognize Indigenous peoples as having their own political systems.

Beyond its connections to culture and land, in Indigenous contexts nationhood is thus a tool for asserting territorial authority and political separation. Like Métis Nation scholar Chris Andersen, I focus on nationhood because it is language that has been fought for by my community and because "nationhood has become an organizing grammar for Indigenous politics more globally. Being recognized in terms of our nationhood demands political and policy conversations that position us as political partners to be engaged with rather than as social problems to be ameliorated."[24] In other words, while settlers often position Indigenous peoples as racialized minorities who need to be assimilated into white society, nationhood is a tool for refusing this narrative and carving out a separate space to address our issues on our own terms. Desires for Indigenous nationhood are thus direct rejections of multicultural policies of diversity and inclusion, such as the all too American narrative of a melting pot or a salad bowl. Nationhood is a powerful vehicle that Indigenous peoples have been using since the beginning of colonialism, to maintain as much authority as we can and bring about our own visions for the future.[25]

Rather than a more analytically static Nation, my focus in this book is the ongoing process of nation building. Nation building does not have a fixed end point or conclusion but is rather a process that evolves to meet existing needs and dreams for the future. In the seminal ethnographic book on Native nation building, Choctaw scholar Valerie Lambert demonstrates how the ideas and icons that legitimize and express the nation are sufficiently flexible and polysemous enough that they can be selected, assembled, and deployed in different ways and with different meanings at different points in time. In addition, such deployments, as the Choctaw case shows, are not fixed but are best understood as claims that are negotiated and renegotiated, institutionalized and reinstitutionalized over time.[26] Building on Lambert's important argument that nationhood is under constant negotiation, I trace the way nation building names the desires peoples have for ensuring their own future. While national desires are never uniform across time or any given population, the themes of language, self-governance, health, and land have been particularly important in Osage nation-building efforts. In all, but especially colonial, contexts, there are always forces that are seeking to undermine nations, and thus nation building is necessarily ongoing. Given all the colonial efforts and structures that have attempted to ensure that the Osage Nation does not exist, Osages' continued commitment to this project is vital.

I have consciously chosen the term *Nation* over *state*, even though much of what I describe in this book could be understood as state building. Much like states, our Nation has an independent government, a robust bureaucracy, and a territory. Chapters 2, 3, and 4 in fact describe each of these core pieces in turn. However, European thought has often reserved the word *state* for political entities that claim a monopoly over certain functions within a territory, including the use of force.[27] In current Osage visions, this kind of external control and violence is not centered. Furthermore, it is this monopoly on violence that marks the colonial state. As Kahnawà:ke Mohawk scholar Audra Simpson writes, "Is it possible for peoples—and here I am thinking of encapsulated communities such as reserves and meaningful but dispersed associations such as 'the diaspora'—to behave as nations do and not desire, at the end of their cultural labouring, statehood? Perhaps the desire may be for an abstraction—a principle, such as sovereignty, for moral victory, or simply for respect."[28] This book takes up this question of what Osages are working toward, if not statehood. I am particularly focused on Osage desires for and strategies of respect, responsibility, order, and layering.

The focus of my last book, *Colonial Entanglement: Constituting a Twenty-First-Century Osage Nation*, was the entanglements of sovereignty. In this book I am more interested in the motivations of nation building. Indigenous studies scholars have long debated the meaning and usefulness of the frame of sovereignty.[29] As I have argued elsewhere, all sovereignty, not just for Native nations, is an entanglement: "Sovereignty operates as an ongoing process of engagement with other authorities. It is an insistence on one's authority without the illusion of full control, a mess of negotiations and interruptions, which almost always lead to further entanglements."[30] Here and in my other work, entanglement offers a way of naming the current situations Indigenous peoples find ourselves in, which are not generally of our own making but which we continue to remake into something both beautiful and uniquely our own.[31] Sovereignty has been a useful frame for me in understanding external relations and limitations, especially in the context of political jurisdiction, but I have found that nation building is a better frame for understanding internal motivations, goals, and strategies.

Given our ongoing experiences with colonialism, which works first and foremost as a set of interrelated structures that attempt to deny Native peoples a political future, we must continually foster our own visions for the future of our Nation. I have chosen to highlight stories about language, self-governance, health, and land because they illustrate some of the most common desires that are currently motivating Osages. There is a danger in focusing too much of our attention on the power of colonialism, as doing so often works to downplay the agency of Indigenous peoples.[32] Such moves further empower colonialism, leaving few openings for Indigenous futures. Unangax̂ scholar Eve Tuck and US scholar Wayne Yang write that a desire-based approach to research "refuses the master narrative that colonization was inevitable and has a monopoly on the future. By refusing the teleological theory of an inevitably colonial future, desire expands possible futures."[33] Here a focus on desires moves us away from narratives of trauma and creates spaces to imagine the future differently. Writing against the far too common narratives that Indigenous peoples are doomed to fail at building contemporary nations or should only operate entirely outside colonial systems, the central goal of this book is to demonstrate that Osages are building our Nation through creative navigation of ongoing colonialism.

This book will detail the many challenges created by colonialism, but I am focusing my lens here on Osage navigation and relationship building, not colonialism's ensnarements. Nation building sharpens our focus on Osage desires for the future, helping to shift us away from colonialism's many entanglements.[34] This is a subtle shift, but one that has significant impacts. While nations are certainly entangled with colonial recognition (such as who gets to be a Nation and what kinds of structures count as national governments), this book is more focused on Osages' desires as revealed by our national movement.

Even within a desire-based frame, nation building must be understood as a deeply conflicted project. I am interested in the processes and tensions within these efforts, not in defining what the Osage Nation has been, is, or will be. I agree with the argument that Simpson makes in her important work in the Kahnawà:ke Mohawk context, that the Nation "is a collectively self-conscious, deliberate and politically expedient formulation and a lived phenomenon."[35] My project is thus not to distill the vast and conflicting desires of Osages into a single or even dual vision for the future. By taking just one Native nation as my focus, I am better able to trace these desires for nationhood in their full complexity, allowing us to clearly see the tensions and challenges at play. While the many Osages I have engaged privilege the same four desires— language, self-governance, health, and land—there are deep disagreements among Osages about how we might best foster them, and whether fostering them is even possible in this colonial moment.

Indigenous studies scholars debate how far back in history we should take the term *nationhood*, with some arguing that it is a distinctly modern entanglement and others exploring the ways that national modalities were present before colonialism.[36] In this book I am focused on nationhood as a contemporary tool Osages have utilized, and even embraced, to ensure our future as a people. I would certainly argue that Osages understood ourselves as a united people and were recognized by others as controlling our territory before and throughout European invasion.[37] If those are the core elements of your definition of nationhood, then we were indeed a Nation. It is important to note, however, that with colonization, our structures, our understandings of ourselves as a people, and even our dreams had to undergo significant shifts. I am interested in these shifts and our ongoing work of using a national structure to carry forward the things that are most precious to us, including my core areas of focus in this book.

The English term *Nation* has been used in the Osage context since at least 1808, when it occurred twenty-nine times in the Treaty of Fort Clark.[38] The term continued to be used subsequently in our six treaties, although most often intermixed with *Tribe*, with "the Great and Little Osage Tribes or Nations" the most frequent formulation. Throughout the treaty period, Osages divided ourselves into multiple groups, the two most common being the Great Osages and the Little Osages. Despite being referred to in these documents as multiple Tribes or Nations, these groups all understood ourselves as part of a larger Osage unit and had strategies to share the territory.[39] What we did not share were leaders, instead relying on regular gatherings (what ethnographers referred to as rituals) to settle disputes and to maintain cohesion as a people.[40]

While it is hard to know how much control Osage leaders had over treaty language, when we began writing constitutions for ourselves, we used the term *Nation*. Both the 1861 and 1881 constitutions utilized the title Osage Nation. As Osage scholar Robert Warrior has written, creating a recognizable national structure was how Osage leaders at this time went about protecting our territory from outsiders and ensuring access to our promised treaty goods.[41] In describing the 1881 Osage constitutional government, the federally appointed Indian agent for the Osage, Major Laban J. Miles, even acknowledged Osages' embrace of *Nation*: "The Osage regard themselves as a nation with a big 'N,' and the government is vested in a principal chief, assistant chief, fifteen councilors, and five district sheriffs, who are elected by the people for the terms of two years. . . . This government is a very real thing to the Osage."[42] Even in the pejorative writing of this colonial actor, it is clear that nationhood was an important tool and perhaps even a form of self-expression for Osage leaders during this period.

Osages continued to assert ourselves as a Nation throughout the twentieth century, despite illegal federal actions that undermined our efforts. The 1906 Osage Allotment Act not only renamed the Osage Nation the Osage Tribe of Oklahoma but attempted to reimagine Osage citizens as shareholders of a corporation led by a tribal council. Osages fought against this diminishment through various efforts, including most notably through the Osage Nation Organization of the 1960s, which rightfully asserted that the 1881

Osage Nation had been illegally terminated by the Office of Indian Affairs and was therefore still a legitimate government. The 1978 federal court case *Logan v. Andrus* confirmed that the secretary of the interior did not have legal authority to abolish the Osage Nation. However, because the tribal council government had been in place for seventy years, it now had authority.[43]

It was not until the end of the twentieth century that Osages were able to reclaim the title of Osage Nation, and this entity was only able to operate for five years. Several Osage annuitants involved in the Osage Nation Organization, including William S. Fletcher, brought the issue of a preexisting Osage constitutional government to federal court again in 1990.[44] In 1992, the case resulted in a court-mandated process that created a new constitutional government, which was viewed by many as an amendment of the 1881 Osage Constitution.[45] The Osage National Council, as the government was called, operated alongside the Osage Tribal Council for five years, with tensions developing over delineation of duties and ownership of assets. In 1997 the Tenth Circuit Court of Appeals reversed the 1992 ruling because the Osage Tribal Council had sovereign immunity and could not have its general governing powers stricken by the US court system. In recognizing the council as the legitimate Osage government, this ruling extinguished the 1994 Osage Nation's constitutional government and returned voting power solely to those holding a share in the mineral estate.[46]

From this one-hundred-year struggle it became clear that the only remedy for the situation was through federal legislation. In 2004 Osages were finally successful at getting legislation through the US Congress that recognized our inherent sovereign right to determine our own form of government and citizenship standards.[47] In the 2004–6 Osage government reform process that followed the passage of this law, many differently situated Osages argued for changing the name from Osage Tribe to Osage Nation. Unlike the easily trivialized notion of tribe, which was imposed on us by the federal government through the 1906 Allotment Act, nationhood better represented our sovereignty and the robust system of government we envisioned.[48]

This book seeks to understand the motivations behind and outcomes of Osage nation-building efforts, especially those that have occurred since the passage of the 2006 constitution. I argue that Osage officials have undertaken deliberate changes to strengthen Osage language, self-governance, health, and land, as these are some of the core elements that we need to thrive as a people, now and into the future. I also highlight in each chapter some of the unique strategies Osages have used to build our Nation. In describing these desires and strategies, I am hoping future Osages and other Indigenous leaders can learn from our past challenges and ongoing commitments, and thus be better positioned to take up the difficult work of Indigenous nation building.

"Moving to a New Country"

Our stories both describe who we are and shape how we approach the world.[49] Through these stories, we often learn where we have come from and develop strategies for navigating the world around us.[50] As Turtle Mountain Band of Chippewa Indians scholar Heidi Kiiwetinepinesiik Stark argues, "Stories are law. . . . Stories lay out the central principles for how people order their world."[51] In other words, stories pass along the strategies that have been used to hold us together. Osage stories document the precolonial moves Osages made in location and material culture while maintaining our language and sense of self as a people. More than that, our stories contain the tools we can use to continue the work of nation building. This section describes these stories, the core theories Osages are deriving from them, and how these stories have been and continue to be enacted through our nation-building efforts.

Many Osage stories describe processes by which Osages have taken control of change to create a new order for our future, a process sometimes referred to as "moving to a new country." These intentional moves are how Osages have often navigated change, including the changes mandated by the US government. Moving is a powerful frame for understanding Osage nationhood, as it is how we have maintained our sense of being a unique people in the face of colonial pressures of elimination and massive change. Rather than seeking to keep practices the same, Osage leaders have used deliberate change to maintain relations with our language, self-governance, health, and land. But moving is about more than deliberate change. Underlying the deliberations are Osage values. Change for Osage people is best made in ways that foster respect, responsibility, order, and layered relations. Osage leaders have repeatedly used these vital relations to create and maintain our Nation.

Twentieth-century Osage Nation writer John Joseph Mathews is perhaps the most cited author when it comes to the Osage 𐓻𐓘𐓤𐓘 𐓡𐓘𐓤𐓘𐓪 (origin stories) and their usage of the phrase "moving to a new country." In describing the origin of the Osage people, he writes, "When the newly-arrived-upon-earth children of the sky, represented by the Wah-Sha-She, the Water People, the sub-Hunkah, the Land People, and the grand division of the Tzi-Sho, the Sky People, came upon the Isolated Earth People, the indigenous ones, the four groups formed a tribal unit, and were anxious to lead the Isolated Earth People away from the earth-ugliness of their village, saying they were thus moving them to a new country."[52] Mathews goes on to argue that this was only the first of many such moves: "The Little Old Men spoke of these moves as one might speak of changing camping places, and each organizational step was a step away from the old, just as they walked away from the disorder of the old campsites."[53] In our stories, moving was never simply a geographical change but rather an ongoing commitment to enact deliberate change to address chaos as it developed in the community. This was the work necessary to ensure that our people would have a future.

Mathews's writing comes from various oral histories, including some from turn-of-the-century ethnologists as well as those he collected himself. US ethnologist and missionary James Owen Dorsey, for example, spent from January to February 1883 speaking with various Osage elders, who described the theme of deliberate change throughout their stories.[54] One of the phrases he recorded and translated from the town criers, who were responsible for running from town to town to share news, was, "They say that you shall tie up the packs today! Wakanda has made a good day! They say that you shall tie up your packs today and remove to a good land."[55] This celebration of moving to a good land highlights how moving was tied to the efforts of ⅄ʌ𝕜𝕆Ⴇʌ, written here as Wakanda, which is the Osage name for God or the ultimate creator being. Moving was not something done in fear, but something to be celebrated. This was not a running away, but an embrace of the path the creator had laid out.[56]

Similarly, Omaha Tribe ethnologist Francis La Flesche recorded oral histories with ⅃Ꙩꙋ𝕆Ⱬ𝕟𝕜ʌ (little old men/leaders) in the early twentieth century. Moving was a common theme throughout these histories.[57] ⅃Ꙩꙋ𝕆Ⱬ𝕟𝕜ʌ observed that the cosmos was constantly changing, and thus embraced change as a fundamental part of their own structures and approaches.[58] La Flesche mentions moving to a new country frequently throughout his writing, defining it as "a term expressive of a slow movement that preceded a change in the government of the tribe."[59] These moves were deliberate changes made in all realms of life that sought to counter 𝕜ʌ⅃𝕟ħʌ (chaos) as it developed, replacing it with a new order. Here and in other Osage contexts, "order" does not signal authoritarian structures but rather an intentional and calibrated system of organization.[60] Each of the different clans' recorded ⅃𝕟𝕜𝕟 ⅄𝕟𝕜𝕟𝕒 repeats this theme of moving in different ways.[61]

During the early colonial period (1673–1880), the sociopolitical-religious structure of the Osage utilized deliberate change as a core strategy of survival. This change was motivated by seeking order, which meant identifying what was causing the community 𝕜ʌ⅃𝕟ħʌ and finding answers to address those challenges. Writing about this period, US scholar Willard Rollings states, "The Non-hon-zhin-ga contemplated and pondered the chaos, and then made the 'moves to a new country,' which meant metaphorically to make the changes necessary to survive. These necessary changes were accompanied by a spiritual rationale and were always placed within a familiar cultural context recognized as Osage and sanctioned by the Non-hon-zhin-ga. In earlier times, the challenges came slowly and the necessary changes were less dramatic."[62] During this time, Osages made intentional changes so they could survive the challenges they were navigating, which included settlers establishing control over trade, the displacement of other Native nations to our territory, disease, white settlers, and Christian attempts at infiltration. Rather than allowing these changes to eliminate the Osage as a people, we continued to use our vital relations and changed in ways that would ensure our future.

During the eighteenth century, this sociopolitical-religious system enabled Osages to expand our territory and population. This Osage strength emerged because the ᏚᎾᏚᎣᏃᏅᎮᎠ were continually modifying practices in search of an order that would best foster unity. They used their size and strategic location between the French, Spanish, and later American traders on the Mississippi River as well as the many resources to the west to, as US scholar Kathleen DuVal writes, "develop one of the largest trading systems in North America and to wield enormous power over both their Indian and European neighbors."[63] Osage strength during this period was certainly built out of interdependence with other polities and vital trade relationships. Through the eighteenth century, the Osage continued to adapt this system to allow us to expand our population, territory, and control.

Further examples of moving to a new country through building vital relations can be seen within our ᏅᏅᎮᎾᎠ (oral history/prayers) shared by these ᏚᎾᏚᎣᏃᏅᎮᎠ. Analyzing Osage ᏅᏅᎮᎾᎠ reveals the growth in the number of clans from fourteen to twenty-four by the nineteenth century. Such changes were likely made to accommodate a growing Osage population, but they also maintained order as trade and wars on all fronts challenged the Nation.[64] The ᏅᏅᎮᎾᎠ also described new "ceremonies" that developed, such as a two-week war ceremony, which not only forced everyone to come together and unite behind the cause but also disrupted impulsive actions.[65] ᏅᏅᎮᎾᎠ show that our clans and practices did not remain static over time but instead changed to meet Osage needs and maintain order.

It is vital for us to untangle our ideas of "moving to a new country" from colonial pressures of assimilation. Assimilation requires Indigenous people to completely disconnect from our unique nationhood, including our language, practices, land, and any sense of ourselves as a community. Moving, on the other hand, is a set of strategic decisions about what kinds of changes we need to make to ensure a future for the Osage as a Nation. At the core this difference is a change in who is making decisions about what is best for the Osage people.

In the nineteenth century, Osages began fending off all those who came for our land. A core part of European settler efforts were missionary and other assimilation attempts to destroy our polities and ways of life. In a letter by Osage missionaries in 1822 outlining the regulation of Indian children, they wrote, "Let Missionary Institutions, established to convey to them the benefits of civilization and the blessings of Christianity, be efficiently supported; and, with cheering hope, you may look forward to the period, when the savage shall be converted into the citizen; when the hunter shall be transformed to the agriculturist or the mechanic; when the farm, the workshop, the school-house, and the church, shall adorn every Indian Village."[66] Such rhetoric plagued Osages for generations, as we were encouraged by federal and religious officials, as well as our own relatives, to leave behind or bury older Osage practices.

When this missionary rhetoric first appeared on the reservation, however, Osages still had the freedom to choose the pieces we would incorporate and leave the rest behind. During most of the nineteenth century, Osages lived a prosperous life with great devotion to a highly developed faith, a healthy mix of hunting and agriculture, and our own well-functioning political order. We were easily able to ignore such assimilationist teachings as misunderstandings on the part of white missionaries and federal agents.[67] In fact, to gain any traction at all, religious efforts had to be made to fit within our worldview, and missionaries had to translate their texts into the Osage language.[68] Even with these significant efforts, until the end of the nineteenth century, Christian religions held little appeal.

A large factor in the continued ability to move to a new country on our own terms was that, until 1875, Osages were able to raise our children in our own knowledges and values. While various Protestant, Jesuit, and Quaker missions arrived beginning in 1821—sometimes even at the request of Osages—we very rarely left our children under missionary care for any length of time. The mission reports are filled with stories of frustration at parents who would not be separated from their children or would only do so for a brief period before returning for them and demanding to take them home.[69] Isaac T. Gibson, an Osage agent, wrote to the commissioner of Indian affairs in 1875 and explained the Catholics' failed efforts: "Five years ago when I assumed charge of the Osages, sixty Osage pupils were in this Catholic School.

Nearly all were mixed bloods. Most of the full bloods were homeless orphans. No chief, or leading man (full blood) patronized the School, which shows the little interest in education and civilization the Catholics had been able to excite in the leading men of the tribe at the end of twenty years constant effort through a great number of Teachers, Missionaries and Priests."[70] As is evident in this quote, mission schools came with entirely new frames that privileged not just Western educational forms of reading, writing, and math but conceptions of civilization and salvation. Agents of the federal government such as Gibson saw it as their job to convert Natives, a job that they believed was harder to accomplish in "full bloods" because they supposedly did not have a biological predisposition to "civilized life."

With the strength of Osage ways of life during this period, the rhetoric of civilization was easy to subvert. During this period, Osages themselves began to pick up on the references to "blood," but it was understood as a marker not of an individual's capacity, or even their actual heredity, but of their actions. "Full bloods" were those who continued to speak the Osage language, were involved in Osage sociopolitical-religious practices, wore "blankets" and other nonwhite clothing, and fought against settler infiltration, especially allotment.[71] "Full blood" thus came to signal a commitment to the Osage Nation and way of life. While missionaries and federal agents misread Osage commitments to our Nation as an inherent biological deficiency, Osages redeployed our language to reinforce our own commitments.

The values missionaries and agents were trying to instill in children during this period were also too divergent from ours to easily take hold. Missionaries' understanding of and relationship to childhood was very different from ours. Throughout the colonial archives, it is possible to see the devotion Osages had to our children.[72] In the 1840s, for example, the French traveler Victor Tixier visited the Osage and later wrote, "The Osage fathers and mothers show an extraordinary kindness and even weakness in regard to their children. . . . The little warrior and the girls give orders and are waited on according to their wishes. When they have children, their turn to obey will come."[73] The disdain and mockery with which Tixier wrote here helps to demonstrate the clash of cultures at play in the early colonial period. European missionaries' discipline-focused treatment was noted by Osages, who during the 1870s would rarely leave their children in missionary schools for any length of time.[74]

Even when children did attend these early schools, Osage life incorporated the mission's practices rather than becoming subsumed by them. One widely circulated story from the 1860s illustrates the general attitude of the period.

Returning home from the Osage mission school run by the Jesuits in Saint Paul, Kansas, 𐓐𐓘𐓦𐓨𐓣𐓪𐓒𐓘𐓒𐓨 declared to the gathered crowd, "It took Father Schoenmaker fifteen years to make a white man out of me, and it will take just fifteen minutes to make an Osage out of myself."[75] He is reported to have entered his father's house as a neatly combed, well-dressed man and "emerged from his parent's longhouse soon after with his hair shaved into a roach and wearing a breechcloth, leggings, and moccasins."[76] This powerful image subverts the common narratives of boarding schools at the time, which used changes in hairstyle and clothing to signal a loss of Indian identity. Even when 𐓐𐓘𐓦𐓨𐓣𐓪𐓒𐓘𐓒𐓨 became principal chief in 1869, he rarely spoke English with Americans but instead used a translator, giving him an edge on outsiders who did not know he understood English and demonstrating his commitment to Osage ways.[77] This ability to use the skills gained in white spaces to serve rather than undermine our cohesion as a Nation is a powerful example of what moving to a new country looked like during this period.

As discussions throughout the rest of the book will demonstrate, Osages have continued our efforts to move to a new country throughout the nineteenth and twentieth centuries, and into the twenty-first, but these efforts have been complicated by colonial assimilation efforts, theft, and violence. While the following chapters will discuss these moves in more detail, with a focus on how they affected language, self-governance, health, and land, it is important to note that my focus on moving the Osage Nation into the future builds on earlier scholarship by Osages. Explaining how Osages were able to quickly transition to a constitutional form of government in 1881, Osage scholar Robert Warrior writes, "A major part of the answer lies not with the cultural practices the Osages were learning from outside their culture, but with the continuation of traditions they had developed over the course of centuries. In adopting their constitution, in other words, they were 'moving to a new country.'"[78] The 1881 Osage Constitution is perhaps one of the best examples of a strategy of "moving to a new country" in colonial times, as it represented a fundamental shift away from the existing government structure in response to the growing chaos created by colonialism.

One particularly noteworthy demonstration of Osages' ongoing commitment to move to a new country occurred in 1922. A newspaper clipping from June of that year describes an Osage man by the name of 𐓇𐓘𐓥𐓾𐓣𐓨 hosting a feast at his house outside Hominy. 𐓇𐓘𐓥𐓾𐓣𐓨 had recently returned from a trip to Mexico where he met with the president, who expressed support for a plan to make Mexico the new home of the Osage. The paper goes on to say that 𐓇𐓘𐓥𐓾𐓣𐓨 "has the idea that this is too much of a White man's country."[79] While such a move never occurred, it is a powerful testament to Osages' ongoing assessment of the state of the nation and conceptualization of what changes could be implemented for Osage people to thrive.

It is important to distinguish this Osage moving from Western notions of progress, which have a predetermined end, be it civilization, democracy, or some other idealized trope. Moving is a commitment to ongoing change rather than a linear path from one place to the next. While the goal of moving is to ensure that the Osage Nation has a future, what this future entails will, by necessity, be constantly changing. As Osage language contractor Veronica Pipestem explained to me, "Inherent in this concept is moving forward, backward, upwards, downwards, and a combination of any of these at any given time."[80] Figuring out how much and in what ways to change is where the vital relations play an important role.

This book also builds on and draws from my previous scholarship, particularly a journal article coauthored with Osage Nation chief supreme court judge Meredith Drent entitled "Moving to a New Country Again: The Osage Nation's Search for Order and Unity through Change." In this article we theorize moving to a new country as a principle that "marks the reproduction of Indigenous values through a process of continuous deliberation and adaptation to foster a unified and healthy government system, even in the midst of massive upheaval."[81] Throughout this piece, we argue that moving means embracing change, fostering unity, and seeking a stronger order. After defining what each of these terms means in the Osage context historically and today, we describe the ways in which they could be further developed within our current structure. The present book builds on this article, looking at how Osages are using the vital relational strategies of respect, responsibility, order, and layering to move the language, self-governance, healthcare, and land into the future.

Other Indigenous studies scholars have also incorporated movement as an important intervention into the way that Indigenous peoples are too often theorized as static or only rooted in place. Muscogee Nation scholar Laura Harjo writes, "Some of our (re)emergence and migration stories are based on our responses to acts of settler futurity that include Indian removal and relocation; however, we also carry other such stories that are based on movement of our own choosing. . . . Conceptions held by Mvskoke and other Indigenous communities disrupt commonly received notions of fixity and place."[82] Similarly, Pohnpeian scholar Vicente Diaz demonstrates how Indigenous peoples' deep connections to place are strengthened through travel, especially travel via water, and that these two aspects, rootedness and routedness, mutually constitute Indigenous systems of knowledge.[83] This book builds on this scholarship to demonstrate how movement is a fundamental part of Indigenous pasts, presents, and futures by sharing the deeply illustrative case of the Osage Nation.

"Turn Them into Something That Could Work for Us"

Scholars in Indigenous studies have written extensively on relationality. It may, in fact, be the core tenet of the field. Goenpul scholar Aileen Moreton-Robinson summarizes much of this research when she writes that "relationality is grounded in a holistic conception of the inter-connectedness and inter-substantiation between and among all living things and the earth, which is inhabited by a world of ancestors and creator beings."[84] Thus, relationality is an Indigenous framework for approaching the world that focuses on creating a balance between all beings, including those that colonialism dismisses as nonsentient, inanimate, or supernatural. Indigenous studies scholars demonstrate how relationality works toward reciprocal relationships and mutual responsibility, whereas colonial relationships are too often based on and working toward extraction, independence, and isolation.[85]

These theories rarely acknowledge how messy and fraught relationality is in practice, since most Indigenous studies discussions of relationality are abstracted from daily life experiences. As Trawlwulwuy scholar Lauren Tynan points out, despite the "mystique and romanticism" that surrounds relationality, it "is not easy, especially when living in a settler-colony."[86] Colonial policies and practices have worked at every turn to disrupt our connections and to insist that we see the world through its hierarchies, rigid categories, and staunch individualism. In this book, I move us beyond the mystique and toward the everyday challenges of engaging the current world relationally.

One important exception to the general tendency to view relationality abstractly is the work of Ermineskin Cree Nation scholar Matthew Wildcat, who looks at the Maskwacîs Education Schools Commission's efforts to build a unified school system across several First Nations communities. In his research, Wildcat uses the concept of relational governance to illustrate the importance of rejecting settler conceptions of sovereignty as exclusive authority over a territory. Instead, he is interested in what becomes possible when various First Nations peoples come together to work on addressing the challenges their communities are facing.[87] While Osage leaders were primarily focused on doing work within the frame of the Osage Nation, rather than working to build regional Native collaborations, my underlying conclusions are very similar to Wildcat's. Effective governance requires "locating responsibility," creating a "relational web," and deciding "what values, philosophies and ultimately laws we are drawing on to make decisions."[88] In the Osage context, I refer to these vital relations as responsibility, order, layering, and respect.

This book's primary theoretical contribution is to deepen our understandings of the ubiquitous Indigenous studies concept of relationality. I have chosen the phrase *vital relations* to encompass the kinds of relationality Osages are working toward.[89] The adjective *vital* means "necessary for the success or continued existence of something."[90] My usage of this phrase signals how Osages understand our relations, even fraught ones with untrustworthy colonial actors, to be necessary for the continued existence and life of our Nation. This book looks at the vital relations that Osages are developing to build our Nation and ensure our future. While Indigenous studies should continue to be a place for what Tanana Athabascan scholar Dian Million calls "intense dreaming," in which we can envision a world not driven by colonialism, it should also be a place to name and discuss the relations our nations are currently enacting.[91] As this world is marked by deep inequalities and conflicting aspirations, relationality must be a commitment to being uncomfortable and working through turmoil as much as it is about envisioning that idealized balance.[92]

My past work has sought to show the limitations the colonial situation has created for our nation-building efforts by naming relations with colonial actors as entanglements.[93] This book builds on that focus, looking at the vital relations Osages are seeking through nation building—namely, respect, responsibility, order, and layering. The way we tell stories matters. Just as it is dangerous to reinforce the notion that colonialism is settled, it is also dangerous to focus our analytical attention primarily on colonialism's entanglements. Framing Osage nation building through vital relations works to expand, rather than limit, both the agency of Osage leaders and the potential for building a future that meets our own unique needs despite and through colonial limitations.

My work builds on Indigenous studies scholars that have sought to name the hard decisions Indigenous leaders are making in the face of colonialism. Leech Lake Band of Ojibwe Tribe and the Lower Sioux Indian Community scholar Scott Lyons's conception of x-marks is perhaps the most widely utilized.[94] The classic example of an x-mark is the literal marking of an *x* on a treaty, where an uncoerced assent was not possible but assent was given nonetheless. He defines the x-mark as "a contaminated and coerced sign of consent made under conditions that are not of one's making. It signifies power and lack of power, agency and a lack of agency. It is a decision one makes when something has already been decided for you, but it is still a decision."[95] Lyons expands this notion of x-marks to incorporate such institutions as current American Indian nations. While for Lyons, today's nations are not based on the same sort of organizing principles that were at work in most American Indian communities before colonization, they have become powerful means for these communities to assert themselves in the present. The concept of vital relations builds on this idea of x-marks, describing how Indigenous peoples are navigating these moments of coerced consent in ways that open up Indigenous agency.

One powerful example of the vital relations Osages are enacting can be seen in how many Osages actively embraced the opportunity to participate in the making of the film *Killers of the Flower Moon*. Based on a best-selling book by the same title, this is a story of arguably one of the darkest moments in Osage history. In the 1920s settlers streamed into our territory in search of oil wealth, taking advantage of the disorder created by extreme forms of colonialism. Settlers swindled and murdered Osages, sometimes their own spouses and in-laws, on a massive scale, to take Osage oil wealth for themselves.[96]

Too often the stories told about this period further inscribe Osages as helpless and ignorant victims who could not foster justice or handle wealth ourselves.[97] This kind of victim blaming is common in colonial contexts, where settlers use stereotypes of Indigenous savagery to justify stealing the land.[98] Rather than addressing the violence that settlers brought to reservations, or better yet the federal policies and practices that had and continued to undermine Osage systems of justice, the federal government labeled Osages as legally incompetent to manage our own affairs, justifying more settler authority over Osage lives.[99] Unfortunately, especially in this context, increasing settler authority only created more violence and theft. Furthermore, despite Osages spending habits as mirroring others in their same income bracket, general mainstream depictions of the time focused on Osage extravagance, implying that Osages were not capable of managing our money.[100] The overarching implication at work here is that Osages were not capable of living in a modern world, thus furthering the logic of elimination that places Indigenous peoples as only belonging in the past.

Attempting to ensure historical accuracy and demonstrate our survival, a broad cross-section of the Osage citizenry and officials entered every available relationship with the film. When Osage Nation chief Geoffrey Standing Bear first heard that Martin Scorsese was going to direct the film, he set up a meeting with him, inviting him to come to the reservation, and then used that visit to persuade him to make the film in the Osage Nation. During this meeting, he said, "We want to make sure your people have everything they need, in terms of Osage artisans, Osage language. . . . Those people are still here in the community and would love to help."[101] Additionally, the Grayhorse community of Osages hosted a dinner for Scorsese and his team where former Chief Jim Gray spoke of this as a moment when Scorsese had an opportunity to change the misrepresentations of Native Americans in Hollywood, especially the savagery and white saviorism that so often plague these stories.[102] Based on these conversations, Scorsese agreed to film the movie on the Osage reservation, and Osages were hired to work on many different aspects of the film. There were, of course, also many Osages who refused to have anything to do with the film, finding the entire project to be at best in poor taste and at worst another powerful example of white people profiting off Osage suffering.[103]

For the Osages who did choose to participate, motivations included the excitement of being around famous actors and directors and the experience that would be gained working on a major motion picture. When I returned to the reservation during the height of this filming period in the summer of 2021, it was hard not to get caught up in the excitement of celebrity spotting and discussions of what it was like to be on the set. While driving down the main street in Pawhuska, it was disturbing to see all the actors playing legal guardians and murderers lined up in front of the Constantine theater as they waited to cross the street to the set. It was moving, however, to see the excitement and passion the project had generated for many of the Osage language employees, who spent time on the set and were regularly visited by the Blackfeet Nation actor Lily Gladstone as she worked on her Osage lines for her starring role as Mollie Burkhart.

There were also deeper desires motivating many Osages' involvement: to do everything in our power to have the story be true to Osage experiences and told with respect. Julie O'Keefe, an Osage woman from Pawhuska who fought for her role as a wardrobe consultant on the film, told me, "Osages have always tried to take control of the forces that came for us and turn them into something that could work for us."[104] Osages were also hired as actors, and they were reportedly able to adapt the script to reflect their own sense of the events.[105] Osages gave museum tours and informally met with the filmmakers and leading actors in their homes. They offered their home movies from the 1920s to the production crew and invited many of those involved to Osage cultural events, meals, and ceremonies. It was a very strange feeling to be circling the drum with my daughter during the Pawhuska ᏁᏬᏍᏗᎪ and having Scorsese, cinema photographer Rodrigo Prieto, and actor Leonardo DiCaprio observing. While such spectators certainly changed the dynamic of the evening, it also felt like something they needed to see if they had any hope of representing our story.

In the end the film only starts to do the work of telling Osage stories; there is still so much more work that needs to be done to fully understand this story. On one hand we must name the structural nature of this violence. This was not just a set of bad actors, but a federal system designed to destroy Indigenous systems of justice and then move into the void created and take land for white settlement.[106] On the other hand, the film does not fully demonstrate Osage persistence beyond this traumatic era. My book thus picks up where the film leaves off, showing both the very real challenges colonial systems have created for us, as well as the ways that the Osage Nation has not just survived this onslaught, but is thriving.

This film is reaching millions of people who would otherwise never know anything about us as a people, and thus it has the potential to fundamentally shape public understandings of Osages, as well as other Indigenous peoples. For many Osages, intervening in the film in every way possible was the only way to stop the cycle of colonial disrespect. As the case studies of Osage language, self-governance, health, and land in this book demonstrate, this film is just one example of how Osages are seeking respectful, responsible, ordered, and layered relations. Through these vital relations, Osages are trying to build a stronger future for our Nation, but we cannot settle for allowing others to do this work for us; we must also do it ourselves.

Each of the chapters of this book is focused not only on a particular area of nation building but also on the kinds of relations Osages are seeking in that space, as well as the challenges of doing that work. In looking at efforts to build relations with our language, I focus on respect. Osages are looking to the language to understand what it means to have respectful relations, are insisting on respect in the face of colonial contempt for our practices, and are using respect to guide how we can build relations with the language going forward. In the context of the Osage Mineral Estate Trust, Osages are insisting on strong relations with a federal government that often ignores its responsibilities, while also seeking self-governance as a way of creating a structure more responsive to our needs. In taking over a federal Indian Health Service facility, Osage leaders are creating ordered relations out of colonial disorganization. Finally, Osage Nation officials are forging layered relations that enable us to buy our land back. I have chosen to use English words to describe each of these vital relations to ensure I am not taking Osage concepts out of context, but each of these chapters looks at how these kinds of relations have mattered to Osages historically and in our cultural realms. Osages continue to foster various forms of relationality to take control over colonial forces and turn them into something that will strengthen our nation.

"Can I Do This and Still Come Home?"

These same vital relations of respect, responsibility, order, and layering have guided the research and writing of this book. My scholarship built out from long-term ethnographic, friendship, and kinship relationships in order to tell stories that open the most possibilities for an Osage future. Indigenous studies scholars have written volumes on the importance of responsibility in research.[107] Summarizing many of these discussions, Moreton-Robinson writes that social researchers must not only understand their relationships but also foster "respect, responsibility, generosity, obligation, and reciprocity."[108] Understanding the ways that research has not only been extractive but also worked to undermine Indigenous desires, Indigenous studies as a field has attempted to carve out research that is responsible to Indigenous peoples. As Pasqua First Nation scholar Margaret Kovach points out, there is no one way in which to create responsible research relationships. Instead, the form reciprocity takes is entirely dependent on the context and the specific nature of the relationships shared.[109]

Vital Relations is grounded in ethnographic research from my time with Osage Nation officials, employees, and citizens since 2004 but is particularly focused on an extended period of research from June 2015 to September 2016, ten years after the passage of the 2006 Osage Constitution. During these stays in Oklahoma, I attended daily meetings held by the chief, Osage Congress, and various boards, divisions, and departments within the Nation. I also had hundreds of informal conversations in person, on the phone, via Zoom, and over email with the key players in these spaces, and I have analyzed archival documents, emails, laws, documents, meeting broadcasts, and online debates. Throughout my research process, including the development of the initial research questions, I have actively consulted with several key Osages, including the chief, assistant chief, Osage Congress members, department directors, and various Osage elders. As I mentioned earlier, I also coauthored an article with the Osage Nation's chief supreme court justice Meredith Drent that informs several key aspects of this book.[110] Whenever possible, Osages cited throughout this book have been sent copies of their quotes, as well as the larger chapters they are quoted in. Almost all have responded with robust feedback, which has led to extended conversations and has shaped and re-shaped the direction of my writing.

One of the ways in which I signal the influence Osages have had in crafting this narrative is through my section headings. Each heading throughout the book highlights one quote that has fundamentally shaped my thinking and writing, which that section will discuss in detail. While these heading quotes occasionally come from Indigenous studies scholars, the vast majority are di-rect quotes from Osages whose statements serve as core theoretical building blocks within the book.[111] Feminist studies scholar Sara Ahmed has pointed out that citations are a "rather successful reproductive technology, a way of reproducing the world around certain bodies."[112] Throughout this book I have sought to reproduce the world around Indigenous (specifically Osage) bodies of knowledge. It is through honoring these ties that I enact respectful relations. Too often our Indigenous communities are treated as data, and published scholarship is treated as theory. These headings are one way in which I respect the daily theoretical work of Osages and this scholarship built out from that knowledge.

My commitments to reproducing Indigenous knowledges through cita-tion are also evident in the scholarship I cite throughout. This book is inten-tionally situated not just within Indigenous studies scholarship but, whenever possible, within the thinking of Indigenous scholars. Rather than employing the typical Euro-American scholarly genealogies for concepts like nation-hood, this book focuses on the ways Indigenous scholars have engaged with these concepts. To acknowledge and highlight this commitment, I have chosen to identify scholars not by their academic discipline but by their connection to specific Native nations or the country in which they are a set-tler scholar. While I have tried to honor how people identify themselves (on their webpages or other online sources), I have chosen to use the official names of the political entities that represent those communities wherever possible.[113]

Due to my citizenship within the Osage Nation, my responsibility is rein-forced, as it is not only me but also my family who are held responsible for my research. Like Simpson, I repeatedly ask the questions, "Can I do this and still come home; what am I revealing here and why? Where will this get us? Who benefits from this and why?"[114] This theorizing "with and as" Osage accom-plishes important academic work not only in terms of shifting the methods but also in shifting the goals of academic production itself.[115] To signal this intellectual move of theorizing "with and as," I regularly use the possessive *our,* rather than the more traditional academically distancing *their,* when referring to Osage histories and practices throughout the book. This term is intended as a disruption of the typically distanced, purportedly objective research paradigm, signaling my own responsibilities in these debates as an Osage. While it might at times be jarring, especially when talking about history, it is an important reminder of my stake in these discussions as extending beyond the research. In highlighting rather than downplaying my relations to this topic, I am consciously upsetting academic norms that serve to hide the power dynamics inherent in knowledge production.

Writing an ethnographic book is fundamentally about bringing order to a mess of human experiences. All research, no matter what the methods, is deeply situated in political and social systems of power.[116] There are no neutral research questions, nor is there a natural way to order the stories shared; rather, knowledge is always working to reinforce or challenge the status quo. "Objective" research is a powerful tool within systems of oppression that has repeatedly been used to discredit Indigenous knowledges and reinforce Western hierarchies of power.[117] Despite and through their claims to objectivity, supposed "rationality" is built out of very particular sociopolitical-religious systems that are deeply tied to colonialism.[118] In other words, colonial ways of seeing the world are often rendered natural and normal through knowledge production. The order we give to the messiness of the world fortifies some ways of being and negates others. Not all things that are observed can or should be shared, and we must make hard choices about what stories we tell. Acting responsibly thus requires enacting refusal.[119] To make such decisions about what stories to tell, I have attempted to build a network of relationships, which can help me not only understand the impacts of sharing certain stories but also be responsible to various Osage perspectives.[120]

Throughout this project I have thus sought to enact a "critical Indigenous consciousness." Navajo Nation and Oglala Lakota Nation scholar Tiffany S. Lee describes critical Indigenous consciousness as not only naming the oppressive conditions that are operating in Native contexts but embracing the position of a Native scholar working to change these conditions with our own communities. She writes, "By serving one's community, one's needs and goals are freed from a dominant, hegemonic position and viewed from an Indigenous perspective, which allows for transformation and is vital for the protection of Indigenous lands, people, culture, and languages."[121] Similarly, my scholarship is grounded in understanding the colonial power dynamics that have created and continue to create challenges for my community and helping us move the Osage Nation into the future.

Such an approach means that validity stems not from one's absence from the research but in fact from our connections to it. As Lambert writes in her work with her own Choctaw Nation, "My ability to carry out this work was greatly enhanced by the fact that my status as a Choctaw opened many doors."[122] My connections are most evident throughout this text in the central role my father plays in several of the stories I share. I would have had a much harder time seeing and naming the unique nation-building strategies the Osage Nation is utilizing if I had not been raised with his insights. My ways of understanding the world have been fundamentally shaped by his experiences and relationships. While he and I frequently had different perspectives on Osage politics, our daily debates helped me to not only fine-tune but expand the arguments within this book. My father passed away while I was writing this book, and thus his knowledge and many life lessons felt all the more precious to hold close.

Furthermore, I have sought to respect Osage stories by strengthening the web of networks I am tied to. As Lumbee Tribe of North Carolina scholar Bryan Brayboy and US scholar Donna Deyhle argue, such a "lack of distance" enhances research.[123] Honoring these relationships has often meant working over multiple drafts of my text with Osages who were represented in these stories, as well as those whose perspectives differ greatly from my own. While a couple of these later conversations were tense, they have allowed me to see a wider spectrum of perspectives and complicate my too-neat narratives. When Osages brought very different perspectives to the fore, it always enriched the story I was able to tell.

While I sought to tell multilayered stories of conflict and disagreement, there is no way I can represent the full complexity of Osage governance in the early twenty-first century. I am limited not only in the space I have to represent Osage stories and the time to witness and hear them but also by Osages' willingness to share with me. There were, of course, many Osages I could not or did not build a relationship with, research or otherwise. Like most researchers, I was naturally drawn to those who could and would linger and talk with me or invite me to visit them. There were others who could not find time to meet with me, would pass quickly by me, or were outright skeptical about me and my research. Being Osage reduced but did not erase the questions circulating about what entitled me to tell Osage stories. These are hard questions, but given the many hours Osage officials, employees, and citizens have spent with me, I feel obligated to share some of the stories they entrusted with me. I hope that other Osages also share their perspectives and stories, complicating or challenging anything they see differently.

The goal of this book is not to capture or even seek a neat alternative to the systems of colonialism we currently operate within but to think through the very real, and nearly impossible, decisions Native nation leaders and peoples are having to make daily. Rather than romanticize or dismiss the realities Indigenous nations are currently inhabiting, this book seeks to share some of the many layered stories within Osage experiences. This means complicating stories that would otherwise flatten diverse Osage perspectives. After reading an early draft of my introduction, Osage Nation assistant chief Raymond Red Corn said, "In my view, your upcoming book's greatest contribution will be a table set with ideas that (almost) any of our elected officials can digest, and put to work."[124] In telling the histories and ongoing efforts of Osage nation building, this book seeks to set the table for future Osage and other Indigenous leaders to continue building vital relations for our futures. Reviewing and assessing these fraught decisions is vital to finding the best possible way forward.

The primary tool I use for sharing this complexity is ethnographic storytelling. Ethnography is a process of observing events and everyday interactions and trying to share those experiences through narratives. While I do understand this as a process of witnessing, I also embrace my role as a storyteller, especially in choosing which stories are most useful to share and what elements to highlight. As Million argues, storytelling is a vital Indigenous methodology that challenges normative histories and visions for the future. She writes, "Stories form bridges that other people might cross, to feel their way into another experience. That is the promise of witness. These feelings, these affects, are part of their power of transformation in politically charged arenas."[125] In sharing everyday stories about contemporary Osage experiences, my goal is to offer doorways into the experiences Osage leaders must navigate as they make the almost impossible decisions about ways to take the Nation forward. *Vital Relations* renders extensive ethnographic research with Osage Nation officials, employees, and citizens from 2004 to 2022 into stories of the vital relations forged to build our Nation in the face of ongoing colonialism.

"They're All Inherently Connected with One Another"

Each chapter is framed by different relational strategies Osage leaders have used in their process of nation building. While I have separated out the threads of the nation-building efforts into chapters on language, self-governance, health, and land, these projects are all deeply interconnected. In describing Indigenous reclamation efforts, Lakota Tribe activist Matt Remle says, "There's no segmenting off of anything. You can't just focus on land, you can't just focus on water, you can't just focus on language, because they're all inherently connected with one another."[126] The creation of a robust health-care system, for example, did not happen before we enacted self-governance, and it is tied to building relations with the land and language. Breaking these chapters into separate themes, however, allows me to focus on the tactics co-lonial agents have used to undermine each of these core pieces of who we are. Additionally, homing in on each area uncovers the specific strategies Osages are using to move the Osage Nation into the future and what we must navi-gate in the process.

Chapter 1, "Language," tells the story of the Osage Nation's relations with our language. Like all languages, Osage was developed within specific political, spiritual, and cultural contexts, and those ways of being and thinking continue to be carried forward through the language. This chapter argues that the lan-guage is a vital component of our nation-building effort and that bringing the language forward requires centering *respectful relations*. While scholars have long seen language as a key aspect of building national identity, this chapter demonstrates that for many Osages, nation building is understood as a tool for keeping alive the important lessons the language has to offer. Respect was a core value contained within our language and lifeways before colonialism and, for many Osages, maintaining a relationship with the language is the best means to stay connected with our unique values. Additionally, respect is an important guide for navigating the continuous changes language is always undergoing, allowing us to ensure that our language has a future.

Historical and ongoing colonial forces have created dire conditions for the Osage language. The US government used outright theft, ecosystem destruc-tion, removal, the supplanting of our government, and assimilation policies to not only shrink our land base but also try to sever our relations with our language and sense of peoplehood. My goal in detailing these challenges within chapter 1, however, is not to reinforce the gross power of the federal govern-ment but to demonstrate that in the face of each challenge, the Osage have cre-atively pivoted. We have continually found ways, often through the development of new technologies, to bring our language forward, even in the face of such disruptive violence. Twenty-first-century nation building, with its expansive revenue streams, has allowed the creation of a robust language program. While the US government almost succeeded in severing the generational flow of the Osage language, creating a moment in the twenty-first century when there were no native speakers, it could not eliminate Osages or our language.

This chapter goes on to detail how the Osage Nation Language Department is bringing the language back into our daily lives through the embrace of various technologies. Hosting classes, creating a writing system, getting this system put into Unicode, and experimenting with a wide spectrum of digital platforms including virtual reality, the language program has embraced innovation while trying to keep respect centered. In sharing the challenges that surround these efforts, my hope is that future Indigenous leaders can use this knowledge to build vital relations with our languages. Discussions with Osage language employees and elected officials clarify not only that the language is understood as a central aspect of the Nation but also that respect is a central aspect of the language. Moving the Osage Nation into the future is thus a process of finding ways to carry this respect forward in the face of massive, colonialism-induced violence and disruption.

Chapter 2, "Self-Governance," describes Osage Nation commitments to self-governance in the face of the many forces that have undermined these efforts. Osage systems of governance have repeatedly been overthrown by the US government's policies and practices. Since our first treaty with the US government in 1805, it has deceived our leadership and failed to honor its promises to protect, support, and effectively manage our resources. Even in the face of such failures, however, the Osage Nation has continually sought to create *responsible relations* with the federal government. Specifically, we have sought to use the federal government to hold at bay our closest, and thus most dangerous, adversaries, such as the State of Oklahoma and corporations. It is thus not autonomy but strong relations with the US government that mark Osage self-governance efforts.

Chapter 2 begins by describing historical Osage commitments to self-governance and responsibility. In the face of federally created waves of violent settlement, rampant disease, ecosystem destruction, mismanagement of resources, threats of termination, and corporate exploitation, Osage officials have continued to strategically use the federal trust relationship toward our own ends. These officials have used the federal courts, the Bureau of Indian Affairs, legislation and grants to hold the US government to its promises and obligations because it is one of our only tools against the threats we face daily, especially from state and corporate actors who frequently disregard our self-governance rights. Meeting Osage needs has repeatedly meant using the US government to gain leverage against, fend off, and receive compensation for problems the government and its policies created for us, especially with extractive industries. Perhaps counterintuitively, this uneven relation of responsibility is what Osages have used to assert self-governance, including the creation of the 2006 constitution, which was enabled by a federal law for which the Osage Tribal Council lobbied.

Following a discussion of these historical relations, chapter 2 uses a February 2016 Osage Shareholders Association meeting to illustrate why, despite the extreme problems that direct Bureau of Indian Affairs management has created for the Osage Mineral Estate, Osage leaders have hesitated to enact self-governance over our extractive industries. While we are forty-five years into the enactment of US self-governance policies that sought to fundamentally shift the federal government's role as trustee away from direct management, there is very little literature on why many Native nations are slow to embrace this shift. This chapter looks closely at the specific concerns of the Osage Minerals Council with self-governance, including the larger Osage Nation's involvement with extractive industries, the Council's commitments to federal responsibility, and the limited capacities of the Osage Minerals Council. While all three of these predicaments stem from federal interventions in Osage governance, Osage leaders continue to insist on responsible relations with the federal government as part of self-governance and thus nation building.

Chapter 3, "Health," chronicles Osage visions for and roadblocks to ensuring our health. This chapter argues that the health of the Osage people is a central project of nation building and that Osage officials are working to meet this need by creating *ordered relations* for its many healthcare programs. In taking over the long-neglected Indian Health Service facility, Osages inherited a cumbersome bureaucracy, outdated and inappropriate equipment, and an inadequate, poorly designed structure. Given the state of governmental programs such as the Indian Health Service, it is almost impossible to imagine Native peoples not wanting to take them over, but in doing so, they must build national organizations that can incorporate dysfunctional bureaucracies into their governing structures. This will not, however, be the first time Osages have sought to form ordered relations out of chaos, colonially induced or otherwise. Using the examples from the Osage clan system and cultural practices, I demonstrate how Osages have repeatedly used deliberative change to create a new order. A similar project is underway as Osage leadership has built their national structure to provide a better healthcare system for our people.

To understand the unique challenges of providing healthcare in Indian Country, chapter 3 interrogates the history of colonial healthcare efforts, including a discussion of how Native peoples have repeatedly tried to intervene in these spaces of colonial paternalism, neglect, assimilation, and elimination.

I then turn to the Osage Nation's twenty-first-century Indian Health Service transition and accreditation process for the newly minted Wahzhazhe Health Center, where Osages attempted to bring order to a neglected space and a cumbersome healthcare bureaucracy through nation building. While increasing the revenue streams can provide improved equipment, services, and even facilities, providing healthcare requires organizing the many separate grant programs into one unified system—a system that can meet the complex health challenges facing the Osage people. Finding the best structure to manage such an unwieldy institution, while centering Osage needs and providing quality care, is a core piece of moving the Osage Nation into the future.

Chapter 4, "Land," focuses on the value Osages saw in land and the methods Osage leadership used to reclaim it. This chapter argues that land is another vital component of our nation-building efforts and that Osages are fostering *layered relations* to reclaim this land. The purchase of forty-three thousand acres of ranch land in the center of the reservation required Osage leadership to commit to a shared vision of the nation, one that understood the land as valuable not only for its economic development potential but for more existential reasons. For Osage Nation officials, the value of this land was intricately tied up with nationhood, as a land base is central to jurisdictional control, and to creating networks of care around our people. Regaining access to our land has meant that Osage children and elders are no longer dependent on external food chains and can more readily access healing foods. The loss of this land had threatened not only our sense of ourselves as a nation but also our ability to feed and care for ourselves. Thus it is little wonder that many Osage leaders understood and continue to understand this land as essential to who we need to be.

Drawing from the discussions Osage leadership had during a host of planning meetings, in personal communications with me, and in public settings, chapter 4 describes the visions of and sacrifices made for this land. In particular, it details Osage leaders' decision to utilize, rather than reject, capitalism as a tool for nation building. I describe the strategic plan for land acquisition, the debates over the purchase of the land among executive and congressional officials, and the visions for the future of this land. This chapter also discusses debates over how this land was to be managed, how the Osage Nation would be structured to best facilitate relations with the land, and how federal funds earmarked to address the global pandemic in 2020 were able to be invested in infrastructure on this land that would foster food sovereignty. This experience demonstrates how Osage leaders are navigating a host of relations to ensure a land-based peoplehood.

Thus, in each of these chapters I detail some of the motivations behind and strategies for Osage nation building in the twenty-first century. These examples demonstrate that moving the Osage Nation into the future involves developing the vital relations of respect, responsibility, order, and layering. As with the chapter's foci, however, these strategies do not operate independently, nor only in the areas the book discusses. In each chapter the reader will see the various strategies working together toward the goal of ensuring that Osages, as a people, have a future. Although in this book strategies have been isolated in each chapter, they are in fact frequently working in tandem. These strategies, especially when considered together, have meant that Osages are not operating in a vacuum or toward isolation but are instead drawing on the tools around us to maintain our unique peoplehood. With the reality of ongoing colonial constraints, the project of nation building is deeply strategic.

"A Vital Aspect of Recovery"

The story of the Osage Nation Primary Residential Treatment (PRT) program is a powerful example of how the vital relations of respect, responsibility, order, and layering manifest throughout Osage practices, including in the help provided to those navigating substance abuse. These strategies are frequently utilized simultaneously to promote Osage nation building. In the seven years since I joined my father in search of treatment for his client, the Osage Nation has built a much more comprehensive set of services addressing the unique needs that addiction creates for individuals and families.[127] Enabling the PRT program to "figure out what is wrong and get Osages the help they need" has not been an easy task for the Nation, but it is certainly one that our future depends on.

It was not until December 2017, two years after it shut down, that the PRT facility would finally be able to start hosting women again. A temporary facility was built using roughly $400,000 that Chief Geoffrey Standing Bear had found in unused federal funds, after various other alternative options had not worked out.[128] This facility, and a separate one for men, remained too small to meet the needs of those seeking treatment, resulting in long waitlists.[129] Additionally, the men's facility was near several bars and a marijuana dispensary. As neither facility had adequate rooms for kids or served minors, many Osages needing help could not be served.[130] There was also no transitional housing, so people often returned to the same triggering and enabling spaces as soon as they were out of treatment. Finally, there was no local administrative space where all the support staff were on hand. To address these issues, Jodie Revard, the Osage Nation's second congressional Speaker, sponsored ONCA 21-58, which appropriated $12 million of the $108.3 million the Nation had received from the American Rescue Plan Act.[131] In 2021 the Osage Nation purchased 320 acres of land on which to build, and the Osage Nation Health Authority Board began working on a design and scope of work for the facility.

Revard said that she hoped this new facility would be a place that would center Osage values and practices such as respect for those seeking treatment. "The spiritual and cultural pieces have to be there, or they are not going to make it."[132] She also insisted that this space needed to foster respect. As we recalled my father, Gene Dennison, who had passed away the month before, Revard remembered how he was able to center respect in his legal practice, especially with those navigating addiction. Revard had worked with my dad during several family legal issues. She told me that no matter what the person had done or what they were up against, he would show them respect. "Whether it was the judge or the returning convict, he built them up and made them feel good. Gene showered everyone with respect, and it was returned."[133] Revard wanted to make sure that anyone going through the PRT was treated in that way. This meant not only designing a premier facility but developing programming that built up, rather than tore down, all those who sought treatment there.

The initial PRT program and the funding for the facility were the result of an Osage insistence that the United States honor its treaty promises to promote the health of the Osage people. Working with the federal government to take over the management of the federal program, using federal funds to run the program as we see fit, and securing federal COVID-19 relief funds to build a structure that meets our needs are all powerful examples of what it means to demand responsible relations with the federal government. In these as well as in other examples, strong relationships, especially monetary relationships with the federal government, are part of the obligations the federal government has to the Osage Nation. In pushing the United States to fulfill its fiduciary responsibilities while operating the programs ourselves, the Osage Nation is best able to meet the health needs of our people.

For a facility like the PRT program's to be successful, however, it cannot stand alone. It must operate as one piece of a larger national support system. Such a system must be organized to promote unity and avoid chaos. It must, in other words, have ordered relations. After experimenting with various structures, the Osage Nation Congress in 2021 passed ONCA 21-31, an act "to establish a structural and procedural framework for a new Osage Nation

Health Care System." This act turned the Osage Nation Health Authority Board into an unincorporated business responsible for all Osage Nation healthcare services, including the clinic and the PRT program. This long-sought new order has enabled the PRT program to be integrated into a broader set of health services that are designed for meeting Osage needs.

Space for treating women was not the only piece the PRT lost when its house on the government campus in Pawhuska was demolished in 2015. The program also stopped offering a sweat lodge, which clients saw as "a vital aspect of recovery."[134] As the Osage Nation ran federal grants, it pulled together a list of best practices of healing from a wide variety of sources, including 12 Steps and cognitive behavioral therapy, but also cultural activities like drum making and a sweat lodge, in addition to examining the historical catalysts for community trauma.[135] By insisting that the PRT "support the establishment and use of culturally relevant Native American customs," the Osage Nation Congress was demonstrating its commitment to fostering layered relations.[136] Members of Congress felt they could best help those in need not simply by enacting Indigenous practices, or a strict adherence to best practices nationally, but by bringing all of these sources together.

This book thus demonstrates that nation building in the Osage context is not about autonomy or purity but about building vital relations. Osage leaders have repeatedly recognized that the Nation is a tool that allows Osage people to operate within very real colonial limitations in ways that ensure our future as a people. Whether it be the State of Oklahoma's schools in which we teach Osage, the federal government agencies with which we continue to forge agreements, the health industries' bureaucracies we are navigating, or the banks from which we seek loans, Osages must act consciously and carefully to step around the many colonial land mines that litter our path. Finding ways to bring forward our language, self-governance, health, and land in this moment, however, requires creative tactics and diverse strategies. In the Osage Nation it has required strategically utilizing many of the things that colonial discourses say Indigenous peoples can't handle or shouldn't be involved with, including technologies, extractive industries, bureaucracy, and capitalism. Ultimately, moving the Osage Nation into the future means enacting our vital relations to foster respect, responsibility, order, and layering.

CHAPTER ONE

Language

"Language Is the Main Artery of the Tribe"

In the summer of 2004, my father convinced me to return from graduate school at the University of Florida to Oklahoma, where I had been raised, to speak with Osage leadership about legislation that was pending before the US Congress. The Osage Tribal Council was advocating for the passage of "An Act to Reaffirm the Inherent Sovereign Rights of the Osage Tribe to Determine Its Membership and Form of Government."[1] This bill would reaffirm Osage sovereign rights that the federal courts had ruled were extinguished by Congress. For nearly a century, Osage government operated with federal intrusion and control into its daily operations that no other tribal nation in the continental United States had endured. Congress had only reaffirmed tribal inherent sovereign rights on one other occasion, the so-called *Duro* fix legislation that reaffirmed that tribes can exercise criminal jurisdiction over all Indians, not just its own citizens. The prospects of enactment of our sovereign rights were uncertain.[2]

My father insisted that once the law was passed, the Osages would establish a government reform process, which I needed to document for my dissertation. I remained skeptical that the timing and logistics would work out. While not as crazy as his idea of building the world's largest roller coaster in Tulsa, which would carry people from the airport to downtown with a loop through Oral Roberts's praying hands, it still felt like a long shot that everything would fall into place within the next couple of years during my PhD study. Though the roller coaster never came to fruition, Congress passed the Osage sovereignty bill, and I was able to do my dissertation research on the writing of the 2006 constitution.

Over that initial summer, Osage leadership expressed full support for my research on the potential reform, but also made it clear to me that it was just one piece of the nation building they were enacting. Since the Thirty-First Tribal Council had been elected in 2002, they had greatly expanded the Nation's revenue through the creation of casinos. From 1906 to 2002, the Osage government had primarily been focused on leasing the mineral estate and holding the Bureau of Indian Affairs managers accountable, with the proceeds from oil and gas being distributed to those with a headright interest. Only $1 million from minerals proceeds was available for operating the Osage government, so the tribe relied on federal funds to carry out federal programs for Indians. This made it difficult to support initiatives envisioned by Osages.

Now, however, the Thirty-First Tribal Council had a chance to create the kinds of initiatives they felt the Nation needed. One of the first programs they created was the Osage Nation Language Department. After I met with the Osage Tribal Council to explain my research, one of the council members, Jerry Shaw, who spearheaded the effort to create the Language Department, invited me to join him in visiting the language program. For Shaw, the Osage language was a core piece of moving the Osage Nation into the future, and something I needed to include in my research.

As I walked into the vacant strip mall office in downtown Pawhuska that day, it was hard to imagine the thriving community space it would become.[3] Osage Language Department director Herman Mongrain "Mogri" Lookout and cultural director Eddy Red Eagle Jr. sat on metal chairs, huddled around one end of a plastic folding table that was the only furniture in the room. Describing the program's founding, Lookout explained, "It took Shaw two years to talk me into creating a language program. I told him I had never done anything like that. Shaw said he could get me training and people. There was nothing here but cobwebs and dust. I didn't know what I was going to do, but I knew Osage."[4] Lookout also knew the weight and challenges of the work he had taken on, and he proceeded with great caution. He was going to have to pull together all the resources he could muster to connect himself and other Osages with our language.

As I entered behind Councilman Shaw, Lookout called us over and pressed Play on the oversize metal tape player. We all listened closely to the crackling voice of Harry Red Eagle Sr. speaking confidently from the other end of what seemed like an impossible distance. His cadence immediately drew me in. While not my first time hearing someone speak the Osage language, it was the first time I really heard its distinctive rhythm and flow. We all marveled at the voice from 1965 and what it brought to us. The tape was one of several that had been donated to the nascent Language Department, which Lookout had invited Shaw and Eddy Red Eagle to review with him. The recording and the other resources Lookout was able to collect provided vital tools for building the language program.

For many Osages, our language is at the core of what it means to build our Nation in the face of ongoing colonialism. For many Indigenous peoples, reconnecting with our languages is a way of connecting with a part of who we are, a part that the US government has attempted to destroy. Given colonial policies, especially mandatory schooling, few Osages after the 1880s were raised speaking the language in their daily lives. By 2004 there were no first-language speakers able to teach the language, and thus Lookout was reliant on his and others' written records and recordings.

When he founded the language program, Lookout was both a roadman for the Native American Church and headman of the Pawhuska district 𐓁𐓬𐓪𐓤𐓬 (annual dances).[5] He was thus deeply invested in carrying Osage practices and values forward. He saw the language as a core part of this work. In the years since 2004, Lookout has often explained his motivations, saying, "The ways we used to live are built into those words. . . . The best way to teach them those ways is to teach them the language."[6] Lookout saw it as the Nation's duty to document and preserve the Osage language and hoped that by teaching the language he could ensure that Osage ways of understanding the world were carried forward.

The Osage language was deeply connected in many peoples' minds with the future of the Nation. In one of the interviews I conducted during the writing of our 2006 constitution, Lookout explained to me that to be a Nation, we had to have three things: a land base, a language, and a culture.[7] Based on his and other Osage feedback, the writers of the 2006 constitution codified a strong commitment to the language, writing in Article XVI that "the Osage Nation *shall* protect and promote the language, culture, and traditional ways of the Osage people."[8] This language was intentionally chosen from various options as the strongest mandate they could put in the constitution. Vann Bighorse, the director of the language program from 2018 to 2022, summarized the motivations behind this mandate: "Culture and language are what makes us a people. Without our culture and language, who are we? We will lose our identity. Language is the main artery of the Tribe."[9] More than just preserving something from the past, languages are frequently named as a central component of ensuring the future of Indigenous peoples.[10] Our Native languages are seen as a vital life flow that sustains the health and even essence of our nations.

This chapter tells the story of the Osage Nation's efforts to reconnect with our language by building a governmental program and explains why this work was prioritized by the Nation, as well as the challenges it entails. I begin by highlighting Osage theories of *respect* as a vital relation our language teaches us. The concept of respect is often used by Osages to define what it means to be in good relations with each other, and thus what it means to carry the Nation forward. Weaving together Osage discussions with Indigenous studies literature, I demonstrate that Indigenous people have our own motivations behind and understanding of language reclamation. Unlike external efforts by linguists, the creation of an Osage Nation language program is enabling us to build a relationship with our language on our own terms. For many Osages, it is what our language teaches us about good relations that will ensure a strong future for our Nation.

I then turn to a history of the onslaught of colonial policies that disrupted Osage lifeways and positioned colonial education, a constitutional government, and English usage as the best path that Osages could take going forward. While these colonial policies and practices were designed to eliminate our language, lifeways, and land base, we were able to use them to ensure our future. I then share the family language stories of several former and current Osage language program employees, demonstrating the ways Osages have remained connected to the language despite these larger colonial trends. Our relationship with the language was fundamentally disrupted, but not severed. Osages have remained committed to the language, especially during community gatherings, and this relationship has helped Osages to maintain self-respect in the face of colonial affronts to our ways of life.

Finally, this chapter discusses the technologies the Osage Nation language program is using to build new relations with the language, including classes, a writing system, and various digital tools. Embracing the latest technologies is nothing new for Osages but rather part of what moving to a new country has long involved. Connecting with the Osage language, however, is deeply challenging not only because of our lack of fluent speakers but also because of tensions over how to best bring the language forward. At stake in these debates is ultimately what it looks like to create a respectful relationship with the language going forward. The core question that Osages and those pursuing other language reclamation projects must answer is, What elements of the language must stay the same, and what can change to meet current needs? To move the language to this new country, Osage language program employees are often turning to their own understandings of what it means to form respectful relations. In sharing these debates, my hope is that future language leaders can understand some of the tensions at play in this difficult work and how some language leaders are making these decisions.

"Always Keep Respect in Front of You"

Osage language leaders frequently name respect as a core part of what the language offers our people and what needs to be centered in building our relations with the language. Respect is thus both an end goal and a tool. It is a motivation for learning and teaching the language, but also a guide for how to go about building the vital relations that will sustain Osages as a people. This section will describe Osage and Indigenous studies theories of respect and how framing the language program around building respectful relations shifts the language reclamation process. Osage language leaders are often refusing a deficit mindset that perceives the language as having been destroyed by colonialism and are instead working to connect themselves and others with the language and its teachings. Such an approach shows us how to respect ourselves and our ways of being in the face of ongoing colonial efforts to shame and eliminate who we are. Respectful relations are thus a vital part of Osage nation building.

Respect has been at the core of many of my discussions with Lookout over the years. He has frequently contrasted Osage ideas of respect, which entails extensive rules, with the American values of freedom and liberty. In the fall of 2022, during one of our weekly Zoom discussions, he succinctly summarized these ideas: "When those English people came over, they had a way of talking, they didn't have anything else here and they weren't respectful. They call it freedom; to do whatever you want. Here things are in turmoil because if it feels good, do it."[11] Before the late nineteenth century, Osage governance consisted of not only village-based leadership but also a separate council that would meet, reflect on the world, and create elaborate protocols to address the things creating strife.[12] In the extreme disconnect colonizers created when they came to the United States, they severed their own relations to place and have attempted to sever ours. Once they were here, colonizers frequently made decisions that privileged their own personal liberty above respectful relations. Lookout worried that without the protocols that Osages developed over centuries, which he framed through the idea of respect, our world was becoming increasingly tumultuous.

As Lookout argued, these distinct values, glossed here as respect and freedom, are so core to Osages and colonizers, respectively, that they are evident in our ways of speaking. Lookout would regularly name these linguistic differences in our weekly discussions and in his teaching. One way in which he talked about this was through evidentiality. "There are a lot more evidentials in Osage. Way more than English, with the 'it' everywhere. That relieves you. . . . There is ambiguity in English. You see this with a lot of politicians never answering questions. They get away with a lot of things."[13] *Evidentiality* is a linguistic term for how much evidence a language requires of the speaker for any given statement.[14] For example, evidentials can mark whether an event was seen or heard and by whom. It is a way that languages demonstrate what kinds of relationships matter to their speakers and what kinds are irrelevant. As Lookout is pointing out here, very few relationships matter to English speakers, especially when compared with the ones necessary in the Osage language.

Another way the Osage language embodies relationality is through the interconnection of its morphemes (word parts that have their own distinct meanings). Linguists categorize Osage as an agglutinative language, meaning morphemes have to be paired together to get the full meaning.[15] English, on the other hand, more often relies on single morphemes that stand on their own.[16] Lookout described this difference: "That seems to be how Osage works . . . to put all the words together to get a meaning. You have different things you can say that mean a lot. . . . English's concept is one word at a time." Lookout frequently described the Osage language as painting a picture, which could not be separated out into its distinct swappable parts like English. What mattered with the Osage language were thus the relationships between things, more than the isolated components. In the very structure of the language, interdependence is central to Osage, while independence is crucial to English. From these discussions, Lookout argued that we needed as a Nation to reconnect with Osage ideas of respectful relations, which the language could teach us.

Many scholars in the field of Indigenous studies have made similar observations about the relational nature of Indigenous knowledge systems.[17] As Kiowa Tribe of Oklahoma scholar Robin Zape-tah-hol-ah Starr Minthorn and US scholar Alicia Fedelina Chávez succinctly put it, "Indigenous epistemology is a system of knowledge built on relationships between things, rather than on the things themselves."[18] Iñupiaq scholar Edna Ahgeak MacLean demonstrates the ways this relationality shows up in the Iñupiaq language, including in the number of demonstrative pronouns used to describe relationships to the land.[19] As in the Osage context, the language is not only an example of what relationships matter but a tool for teaching how to enact relations of respect in that context.

Lookout was not the only Osage who placed a high premium on relations of respect. Red Eagle discussed in-depth the importance of strong relations of respect with me in July 2016. Describing Osage governance before the twentieth century and why it worked so well, he explained, "There was something beyond trust and biological relationship, stronger than blood. That is ꝄꞦꞨꞨ. . . . Everybody knew what they needed to do and they had their role. The communication was awesome. That deep relationship made it fluid and trustworthy."[20] The Osage idea of ꝄꞦꞨꞨ is most often translated as "respect," but it is referring to a system of relationships within the clan structure that help people to understand their role in the larger order. To communicate in Osage, you have to both understand your relationship to the speaker and speak using the protocols mandated by that relationship. Built directly into and mandated by the language, ⵙⴱⵍⵔ is another way the language provides a guide for what is involved in respectful relations.

The Osage clan structure undergirded our sociopolitical-religious life before the twentieth century. Oral histories of the Osage Nation describe the sociopolitical structure of the Nation as consisting of multiple groups, including the ⵙⴰⵌⴰ (Earth People) and the ⵒⵏⵣⵔ (Sky People). Within these groups there were multiple clans representing the spectrum of life on earth. Each had their own designated role to play and specific location within the geographical layout of the houses in each village. The ⵤⵔⵌⵔⵣⵏⵌⴰ (little old men/leaders) also assigned each clan a specific role to play in yearly ceremonial gatherings, so that they all had to come together, resolve any standing disputes, and work together.[21]

To be a whole person, Osages needed to understand their relations to each other and the world around them, which was accomplished through clan names. Red Eagle, who named me and my family members, described the importance of being part of these clans to Osages historically and today. Until you had a name, Red Eagle explained, you were not considered a person, because no one could understand their relationships to you. With that naming comes a dense web of relations. In your family, the name shows birth order and the attributes you were intended to have.[22] My daughter and I were given the name ⵏⵓⵇⴺⵔ, which Red Eagle translated as "looking at the eagle." During our naming, he described how the first daughter is supposed to be in communion with the eagle and then tell the community what she has learned. He went on to say that some people understand first daughters as bossy, but that is their role in the family structure.[23] In the Nation, the clan name also gives you a set of relations and roles. Clan names have been a powerful way in which Osages have maintained an understanding of our place in the larger order of the Nation despite ongoing change. It was how respect was generated and brought forward.

This idea of ⵙⴱⵍⵔ is at the core of the phrase "relations of respect." I am using this English phrase to avoid taking ⵙⴱⵍⵔ out of the context of the Osage clan structure but still honor the teachings it offers.[24] Describing what it means to be in good relations within the Osage context, Red Eagle privileged the idea of respect. "The word 'respect' was used universally by eldership to convey 'humbleness' in relation to God's sacred creation(s). With these ⵙⴱⵍⵔ, and even within oneself, the goal was to live the attribute of respect in daily practice. Hence, the common phrase, 'Always keep respect in front of you.'"[25] Respect is something to strive toward and be guided by. Understanding the limits of what you know while remaining committed to getting it right signals modesty's respect and persistence. Respect is thus a core piece of what this book theorizes as the Osage Nation's vital relations.

This notion of relations of respect also mirrors more general discussion in Indigenous studies about being "relatives with responsibility." Pasqua First Nation scholar Margaret Kovach writes about the importance of relational responsibilities in Indigenous communities, noting that "responsibility implies knowledge and action. It seeks to genuinely serve others, and is inseparable from respect and reciprocity."[26] Knowledge is required to serve others, because without that knowledge your actions might cause harm. Core to respectful relations, then, is constantly reflecting on the impacts of your current protocols and making sure that they are fostering a just world. In this way, the local needs of the nation are privileged rather than undermined through the enactment of respectful relations.

Like Lookout, Red Eagle saw the Osage language as the main tool for our Nation to understand and bring respect forward. As he explained to me, "The Osage language is what ties all this together. It is the conduit. If you take the language out, then you lose that knowledge."[27] There is extensive literature in the field of Indigenous studies that demonstrates the widespread belief across many communities that languages contain unique worldviews, ways of thinking, and connections across time and place.[28] While this literature tends to be deficit focused, naming all that we are losing without the regular usage of these languages, Red Eagle is instead focused on the future potential of the language as a teacher. Not only is he arguing here that the language is our primary teacher for ideas of respect but, in naming the language as a conduit, he is arguing that the Osage language has a vital life even though we have no fluent speakers. Fluent speakers are only one marker of how a language's life can be measured.[29] Osages have maintained a relationship with the language through active study as well as through ceremonial and community event usage. Languages can connect us with important teachings and thus have a powerful existence outside of daily life usage.

In finding ways to stay connected with our language, Osages are demonstrating the inaccuracy of linguistic pronouncements of language death. Miami Tribe of Oklahoma scholar Wesley Leonard directly critiques linguists who describe languages without first-language speakers as "dead" or "extinct." He writes, "No longer do we accept the 'e-word' (extinct) to describe *myaamia*; we instead use the term *sleeping* to refer to its status during its period of dormancy, noting that this term is not only more socially appropriate but also more accurate in that our language was never irretrievably lost."[30] Losing the last first-language speaker is in no way equivalent to losing the last animal in a species. The concept of extinction assumes not only that there is no way to reverse these processes but that such loss happens naturally or is the fault of Indigenous peoples ourselves.[31] Such terms contribute directly to settler colonialism's project of elimination, furthering the rhetoric that Indigenous peoples have gone or are going extinct.[32] Signaling the ongoing and future potential of this work, I frame the Osage language program's efforts as building respectful relations with the Osage language.

The phrase "building respectful relations" foregrounds the importance of having Osage language leaders as the ones defining the research and teaching priorities for the Osage language. Describing the work of non-Osage linguists, Lookout frequently lamented their focus on translation, extraction, and categorization. "Linguists structure your curriculum on translation alone. It doesn't work. You can say that, but it is different. . . . I can say a lot of things that won't correlate in English. . . . When I teach, I am trying to get that abstract meaning to people. I am working to bridge that gap."[33] He worried that those who aren't raised in the community and are relying on English-language translation alone can only bring English frames, and thus values, to the language. Relying on translation would make it impossible to use language to transfer deeper lessons about respectful relations to the Osage people.

Osages are not alone in rejecting hierarchical approaches and goals set by linguists and other outsiders.[34] US scholar Richard Henne-Ochoa, Cowichan Tribes scholar Emma Elliott-Groves, and their coauthors reject the ways that linguists have too often turned Indigenous languages into codes removed from their cultural contexts, describing this as another form of erasure.[35] They discuss the importance of linguists working with languages to engage Indigenous ways of knowing and being, contending that "those engaged in language reclamation efforts need to recognize and understand community-based knowledge, including relational dynamics, and how these understandings facilitate Indigenous language learning and education more broadly. . . . Discourses of respect teach everyone about the social structures of their place in that community."[36] Not only do languages teach what respect looks like in a particular community, but building respectful relations is an important method that Native nations' language programs are insisting on more often.

As more Native nations create their own language programs, they are taking control of both the methods and goals for their relationships with our languages. In the context of the Miami Tribe of Oklahoma's language program,

Leonard writes about the importance of moving away from linguistically driven models that focus on grammar in favor of programs based on community history and current needs.[37] Similarly, Cheyenne River Sioux Tribe scholar Tasha Hauff writes about the Standing Rock Sioux Tribe's language program, asserting that "a tribal government can function as the central organizing force that can ascertain community wants and needs and then flex political muscles so that those needs can be met."[38] Native-nation-led language programs seek to more directly address the larger colonial context that has created language disconnection, and they do so by continually recentering respect for the language and its teachings. This chapter will use this frame of respectful relations to understand the work the Osage Nation language program is undertaking in the face of ongoing colonial efforts that have attempted to foster disrespect.

"An Extraordinary Social Device"

Throughout our history, Osages have made significant changes in location as well as lifestyle while maintaining our distinct language and sense of peoplehood, a process Osage scholars have long narrated as "moving to a new country."[39] While debates about Osage origins continue, the most common history told of the Osage is that we are part of the Dhegiha Siouan language group, which, around A.D. 400, lived in the Ohio River valley.[40] Dhegiha people then began traveling down to the Mississippi River, ultimately moving into the area that has become known as Cahokia (current-day Saint Louis, Missouri). While other members of the Dhegiha language group left earlier, Osages did not leave the area until around 1300, moving into the central and western portions of what would become Missouri, where they were when the French began exploring the area in 1682.[41] Such changes in location had limited impact on the Osage language, which stayed very close to other Dhegiha and related Siouan languages.[42]

Contrary to the popular myth that Indigenous peoples don't embrace new technologies, archaeological evidence tells a different story.[43] Large early colonial Osage village sites in the central Missouri area all contain substantial trade goods, signaling Osages' full embrace of trade and diverse technologies. The European technology introduced at these sites includes pottery decorated through impressed fabric, guns, traps, horse bridles, iron knives, axes, awls, brass, and iron kettles.[44] While our language remained very similar to that of other related Dhegihan groups, our technologies differed. It was the Osages' ability to assimilate technologies to our own needs that enabled us to maintain our language and our peoplehood. Innovation and change have always been a fundamental part of what ensured an Osage future.

Throughout this period, the Osage language and lifeways were taught through immersion and ceremony. Ceremonial practices offered core educational lessons, especially about the value of the community and the role individuals were to play in that community. Naming practices, for example, demonstrated the child's place within family, clan, and thus the Nation, with specific roles being assigned based on birth order, location within the clan, and clan role. As anthropologist Garrick Bailey writes, "From sunrise until sunset, from birth to death, in all endeavors—war, peace, hunting, farming, child rearing—Osage life was one continuous flow of rituals."[45] The robust calendar of rituals offered plenty of opportunities to learn one's place, the values of the community, and how to best maintain proper relations of respect. These practices allowed Osages to navigate many obstacles while maintaining our language and cohesion as a community.

Colonial disruptions to our language and lifeways began as incomprehensible land theft. At the end of the eighteenth century, Osages controlled much of the land in what would later become Oklahoma, Kansas, Missouri, and Arkansas. From 1808 until 1839, seven treaties stripped Osage control over ninety-six million acres of land, representing 75 percent of the Osage land base; in return, we received only $166,000 in cash, annuities, livestock, and farming supplies.[46] The end of treaty making did not stop Osage land theft but instead further facilitated it. After years of negotiation and stalling tactics on the part of Osage leaders, the federal government again forced Osages to move to a smaller territory in the 1870s, this time a 1.5-million-acre reservation in Indian Territory. Furthermore, the bison hunts that had been a staple of Osage sustenance, survival, and lifeways were no longer feasible. Not only were Osage hunts limited by the vast land theft and direct orders from the commissioner of Indian affairs that forbade the hunt, but intentional overhunting by white people reduced the bison population in the nineteenth century from at least 30 million to just 456 wild bison.[47]

These losses of lands and lifeways were substantially exacerbated by colonial diseases (influenza, cholera, smallpox, measles, and pneumonia), which decimated the population and left just 1,950 Osages in 1882 from approximately 10,000 in 1830.[48] Such cataclysmic losses were a direct result of colonial policy that forced other Native peoples onto Osage land and failed to enforce promises to keep white settlers out of Osage territory. Before being forced onto the small reservation base, Osages had been able to avoid serious outbreaks by dispersing across large territories in smaller groups. Furthermore, the stress of removals, diminishing food supplies, and the withholding of government-promised rations further exacerbated Osage health problems, weakening immunity and increasing the likelihood of fatalities. Not only did this 80 percent loss in population have a marked psychological impact, but it meant that the existing sociopolitical-religious structure was no longer feasible, given the loss of knowledge keepers and hereditary leaders.[49]

In the face of this colonial devastation, Osages responded with a more extreme move to a new country, replacing our hereditary political system with a constitutional government. This happened in fits and starts from a first, abandoned constitutional government in 1861 to a more fully embraced one in 1881.[50] Such an extreme move was made under the direct pressure of various Indian agents and had almost immediate impacts on education and Osage language usage.

A significant step toward embracing a new constitutional government occurred in 1876, shortly after Osages arrived in the diminished reservation land in what would become Oklahoma. Agent Cyrus Beede recalled finding the existing Osage government in disarray due to a variety of factors, including an unsuccessful bison hunt, the federal government's inexplicable failure to deliver most of our treaty provisions or disperse the interest from land sales, our resulting inability to pay off the over $12,000 in debts to traders, and the recent death of hereditary chief Pawhuska VI. Responding to this ꞰᴧᴐᴨꞪᴧ (chaos), Beede writes, "one of my first efforts was to create harmony therein, and to this end I recommended that they choose a governor from among the leading men of one of the two factions and a chief counselor from the other, and that a business-committee of five leading men be appointed, representing both parties, to be associated with the governor and chief counselor in the transaction of all necessary business with the agent and the Government."[51] This supposed "harmony" was created at the expense of the system of band chiefs who had generally operated independently and outside the control of the agent. Such moves to consolidate dispersed authority into one tribal government was a strategy federal officials utilized throughout Indian Territory to gain more control.[52] Beede went on to write that this system enabled him to transact necessary business, delivering several Osages suspected of horse theft to Fort Lewis for prosecution.[53]

The direct link between establishing a government recognizable to the US government and the enforcement of US laws is vital to note, as it represents a shift not only in how crime was punished but in what constituted a crime within the Osage Nation. It also demonstrates that officials in these positions were quick to do the bidding of the Indian agent, a fundamental shift from previous systems of Osage government. Unsurprisingly, mission-educated English-speaking Osages were the ones who came into leadership positions during this time.[54]

Another, more Osage-driven catalyst for both a constitutional government and English-speaking leadership came in 1879 when an Osage delegation was able to successfully lobby for themselves in Washington, D.C. The existing system of rations created by the federal government was not only unreliable and inadequate, but it failed to meet the treaty promises. Osages resented that all our payments were being delivered as rations, requiring Osages to walk up to twenty miles to be "fed like dogs."[55] Osages sent a delegation to Washington, D.C., which was able to successfully lobby for direct payments of $160 to each man, woman, and child annually. These funds made Osages less dependent on farming and other agent-initiated activities, as it provided them with ample funds to feed, clothe, and care for themselves outside the agency. Such a success demonstrated to Osages that English-speaking leadership could succeed where the existing Osage government structure or a reliance on federal agents alone could not. The individual payments also directly undermined the existing Osage leadership and government structure, as band chiefs had previously been charged with distributing funds and rations.[56]

As in earlier moments of community ᖾᐱᒡᏂᐱ, many Osage leaders during this period embraced change to restore our vital relations. During a general council meeting in the winter of 1881, a large committee was created to draft a new constitution. Part of what Osages advocated for at this time was a new means to settle our own disputes, pass our own laws, and enforce these laws.[57] Two members of the committee went to visit the Cherokee, whose constitutional government was at this time recognized and largely trusted by the federal government to manage its own affairs. A fundamental part of this move to a new country, like those that came before, was observing the world to find the tools necessary to carry our vital relations forward. Ultimately, the Osage constitution used the Cherokee constitution as a guide but included some additional provisions and excluded others, especially those that would have outlawed existent Osage practices.[58] Osage scholar Robert Warrior has written about the 1881 constitution as a powerful example of moving to a new country. Warrior points out that the process of refashioning, while sometimes appearing as "mimicry," was done to ensure the continuity of "a self-determined, self-imagined, autonomous Osage Nation."[59]

While the 1881 Osage Constitution was a vital tool that carried the Osage Nation forward, it could not stop, and may have even facilitated, federal policies such as colonial schooling, which directly affected the Osage language. In 1884, just three years after the passage of the constitution, Agent Miles was able to convince the government to pass a mandatory education bill, which withheld from any noncompliant families the annuities Osages were now dependent on after the demise of the bison hunt.[60] Describing this law, Bailey writes, "Laws were passed to make agency policy legal or at least give it some semblance of legality."[61] While many Osages embraced the constitutional government as a system to give them more control over their own lives in these chaotic times, this government also facilitated many of the devastating policies Osages had long been fighting against, such as colonial schooling.

This mandatory education had the immediate intended effect, ensuring that most Osage children raised after 1883 were fluent English speakers. Writing about the success of the mandatory education law, Agent Miles states, "I have long believed that to educate the Indian was the only way to solve the much perplexed Indian problem. . . . In one generation the Indians would be an English-speaking people. . . . They would be ready for citizenship."[62] Education, fluency in the English language, and US citizenship were all part of the federal government's effort to eliminate Indigenous peoples from the land settlers would then claim for themselves. Commonly referred to as assimilation, the logic held that settlers could do away with Native practices if they could destroy their political hold on the territory.[63] Mandatory schooling, with its focus on English education, had a devastating impact on the language. Children were taken out of the community system of education in which the Osage language and vital relations were embedded.

The enactment of the 1881 government was not the only move Osages made during this period. Osages created a host of new practices that were intended to carry us and our language forward. Whether it was the ᏁᎶ̇ᏍᏦᎩᎾ, weddings, funerals, namings, Native American Church ceremonies, or community meals, Osages maintained a sense of self by bringing our vital relations and language forward in these new spaces. Anthropologists Daniel Swan and Jim Cooley argue that "our examination of Míchi(n) weddings and the Ilo(n)shka [dances] identifies the values of order, deliberate action, and sacrifice for the greater good as consistent factors that have governed Osage Society over the past two hundred years."[64] These values are core elements of Osage understandings of respect. While navigating settler-colonial structures has meant that Osages have had to change our practices drastically over time, the principle of moving guides us to seek change in a deliberative way that upholds rather than destroys our language and respectful relations.

The 𐓵𐓘𐓸𐓤𐓘 are a powerful example of moving to a new country and have been a key setting in which the Osage language has continued to be spoken and respectful relations taught.[65] 𐓵𐓘𐓸𐓤𐓘 began in the mid-1880s when the Grass Dance was gifted from the Kaw (Kansa) and Ponca. As part of this process, Osages incorporated various aspects of older religious practices to create our own dance. In an interview with Dan Swan, an Osage elder from Hominy, Leroy Logan explains, "They put those Waxobes in there. Those sacred bundles, sacred medicines, things they understood about, they put them in the Ilonshka. They used that dance that way, [to] take [the] place of what they had."[66] Swan goes on to cite other elders who spoke about the "medicine in this drum," as well as the "strict rules and regulations" and the "ceremonial division of labor found in the Osage tribal religion" the dance follows.[67] In similar ways, the Osage language was woven into the dance, especially in moments such as the passing of the drum, bringing a new male into the dance, or gifting during the family songs.

This ceremony continues to the present day, taking place in our three villages, most frequently during the month of June. For over 120 years, Osages have united to celebrate our community and, in doing so, have taught new generations respectful relations. Sharing what he was taught about the dances, Osage leader Fred Lookout said, "We were told that a select group . . . created an extraordinary social device that transmitted a powerful spiritual foundation. It encompassed such force that today it is the basis for the perpetuation of all of our Osage values."[68] 𐓵𐓘𐓸𐓤𐓘 has become a core tool by which Osages pass on our language, knowledge, history, philosophy, and respectful relations to younger generations.

In particular, the dances became a key place where the language was expected to be spoken. In describing his own language journey, Osage graphic designer and photographer Ryan RedCorn explains that around the year 2000, Lookout gave a speech during 𐓵𐓘𐓸𐓤𐓘 saying that if Osages did not invest in learning the language now, it was going to be lost forever. "That got everyone going. It made the difference to me. I could not imagine the dances without the language."[69] 𐓵𐓘𐓸𐓤𐓘 thus became a vehicle that not only carried the language forward but, in the minds of some Osages, necessitated its continued existence.

Osages have long used the strategy of moving to a new country to maintain respectful relations with our language. Throughout our many adaptations, we have ensured that the language played an important role in our lives, helping to guide us in our many decisions. During the late nineteenth and early twentieth centuries, when colonial disruptions reached a fever pitch, Osages embraced English as part of our survival strategy. While during this period our relationship to the Osage language waned, it still held an important place in many Osage lives through our unique practices. Turning from this more general history to family histories, the following section will demonstrate how specific Osage families overcame these colonial pressures.

"Something That Is Going to Do You Some Good"

Osage family language histories provide a window into the variety of experiences Osages have had with the language and important examples of what it has meant for different families to move the language to a new country. While everyone I spoke with named the pressures their families faced to learn English, Osage families responded to these pressures in different ways. This section narrates several family histories of Osage Language Department employees. These stories demonstrate not only the kinds of ongoing relations Osage families have had with the language but also the shifting understandings of what was going to be beneficial for Osages. In the face of colonial pressures to shame Osages for our language and practices, these Osages have committed their lives to building respectful relations with the language.

Herman Lookout, like most Osages born in the 1940s, did not grow up speaking the language, despite being surrounded by his parents and grandparents speaking it.[70] In addition to his being in English-only schools, his parents also spoke English to him at home. While they never discussed their exact reasons, Lookout suspects they wanted their children to learn English so they wouldn't be taken advantage of by the growing non-Osage presence on the reservation.[71] Despite the Osage reservation land only being distributed among the people listed on the 1906 Osage allotment roll, the 1920s oil boom on the reservation brought many non-Osages to the area, quickly shifting Osages to a minority in our own territory.[72] The reality of Osage vulnerability became clear during the 1920s Reign of Terror. At least sixty Osages were murdered, and millions of dollars were lost to price-gouging shop owners, corrupt legal guardians, murderous spouses, conspiring town officials, and indifferent and complicit law enforcement.[73] Education and the English language became vital tools for arming future generations of Osages against such corruption and violence.

While Lookout first began actively studying Osage when he was in his thirties, the prevailing attitude of this time was that the language was not where he should focus his efforts. His parents were still around, and he was able to learn from them and his other relatives. One day, however, when he went to his uncle to ask him about some Osage words, his uncle told him: "The Osage language is dead, let it go. Let it die. Go learn Spanish, learn French, something that is going to do you some good."[74] While the Osage language continued to have life, especially at community events such as ᓄᒼᨱᔕᎵ and funerals, his uncle's words discouraged Lookout enough that he put his language study away, at least for a while.

Despite putting his books away in the 1970s, Lookout never shook the desire to connect with the Osage language. Taking language classes when he could, he was able to keep his learning going. Then, during a New Year's Eve hand game in 2000, Red Eagle challenged everyone in attendance to learn the language.[75] As discussed earlier, for Red Eagle, language was at the core of Osage cultural practices. He would frequently profess, "English can't get you there. Osage can."[76] This insistence that the language was a core part of Osage ways has motivated generations of Osages to connect with the language. After spending the whole day and night talking and planning, Lookout worked with Red Eagle to bring together a group of Osages who wanted to learn to pray. Lookout had learned to pray from his father and was confident in his ability to pass on those protocols. Once they learned the core elements of an Osage prayer, this group wanted to learn to speak conversationally. Lookout was determined to learn along with them. He collected and taught sentences from native language speakers who had spoken Osage exclusively in their youth.

During this time Jerry Shaw, an Osage running for the Thirty-First Tribal Council, approached Lookout, saying that it was time to put Osage ways into the government.[77] From 1906 until 2004 when Shaw was elected, the Osage Tribal Council had been focused primarily on the mineral estate, jurisdictional issues, taxation, and federal grants. The Thirty-First Tribal Council made significant changes, creating language and culture departments, opening casinos that drastically increased the tribe's revenue, and reforming the government.[78] Shaw eventually convinced Lookout to apply for the newly created director position and create the Osage Language Department.

Because of the important space Lookout and other language program employees have created, current generations of Osages are now being raised to understand that the Osage language will in fact do them good. During a 2019 language conference entitled "Our Dhegiha Children," Lookout described how, while many Osages are building a relationship with the language, the younger people are even more driven. They are demanding the things his generation had been told to leave behind. Lookout has devoted his life to shepherding core Osage spaces such as the Native American Church and 𐓣𐓧𐓪́𐓯𐓤𐓘, ensuring that the language continues to have a key place in them. As will be discussed in the remainder of this chapter, his work with the Osage orthography and his continued dedication to building the Language Department are what have enabled him and others to build respectful relations with the language.

One of the first employees Lookout hired was Debra Atterberry (then Littleton), an Osage woman who had grown up hearing her older family members speak the Osage language fluently.[79] While she did not seek out a relationship with the Osage language, the language found her. At a cultural event in late 2004, Lookout approached Atterberry, saying he needed her help creating symbols to represent Osage sounds. Atterberry was skeptical of what she had to offer, as she was not a trained linguist, nor did she speak or study the Osage language. She had taught for fifteen years, teaching first graders to read and business professionals to write shorthand. While these are not the kind of experiences usually sought after by language departments creating a writing system for the first time, Atterberry's deep connections to Osage practices and her unique set of skills all proved very useful in developing the Osage orthography.

After working at the Osage language program, Atterberry went on to be elected to the Osage Nation Congress before serving in various roles for the Chief's Office. Her primary project was the creation of the Osage Nation's own school system, which actively incorporated the Osage language. Atterberry is now running Project PISTONS (Providing Instructional Supports to Osage Nation and Schools), a program that supports Osage County school districts' prekindergarten students through third graders in their reading journey. This program crucially incorporates reading in the Osage language, specifically using the orthography Atterberry helped to create. Despite her original skepticism about working with the language, it continues to be a core part of all the work she does.

As random as Atterberry's path with the language felt to her, I recently came across a letter that demonstrated to both of us that it was, in fact, envisioned by her great-great-grandfather 𐓷𐓘𐓯𐓪𐓯𐓛. In 1881 𐓷𐓘𐓯𐓪𐓯𐓛 decided to send his son, Louis Bighorse, to Carlisle Indian School. Writing to his son in 1883, 𐓷𐓘𐓯𐓪𐓯𐓛 envisioned exactly the kind of work Atterberry would devote her life to. In the letter, 𐓷𐓘𐓯𐓪𐓯𐓛 tells his son that he sent him to this school so "that you would understand books." He goes on to say, "So I planned for you, my son. As soon as you have learned how to use books, send me a letter with my Osage name written. . . . Those here, in the Osage land, know nothing.

Even he, who is a very important man, is not apt to accomplish anything."[80] ⅄⅄₷Oₑ₷Ɑ sent his son to boarding school not because he was forced to but because he wanted his son, and Osages more generally, to learn how to use English and the knowledge contained within books. ⅄⅄₷Oₑ₷Ɑ recognized that these were necessary tools for navigating the current world.

Importantly, however, this is not a story of assimilation but of moving. ⅄⅄₷Oₑ₷Ɑ's request to see his Osage name written signals a desire to maintain his and Osages' unique identity in the face of colonial pressures. Boarding school here becomes a key location where Osages are sent to gain the skills necessary to lead the Osage people. Given the challenges faced by Osage leadership at the time, literacy was a vital tool for ensuring the future of the Osage Nation. Books were a new technology that Osages were eager to embrace.[81] Even so, what the father wanted was to see his Osage name written. Atterberry's path of teaching children to read, creating an orthography to write the Osage language, developing a school in which Osage children can be taught both how to use books and how to write in Osage, and then taking that knowledge to Osage children outside the school system is a powerful manifestation of the vision ⅄⅄₷Oₑ₷Ɑ laid out in this letter to his son. While it is easy to see the disconnect boarding schools created with the Osage language, this family history demonstrates ongoing relations of respect with the language despite and through schools.

Other Osage families actively worked to ensure that the Osage language and practices would be carried forward. Veronica Pipestem, who began working for the Language Department in 2007 as a curriculum specialist but who has been on contract periodically assisting language instruction since then, described her ancestors' various strategies for ensuring that core aspects of Osage ways were part of each generation's life. Pipestem said that her great-grandfather Wilson Kirk helped to bring the older ways into ΩᏞOₑ₷ᏦᏛ. Her family is part of the Osage Grayhorse district and played an important role in accepting the drum from the Ponca to create the dances. Her grandfather Francis Pipestem served as headman for the dances, as did her father, F. Browning Pipestem. She understood how her great-grandparents' generation put the old ways into new forms as an act of love. They did not want to give later generations the impossible task of enacting practices that had been built to support a different way of life, but they were not willing to entirely let go of these ways either. This is what building respectful relations looks like in practice.

This commitment to finding respectful ways to bring Osage practices forward also influenced her family's language journey. Pipestem's grandmother

Rose Pipestem insisted on only speaking Osage to her son, directly in the face of fears that his education would suffer.[82] It was not until age eight when they sent him to the Chilocco Indian School that he learned English. From this strong grounding in who he was, Browning Pipestem grew up to be a nationally recognized lawyer who worked for the Bureau of Indian Affairs, the Native American Rights Fund, the Navajo Nation, the University of Oklahoma School of Law, and the Oklahoma Court of Indian Offenses.[83] He was able to pass Osage ways and aspects of the language down to his three children, Wilson (Wolf), Francis (Rock), and Veronica.

Veronica Pipestem has attempted to enact this ongoing work of moving the language to a new country through her work for the language program. This work, however, is at times marked by sadness. "I am never going to speak Osage like Rose Kirk Pipestem; I can only speak it the way I speak it. I can aspire to try to speak like her, but I am going to speak Osage the best way I know how."[84] Mourning for what has been lost, combined with a commitment to continue carrying the language forward, marks some of the conflicting emotional forces at work in building respectful relations with the language.

At the core of all the family language histories shared with me was love and care for Osage children. Speaking about how her mother and aunts grew up bilingual, Janis Carpenter, the principal teacher of the Osage Nation Language Department, said, "They wanted them to learn English for good reasons, not bad ones; to be functioning adults."[85] As the Osage reservation had become majority English speaking, it was important to Osage parents that their children were educated and spoke English, so they could thrive in the world around them. Carpenter's Osage grandfather, who had started attending boarding school at age twelve and then went on to graduate from Hominy High School, always encouraged her to pursue her education. It was with a pride in who she could be, not any sense of shame, that her family encouraged her to attend Tulsa University and become a public school teacher. The skills she learned ultimately enabled Carpenter to play a key role in moving the Osage language into the future.

As she grew up, Carpenter assumed that the language was always going to be there, but as her aunts began to pass away, she realized that it was going to require active study, preservation, and instruction. "It was hard to realize that nobody was talking Osage anymore. . . . We see and feel the sadness of this loss today in ways I don't think those earlier generations did. We now know what was being lost."[86] Six weeks after retiring from the Sand Springs Public Schools, she went to work for the Language Department, teaching Osage in local high schools. After years of not hearing the language at dances and funerals, she had begun hearing it again from Language Department students and knew that this work was essential. She is now coordinating the department's curriculum efforts in teaching not only these high school classes but also community classes. She is also working on an Osage textbook, as well as an online immersive experience. From her firsthand experiences working with high school students, Carpenter has seen how much self-respect the language, particularly the orthography, offers students. She has seen these students become young adults in the community who are using the language with their families, on social media, and at Osage events.[87] While the Carpenter family's language story is certainly marked by loss, it also demonstrates the ongoing connection and value of the language.

Some of the students in these high school classes have gone on to join the staff of the Osage Language Department, including Christopher Cote. Cote has been driven his entire life to reclaim the language and is a good example of this younger generation the Language Department has helped. At an early age his family explained to him that being Osage was something more specific than just being American Indian; that American Indians were not a race of people but many different nations. From these teachings, he was inspired to learn everything there was to learn about being Osage. He grew up in the ᴨᴄᴏꞟꞣʌ and had an Osage name, but he turned to language to deepen his understanding of what it meant to be Osage. He was able to learn from his uncle Talee Redcorn, one of the core members of Lookout's early language class, as well as the community and high school classes the Osage Nation Language Department offered.[88] Cote, now in his mid-twenties, started working at the Language Department in February 2017.

In discussing his family's language history, Cote talked about the privilege he had because he never felt pressured by his family to blend into American society.[89] He contrasted this advantage with earlier generations of his family. "My [great-great-]grandfather didn't want her [my great-grandmother] to speak with an accent because it would put more stigmatism to her life. They wanted her to be able to function in a modern [world] . . . but that's not where we are now. It's like the funnel is completely opposite. Now, the younger generation is hungry. They want to know Osage things, they don't want to be identified as Osage-American; they want to be identified as Osage."[90] Generations of his family had been able to survive and even thrive in the face of colonialism. Now the Nation had created a place where he could make a living learning and teaching the language, and he felt privileged to build a strong relationship with the language.

As these five family histories illustrate, Osages have not lost our language, nor, despite the lack of fluency, is it extinct. Colonial pressures, especially efforts to assimilate American Indians by shaming our practices, has, however, put a great deal of strain on our relationship with the Osage language. Many Osages feel this loss personally, but this serves as a motivation to build respectful relations with the language. Osages have creatively responded to colonial pressures by finding ways to both succeed in the changing world and bring the Osage language forward.

"I Want It to Go into the Future"

Even with the renewed commitment to learning and speaking our language, however, it will not be easy to move the language to this new country. This chapter will now turn to some of the challenges playing out as Osages attempt to build relations of respect through the language. From the creation of the Language Department, Lookout and other language instructors have debated whether the language program should be primarily about documenting the past language structure or creating a modern spoken language that can easily be taught to English speakers. While these two approaches appear to be in tension, both are ultimately required to ensure that the language can go forward. Language instruction is a vital tool for creating new language speakers, but this is a tall order for a language without fluent speakers. Language classes, whether taught in the community, local high schools, or the Osage Nation's 𐓷𐓘𐓤𐓪𐓨𐓤𐓘 𐓘𐓤𐓪𐓩𐓘𐓧𐓮 (Our School), pose a challenge, as teaching takes energy away from more advanced learning. Finding ways to ensure that Language Department employees have time and space to advance their own knowledge is vital to the future of the language.

Observing the fledgling state of the Osage language program during my initial visit to Lookout's office, I volunteered to help develop their technology and media. Given my bachelor of science in visual communications and experience setting up an ethnographic media lab at the University of Florida while I was doing my graduate coursework, I was familiar with computers, video, and sound technology—at least enough to help the office get equipped with a few essentials and learn how to use them. I provided some basic tutorials for a staff member on how to use their dictation software and DVD player and helped Lookout design a soundproof room they used for recording. I returned at the end of the month, throughout my dissertation research, and any time I have been in town since 2005 to discuss new equipment, participate in staff trainings in Final Cut Pro and filmmaking, and assist with language audio recordings and videos. I have listened closely to their struggles, debates, and accomplishments over these two decades. I have also seen how the language program embraced technology as a tool for bringing the language forward.

From my first visits, the massive challenges Lookout and the Osage language faced were readily apparent. The Osage Tribal Council was putting a lot of pressure on the department to teach classes: they had almost two hundred students enrolled for fall 2005 but were still trying to understand the structure of the language themselves and did not yet have a curriculum in place.[91] While Lookout had been working with a group of his students who were willing to teach introductory classes, he worried that they did not have enough of a handle on the larger structure of the language to begin teaching it and did not yet have the tools in place to teach the language to so many individuals. Many of the tapes he had were muffled and only contained speeches, leaving few resources to learn about conversational Osage.[92] As he described to me in 2005, "There are a lot of missing pieces. I don't feel like I can get back to the pure language. Even those that have documented the language have put it into white man's language."[93] Lookout's lasting concern, that he would not be able to restore the language to its precolonial form, is a devastating truth. Given the rupture that colonial policies created, there is no way of going back. In his frequent discussions of "English as big medicine," he pointed out how English corrupted Osage thought and speech, making the structure of the language even harder to see or teach.[94]

Colonial practices leave a devastating wake. Not only are languages shot through, missing vital pieces that once held them together, but contemporary enactments are easily made to look suspect and inauthentic, especially to ourselves. One of the earliest and most direct critiques of colonial authenticity comes from Vine Deloria Jr., who writes, "Indian people begin to feel that they are merely shadows of a mythical super-Indian."[95] This "mythical super-Indian" is a direct result of the research of anthropologists, which has too often focused primarily on precolonial, supposedly disappearing practices that were seen as "pure" and "authentic." Additionally, authenticity is also directly linked to colonial policies that held that they could "kill the Indian inside him and save the man" by sending Natives to boarding schools.[96] In both contexts, change could only mean moving further away from supposedly pure Native practices.

The reality of Native experience, even with colonial schools, has always been far more complex, involving negotiation and adaptation.[97] As the last section chronicled, various Osage language program employees described how their parents, grandparents, and even great-grandparents embraced schooling and English as part of what would enable Osages to thrive in the changing world. Osages have long utilized a philosophy of deliberate adaptation, or "moving to a new country," to consciously create a new order that would carry values forward.[98] Despite this reality, one of the legacies of assimilation policies is the lasting assumption that colonial impacts are permanent and totally corrupting. In creating a precolonial moment of "authenticity," narratives of assimilation create a "disdain for hybridity," in the context of the Osage language a shaming of anything that appears touched by English.[99] While "moving" offers us the ability to draw on the larger world in a way that helps us ensure our future, assimilation narratives assume any change is fatal. The danger of accepting narratives of purity and assimilation is that they work to make settler colonialism's logic of elimination a self-fulfilling prophecy.

Curriculum specialist Atterberry (then Littleton) responded in 2005 to Lookout's concerns about offering classes by pointing to several Osage practices that were not precolonial, such as the Native American Church and the 𐒰𐓊𐓆𐓘, but were nevertheless carrying the Osage people forward. She wondered why they couldn't do the same thing with the language. She argued that our understanding of the Osage language might be fragmentary and infused with English worldviews and linguistic understandings, but they could bring Osage values back into the language as they taught it. "Osage culture can be brought into the language plans. . . . We are in an extreme situation; we are going to lose all that we do have if we don't start teaching it."[100] What Atterberry was ultimately arguing for was moving the Osage language to a new country by determining how to foster respectful relations with the language. Based on her comments and other conversations, as well as pressure from the Osage Tribal Council and the public, Lookout was convinced to teach the language.

Despite knowing the limitations and concerns, I was one of many Osages who eagerly awaited language classes, which were scheduled to begin on August 17, 2005. I was amazed at how different the space felt as I walked into the Osage language program office that first evening just a little over a year after my first visit. With almost one hundred students across the three classrooms, the energy and excitement were palpable. There were also language classes happening at other locations, including the two other Osage districts of Hominy and Grayhorse. Those evening classes felt very different from the many Osage Tribal Council and Osage Government Reform Commission meetings I was attending during this period, which were frequently marked by tension and anxiety. The shared sense of devotion during the language classes was very similar to the feeling of helping the cooks during 𐒰𐓊𐓆𐓘.

There was a humbling sense of participation in something larger than yourself that was infectious.

In addition to offering community classes, the language program also worked during this period to bring the language forward by teaching it in local high schools on the reservation. The logistics involved in such a process were a significant hurdle, and it took parent pressure to create the necessary momentum. In August 2007, a concerned parent invited Lookout to attend a Skiatook School Board meeting.[101] Lookout was unable to attend, but in his place he sent Billy Proctor, who arrived at the meeting not knowing what to expect. The parent was raising his Ponca and Kiowa kids in Skiatook and used this meeting to take the school to task for not doing enough for Native kids, especially by failing to appropriately use federal funds that had been earmarked to support these children. When the superintendent asked the parent if he had any solutions, or only problems, he said that the Osage language program was ready to teach the language in their school. Surprised, Proctor agreed, despite the lack of certified teachers, accreditation process for the language, or even curriculum. Proctor and Veronica Pipestem worked quickly to get licensed, develop curriculum, and create a process of language accreditation, beginning to teach in the school just a few weeks later. Proctor described his goal for this class as "flipping the boarding school history on its head and converting everyone, even non-Osages, to speakers."[102] Most current Osage language program employees came out of this high school program, demonstrating how successful these classes are in building Osages' relationship with the language.

Despite the widespread enthusiasm for the language classes, Lookout continued to be concerned by the way many of the instructors were teaching their classes. He worried that by breaking the language down into individual words, even when the instructors relied on images rather than English, they were imposing an English understanding on the Osage language.[103] Lookout explained, "The Osage language does not represent things as single separable ideas, but through a sequence that paints a full picture. It is like when you come upon a scene and take the whole thing in with one glance."[104] His primary concern was that language learners would keep thinking in English, just substituting Osage words. He wanted to ensure that the relationship Osages were building with the language was grounded in respect, and this could not be done by memorizing vocabulary.

Lookout's concern that English language speakers would struggle with fully understanding Osage language structure stuck with him throughout his many years working at the Language Department. In 2021 he described this problem as one result of a much larger project of English colonization globally, which was even affecting places as far distant as Japan. "We don't have many models left of other kinds of order. All languages are turning their order into English. The Japanese have come here to find out how we are doing it. We are trying to find Osage order, but that is an abstract world no one alive has been in."[105] Throughout our conversations over the past two decades, Lookout described feeling consistently hindered by imperialism. The devastating impacts of colonialism not only marked a limit of what was knowable but at times imbued Lookout with an unshakable fear that reclaiming the language was ultimately an impossible task in the face of the hegemony of English.

The threat of language loss can feel like an overpowering force, creating its own momentum. Over half of the world is already speaking one of only thirteen languages. As Canadian scholars Aidan Pine and Mark Turin write, "Even conservative estimates paint a picture of near catastrophic endangerment levels, with half of the world's remaining speech forms ceasing to be used as everyday vernaculars by the end of the twenty-first century."[106] However, as the authors conclude, Indigenous peoples are proving that these odds can be beaten. Using a host of new tactics, including digital archiving software, language nests, and smartphone apps, Indigenous peoples are building our relations to our languages. The success of these efforts comes from persistence in the face of ongoing colonialism, as many communities see these languages as containing vital elements for community health and nation building.[107]

In the face of colonial pressures and fears, Lookout has persisted in studying and teaching, continuing the daily work toward his vision of building Osages' relationship with the language. On October 19, 2005, Lookout spoke to the Osage Tribal Council as part of his report on the status of a new building design. He spoke about his desire to bring forward the language from when the Osages passed into Kansas, but acknowledged that this was not the life Osages are living today. "I was asked, though, how can you talk the old language when you don't live it? And that is a good question; how can you? We have a latent language. Nowhere is Osage the primary language spoken in a home. I want the language in the home."[108] Having a language spoken daily in the place where children will most likely acquire it is a vital step for any language to go forward.

The fundamental difference between assimilation and moving is a commitment to building respectful relations with past practices and values that can guide us into the future.[109] Lookout went on to describe his vision for the language program: "We are retrieving the things that have been away. I believe that God is with us, because everything we have needed has come to us. . . . When we get the language back, I want it to go into the future."[110] Such a belief, that we have been given what we need to ensure that the language has a future, shifts the focus from the overwhelming nature of colonial theft to the resourcefulness of Osage potential. Moving thus remaps how we understand where we are and thus where we can go. In describing his hopes for the language, Lookout was moving away from the pressures of colonial authenticity that position the Osage language as only a past practice toward something that could make sense to people in our daily lives today.

"Orthography Is Sovereignty"

The most powerful example of Lookout's efforts to bring the language forward is the department's creation of an orthography. Lookout quickly realized that the largest impediment to teaching the Osage language was writing down the sounds. While there were various dictionaries and documentation efforts, there had been nothing standardized or easily accessible. Osage words were spelled inconsistently, sometimes using the International Phonic Alphabet, which most Osages could not read. Lookout explained that in his own research or classes, he would just write the words down the way he heard them, but when he looked at them later, he was not able to pronounce them consistently. His vision was to create symbols that would only have one sound, so there would be no confusion.[111] While other Native language programs, such as the Wôpanâak Language Reclamation Project, utilize an English alphabet to create a standardized orthographic system, the Osage language program created our own new symbols to solidify the separation from English.[112]

In 2004, Lookout and Atterberry worked collaboratively to develop new symbols representing each of the discrete Osage sounds they identified. These symbols usually began with a character from the English alphabet, but were modified to better represent the Osage sound. The h, for example, was tilted and given a more aspirated flowing quality, becoming "𐓷." Certain English letters were combined into a single symbol, representing their frequent combination in the Osage language, such as br becoming "ʀ" or sh becoming "ᘓ." Finally, some sounds were a blend of two English sounds, such as the "ᑫ" that sounded somewhere between the b and p in English sounds. Unlike English spelling, which requires a great deal of memorization and study, the Osage orthography allows for a more direct link between symbols and sounds.

This approach of drawing from the tools around us (in this case the English alphabet) to bring forward older practices and values is another powerful example of how respect must be centered in moving to a new country.[113] Reflecting on this project, Lookout said, "The sounds weren't being captured; you had to know the language, to know the sounds. English letters did not work for Osage. We did take a lot of liberties from English because we know how to pronounce from those letters." Like other moves, the orthography gave the language a new form to match our contemporary needs. Furthermore, a written form moves the Osage language away from the dangerous contingency so many oral languages face as they attempt to stay alive in a world inundated with written and digital communication.[114] The orthography allows the language to take a form in this new world that honors its unique sounds.

Of course, some Osages were skeptical of the new orthography. For those who had not yet learned the sounds, the new symbols made familiar Osage words impenetrable. One situation in which I saw this play out was in the writing of the 2006 constitution. The constitution included several Osage words, as when the spring and fall congressional sessions were named after the early division of the Osage into the 𐓷𐓓𐓟 (Sky People) and 𐓧𐓘𐓯𐓤𐓘 (Earth People). As part of their drafting process, the writers sent an early version of the constitution to the Language Department asking for their approval of spelling and usage.[115] Lookout responded that they would only help with the words if the writers agreed to use the new orthography. The drafters worried that the symbols were not finalized, that 99 percent of Osages would not understand it, and that the Osage Tribal Council had not given approval to the system yet. Such responses are common critiques of any new system put in place, which always takes time to enter general usage and acceptance.

During this initial conversation, one of the drafters took a particularly strong stance against the orthography, and the efforts of the language program more generally. In a similar vein to Lookout's concerns about teaching the language, this commissioner was concerned that Osages were moving away from the "true" language. They explained that Osage parents had used their thumbs to round their children's palates, allowing them to properly speak the language, and that no one was still doing that. They concluded, "So I don't pay any attention to these people who get involved in the language because they can't get it back to the way it was. We can only create a new language and that's what they are doing; and there's people mad at them for this."[116] This devastating critique gives in completely to colonial destruction and ideas of authenticity. Such a position, if embraced widely, would eliminate the potential for the Osage language to have a future.

About a month after this meeting, the drafters met with Red Eagle, who again took a strong stand advocating for the language.[117] After the drafters explained their concerns, Red Eagle said,

> I see this differently. I would put the whole thing in Osage. Our language says this better. We have put a lot of effort into saving this language and this is an opportunity to share it. Unlike in the past, for our language to be preserved now, it has to be written down. Because our Osage ways have been minimized, we need this document. This document is the best way we know in this world we are now in to direct our madness. Our ways are above that. Now our tribe is saying we want our ways back through our sovereignty.[118]

Connecting the writing of the 2006 constitution with the fostering of Osage ways, Red Eagle made a compelling case not only for bringing the Osage language into the document but for the constitution as a tool for building respectful relations through the language. The goal of the document, as Red Eagle saw it, was to create a space for Osage ways to thrive again. This powerful speech, along with the council's official adoption of the orthography and the realization that the constitution could be updated as the orthography changed, encouraged the writers to include the Osage language in the 2006 constitution. Over time the orthography has grown in acceptance and is now widely utilized across the Osage Nation.

The orthography has continued to evolve, and there are still active debates about how certain sounds should be represented. Some of these changes have been motivated by design needs, such as when the language was put into Unicode. Osage language web specialist Mark Pearson worked tirelessly to secure the support of Scotland-based "alphabetician to the world" Michael Everson, who successfully put the orthography into Unicode in 2014.[119] As part of this process, Everson worked not only with the language program but also with Osage leaders, Osage linguist Cameron Pratt, and Osage graphic artists Ryan RedCorn and Jessica Harjo in order to finalize the orthography. In Everson's proposal to the Unicode Technical Committee, he wrote about their three-day working seminar as a time when "questions of linguistic issues, graphic design and fonts, and character encoding were discussed at length."[120] Putting the orthography into Unicode has, like earlier moves with the language, demonstrated Osages' embrace of technology to give the language a future.

Securing the orthography in Unicode has not, however, ended the challenges to and debates surrounding it. Pearson had to convince companies such as Google, Apple, and Microsoft to support the orthography on their devices, which continues to be an ongoing challenge with system updates.[121]

Other debates about the orthography have concerned representing the nuances of Osage sounds. There has been an intense, multiyear, ongoing debate that has consumed a great deal of the Language Department's time about whether to add additional markings for aspiration. While these markings complicate the language, they aid in pronunciation. As curriculum specialist Janis Carpenter told me in July 2021, "I think the orthography is a good teaching tool. It really opens doors and allows people to read the language and hear the sounds. We still have some issues on how to write things. We need to come together and collaborate on how to go forward."[122] As with other moves to a new country, the orthography is ideally something that will change as new needs are identified, acting as a vehicle to carry the language forward respectfully.

Osage orthography has allowed the language to take on new forms, including new signs around the reservation. People can now easily use it to communicate in Osage online and through our smartphones. The Language Department also developed several apps, making the language more accessible to younger Osages and Osages living off the reservation. Canadian scholars Patrick Moore and Kate Hennessy considered a similar effort by the Tagish First Nation in British Columbia: "Native communities are using digital technologies to regain control of their language resources, while conceptualizing Indigenous ideologies to use in restoring these languages."[123] The Osage Language Department fully understood the orthography as a potent refusal to disappear and an assertion of sovereignty, even making shirts that proudly declared, "Orthography is sovereignty." In the context of the Osage Nation, a fundamental piece of asserting sovereignty is ensuring that the Osage language has a future. Our orthography is a powerful piece of building this relationship.

The orthography is more than just a tool for pronouncing and reading the language; it creates special connections to both the language and being Osage. Osage scholar Jessica Harjo writes, "The orthography itself, as a form, gives the Osage community a tremendous sense of pride and empowerment."[124] In her work Harjo has designed a typeface for the orthography based on Osage dance movement, art, and ways of life and has developed stencils for use in children's Osage language classes while also utilizing the orthography in her design practice. Her work is a powerful example of the role that design can play in building respectful relations with the language.

"You Must Pull the String Back to Go Forward"

Orthography, of course, is just the beginning. There is a great deal of effort that is required to build respectful relations with the language. As the language program has grown and expanded, additional language instructors have been hired. They have added their efforts to Lookout's and have their own visions for what the next steps are for the Osage language. There have also been efforts outside the language program, particularly through the development of 𐓰𐓘𐓬𐓪𐓮𐓤𐓘𐓘͘𐓤𐓪𐓰𐓘𐓬𐓣, to pass the language on to the next generation. This final section will discuss these efforts that are continuing to move the language to a new country.

In late July 2021, Veronica Pipestem and I, perched at the kitchen bar stools in my parents' garage apartment, took refuge from the summer heat and the latest resurgence of the coronavirus that made us afraid to meet publicly. For Pipestem, moving the language to a new country meant finding new methods of bringing Osage ways forward in a shifting world. While mourning the many practices and parts of the language that colonialism had disrupted, she argued that modern technology might be one tool to bridge these gaps. She offered the example of building our relationships with other Dhegiha language speakers. Whereas we used to be able to spend two weeks visiting and talking with neighboring tribes and solidifying those relationships, an online meeting platform such as Zoom could now be a tool to stay in regular conversation. [125]

Language instructor Christopher Cote also discussed creating a language that could serve current Osage needs.[126] As we sat in his office in Pawhuska, Oklahoma, I asked him what he meant by creating a "modern" Osage language. He pointed up at the felt banner on his wall containing the mission statement for the language, which read, "Our Mission is to revitalize the Osage language to its purest form, and to teach our people to speak Osage within the realm of our unique ways and in daily conversation—our endeavors will be unwavering; our future depends on it." He and others in the department had been discussing how the mission statement needed to be updated. He explained that the longer he worked with the language, the more he realized that it was alive. There was no moment in history in which there was a pure language, only constant change. "There are going to be things that we don't understand because our lives are so different. But we are going to go forward. There are also things in our life now that they knew nothing about. We will need to come up with words to describe those things. Think of it like a bow, you must pull the string back to go forward. We must look into the past to go forward. They left what we need here for us."[127] In saying that the things we need to go forward have been left for us, Cote was helping to shift the ground. Focusing on future potential rather than just colonial loss is a fundamental aspect not only for languages but also in building our relations of respect more generally.

During July 2021, I also chatted with Braxton Redeagle, an Osage from Pawhuska who had worked for the Language Department for more than a year and a half. It was at the end of the workday and all other language employees had left the office, but Redeagle's intense passion and devotion kept us talking long past four thirty that afternoon. Describing his own journey with the language, he said, "I was originally motivated to be able to talk and pray for people when called upon, but now I want to move the language into everyday contexts and spaces."[128] He was not convinced that the Osage language could only be understood in Osage cultural contexts and believed that speakers could use the same structure of describing the scene to create new words and phrases that would fit within the current context. He thought that the linguistic work that had been done was enough to understand the structure of the language, if they could only carve out enough time to focus on studying the language and building out the models of the language rules. Like Pipestem, Cote, Atterberry, and many of the other Osages who have worked to reclaim the language, Redeagle was committed to moving the Osage language to a new country.

While the numbers of students in community classes fluctuated over the years, during the pandemic the Nation invested in a very successful media campaign with the tagline, "Stay home, stay safe, learn Osage." The growth in high-speed internet access among Osage citizens and the ease of teleconferencing brought about through Zoom made the language far more accessible, resulting in 950 Osages signing up for Zoom classes.[129] Additionally, another thousand people were enrolled in a self-paced online language class. Even after most pandemic restrictions eased, interest in online classes remained high, again demonstrating Osages' embrace of technology as a tool to build their relations with the language. Despite the many existing colonial tropes about Native peoples' rejection of modern technologies such an embrace is nothing new for Osages or other Indigenous peoples, whose knowledge systems have continually modified foreign technologies to meet our own needs.[130]

In 2022 Redeagle became the director of the Osage Nation Language Department when Vann Bighorse was promoted to the new position of cabinet secretary of language/culture/education. In July 2022, Redeagle and I discussed his visions for the department, particularly for community classes. Noticing that many of the students were not progressing beyond introductory classes, Redeagle planned to try a new structure that was based less on vocabulary and more on ways of thinking in Osage. These shorter classes would be focused on a particular theme and delve deeper into the structure of the language. Redeagle envisioned these focused lessons not only helping students understand the underlying structure of the language better but also engaging students further in topics they cared about. This approach would then raise the confidence of the students and eventually widen the pool of potential teachers. He also envisioned implementing regular assessments of both the students and teachers to find out whether these changes were effective.[131]

Another effort that has attempted to build relations with the Osage language is ᎠᏆᏍᎦ ᏁᏉᏓᎯ. The Osage Nation's own private school is a core aspect of Chief Geoffrey Standing Bear's vision, and he has continually insisted that language immersion be a key priority within the curriculum. The school opened its doors in 2015 with nineteen zero-to-five-year-olds, and it has added a grade every year. Not only has language instruction been built into the curriculum, but parents and family members have been heavily incentivized to enroll in community language classes through tuition reductions.[132] Such a policy is a powerful reversal of the 1883 law that forced children into boarding schools, demonstrating the ways that nation building enables a direct challenging of colonial policies and mindsets.

Despite being one of Standing Bear's most prioritized initiatives, the school faced several challenges early on, including frequent turnover in teachers, students, and administrators as well as funding challenges from the Osage Nation Congress. Additional challenges came with the language immersion curriculum that Standing Bear envisioned as created and implemented through the Osage language program. The biggest source of tension between the Osage language program and the school was the short timeline for the creation of the school. Standing Bear insisted that the school open its doors just one year after he took office because he worried that the planning was stalling the implementation of the program. During the summer before opening, language program staff frequently complained to me that they did not have the necessary curriculum, they had not been hired to work with babies and young kids, and they did not feel prepared to teach through immersion. Eventually, Standing Bear acknowledged these challenges and created a clearer separation between the language program and ᎠᏆᏍᎦ ᏁᏉᏓᎯ, with the main link being that language staff would work directly with the teachers of the school so that they could develop their own language capacities and build the language into their curriculum. Additionally, one former language employee was moved fully to the school, offering daily language classes to all the students and helping to develop the school's curriculum.

In 2021 the school achieved the important milestone of accreditation. The accreditation agency was impressed by the number of Osage Nation services that had been woven into the school, including "a Counselor, a Clinic, an Education Department that provides STEAM [science, technology, engineering, art, and math] lessons and after school tutoring, a Prevention [Department] that comes in once a week and provides lessons on drug and alcohol awareness for children, a Language Department that provides Osage Language instruction to our teachers and parents, a Culture Department that provides cultural trunks and lessons for our children, a Museum nearby that offers a look at our rich past and cultural heritage."[133] When I spoke with Superintendent of the school Patrick Martin shortly after accreditation, he explained that his goals thus far had not only been to incorporate as many Osage resources as possible but to also build up the academics and make the school a friendly environment.[134] He said that COVID-19 had made both academic rigor and Osage language instruction difficult to achieve, as online classes and required masking during the pandemic had presented extreme challenges for learning. He also sees the children growing and the school becoming more of a space for learning, with the Osage language and general academics taking root. He later explained, "The children take the language instruction for granted, but they also realize that they are part of something very special that the Osage Nation is providing them."[135] The ability to take the language for granted is exactly what makes the school so special.

Despite its many challenges, DΛÞOꞔʞΛ ΛʞODΛÞΩ is a powerful example of Osage efforts to move the Osage language to a new country. It demonstrates the financial and labor investments the Osage Nation has made in building respectful relations with it. Describing this effort and the broad support Chief Standing Bear has shown for the language, Lookout reflected, "Linguists think that fluency and speakers is the biggest thing, but there needs to be something that names what we have. Chief has done this, he has stirred up interest. More people are interested in taking classes. You can go to ΩⵎOꞨʞΛ and see two kids that don't know each other talking in Osage. They might not be speaking fluently, but they understand each other."[136] In the face of the extreme colonial disruptions of the nineteenth and twentieth centuries, the Osage Nation is taking vital steps to move the language to a new country.

There are many challenges that such language efforts face, including the way colonial authenticity works to discredit Indigenous futures. Centering respect for our language, however, is a powerful antidote to such colonial forces. Reclaiming a language in the face of colonial theft is tiring, expensive work that is not only slow moving but fraught with challenges. In the context of the Osage Nation, it means reframing how we understand moving to a new country, so that the language and all that it contains is not left behind. As Eddy Red Eagle told me, "We thought we had to vacate our Osageness and go into societies today, but we don't have to. Well, we can't. It has slowed our progress of our tribal attentions. But if we get back to the intention embedded in those names, then we can go into society as a whole and contribute. It all has to be understood through the language, but we have to be patient with it."[137] Here Red Eagle articulates how moving means that we have to find a way, embedded in our own systems of respect, to bring the language forward. For ultimately, as the Osage language mission statement lays out, "our future depends on it."

Self-Governance

"Right Now, They Don't Understand Their Responsibilities"

On a Sunday afternoon in late February 2016, my father and I joined around twenty concerned Osages and Osage Nation officials for a meeting of the Osage Shareholders Association (OSA).[1] The OSA was founded as a grass-roots group in 1994 to monitor the US government's and the Osage Tribal Council's (later the Osage Minerals Council's) ongoing management of the Osage Mineral Estate.[2] This meeting, like all OSA meetings, was both a testing ground for community sentiment and a place where new ideas were pitched and debated outside the constraints of formal meetings. While the OSA did not have any official authority to shape policy, their sentiments did frequently sway decisions and elections. Unlike some of the OSA meetings that attracted upwards of one hundred people, this was a smaller gathering. Those present included two members of the Osage Nation Congress, three from the Osage Minerals Council, and Principal Chief Geoffrey Standing Bear. It thus became an important informal space for communication between these often-siloed governing bodies of the Osage Nation to navigate some of the many challenges facing the Osage reservation's subsurface mineral estate.

Although I will not inherit a headright, a term for those who receive payments from the Osage Mineral Estate's profits, until both of my parents pass away, I was welcomed into OSA meetings not only as a researcher and writer but as someone who had a vested interest in the future of the mineral estate. My grandfather, who was listed on the 1906 roll, was what Osages call an original allottee. Based on this status, he received 640 acres of land, quarterly payments from the minerals produced from the reservation, and a vote in the Osage Tribal Council elections when he turned eighteen. He had divided his share equally between my father and aunt so that when he passed away, they would each receive half of the lands my grandfather had not sold, a half vote in the elections, and half of a share of the profits from the minerals extraction. As a headright holder, my father would join me at these intermittent OSA meetings and would sometimes engage animatedly in the day's discussions about what was needed to generate more profit from the Osage Mineral Estate.

The Osages attending this February 2016 OSA meeting had many conflict-ing opinions, but everyone agreed that the Bureau of Indian Affairs (BIA) was failing to fulfill its duty as *trustee* for the mineral estate. Historically, Osages have understood the US government as obligated to protect and di-rectly manage Osages' natural resources. As this chapter will chronicle, this notion of the "trust relationship," as it is termed, can be traced back to older Osage understandings of the vital relations necessary for survival, hard-won treaties promising protection, and the 1906 Osage Allotment Act (34 Stat. 539), which set out the unique responsibilities the federal government had in over-seeing and managing the Osage Mineral Estate. Underlying all these assump-tions is a commitment to the trust relationship, not as it has ever operated but as we envision it.

In explaining our trust relationship with the federal government in No-vember 2021, Osage Minerals Council chairman Everett Waller made clear to me that the trust was more than a tool, that it was in fact alive. He explained that Osages had long been nourishing this relationship because our very sur-vival as a people has depended on its strength. "We have always demanded more from the trust. It should be growing as we grow. I am trying to make it better, just like my family has done for generations. . . . But the federal gov-ernment needs to grow as well. Right now, they don't understand their re-sponsibilities."[3] Despite the continued failures of the US government to live up to its obligations, many Osage leaders have remained committed to foster-ing relations of responsibility.

After we shared a potluck-style meal, Susan Foreman was the first to speak. She was a headright holder with a career in natural gas marketing who would two years later be elected to the minerals council. Her speech was filled with passionately delivered and detailed examples of the many failures of federal responsibility. The primary target of Foreman and the others in attendance was Robin Phillips, BIA superintendent at the Osage Agency. Production was down, and would soon plummet, because Phillips had completely halted drilling-related permitting while she unilaterally developed her own environ-mental assessment process. Phillips was now sitting on over four hundred permits to drill for oil and natural gas, which Foreman argued was driving companies to take their business elsewhere. Furthermore, Phillips was also insisting that all well data be kept confidential unless accessed through Free-dom of Information Act requests. These were data that had been readily acces-sible to anyone, including the oil producers, but Phillips stated that she now believed this to be proprietary information that even the minerals council should not be allowed to access without heavy redactions.[4] Phillips had refused to explain her reasoning and no one in the meeting had a clear sense of her rationale. As Phillips was the individual most directly charged with ensuring and maintaining the federal government's responsibility to the Osage Nation, it was clear to all present that there was a fundamental breakdown in this vital relation.

While the nature of this rupture perplexed and frustrated Foreman, she was not completely without hope, citing evidence that minerals council involvement could change the situation. She described how the minerals council had managed to halt what she saw as devastating negotiated rules from being enacted by the BIA, and the new environmental impact statement had also been sent back to the drawing board because the minerals council had not been fully involved in the process of its creation. The major problem, Foreman explained, was that the BIA did not have the staff to oversee all the negotiated regulations and environmental impact statement issues in the Osage. "It bogged down their whole system. I think their intention is to shut it all down. Why on earth would we want the BIA to manage when they have proven they can't do it?"[5] In conclusion, Foreman asked why they couldn't take it over and do it themselves. Here she was suggesting not only that local BIA changes were devastating, and that the BIA had long been poor managers of the mineral estate, but that the Osage Minerals Council needed to take control of the mineral estate away from the BIA.

The collective gasp of concern following Foreman's question was audible. In the context of OSA meetings during this period, protecting mineral assets was synonymous with holding the federal government accountable in its job of managing the mineral estate. Many in the room saw Foreman's call to do it ourselves as letting the federal government off the hook on their promises of protection and oversight enshrined in treaties and the 1906 act. Osages had long been fighting to maintain, not sever, this federal responsibility. Despite and because of ongoing federal mismanagement, there was great skepticism about the Osage Nation managing the minerals ourselves.

The story of the Osage Mineral Estate is a powerful demonstration of why so many Native nations have been slow to enact self-governance policies but are now turning to them to address the extreme failures of colonial mismanagement. Self-governance is a federal policy dating back to the 1970s that seeks to fundamentally shift the federal government's role as trustee away from direct management, allowing Native nation governments to be managers of our own resources and programs. This chapter describes why mineral estate self-governance has been delayed but is finally gaining momentum. While the Osage Nation has been committed to building and maintaining responsible relations with the US government, the ongoing challenges are demonstrating why we need to shift management responsibility to the Osage Nation.

The chapter begins with a discussion of the different spaces in which federal responsibility has been solidified as an important tool for Osage survival, including older Osage understandings of that responsibility, the treaties that enshrined it, and the 1906 act. After discussing the development of this vital relation of responsibility, I turn to a history of the Osage Mineral Estate. This includes failed treaty promises of protection, repeated waves of violent settlement, federal limitations in governance, constant threats of termination, massive mismanagement, and ongoing corporate exploitation, all of which demonstrate the lack of responsibility shown by a wide host of US actors. While this story clearly demonstrates the many failures of the trust relationship, it also chronicles how Osages have strategically navigated such failures to ensure our future. For many Osages, the United States' extreme failures, alongside ongoing promises of protection, work together to reinforce the idea that not only does the federal government have an obligation to manage the minerals, but it is the only agency that can do so.

Following a discussion of these efforts historically, this chapter returns to the February 2016 OSA meeting, describing how, despite the vast problems the current trust relationship is creating for the Osage Mineral Estate, Osage leaders remained divided over what it means to hold the federal government to its promises of protection. In 2016 many Osage headright holders remained deeply concerned about entering into self-governance agreements, preferring to leave the mineral estate in BIA hands despite a growing list of issues. This chapter will look closely at their specific concerns with self-governance, including the larger Osage Nation's involvement in minerals governance, their commitments to federal responsibility, and the limited capacities of the minerals council. Building relations of responsibility has been key to Osage success historically, and such connections continue to feel essential, especially in minerals management. As the ongoing frustration with the trustee continues, however, moving the Osage Nation into the future is requiring Osage leadership to reenvision our relation with the federal government away from management and toward supporting our self-governance.

"A Moral Obligation of the Highest Responsibility and Trust"

This chapter utilizes the phrase *relations of responsibility*, rather than the more common language of a *trust relationship*, because of the massive distrust that marks Osage engagements with the federal government. Given the federal government's continued failures to live up to its promises of protection, it would be absurd for Osages to trust it.[6] Despite this history, however, many Osages continue to insist that the federal government should not be let off the hook for its responsibilities, which are colloquially known as the trust relationship. I have chosen the phrase *relations of responsibility* as a way of naming the intentional relationships Osages have fostered with a host of federal agents. These relationships, while failing to meet Osage needs or expectations, have still been a fundamental part of ensuring that the Osage Nation goes forward. Accountability is a fundamental part of what Osages are frequently seeking in our relationships with federal actors, especially in the face of their ongoing failures. I understand responsibility, however, as a larger category that includes not just accountability but also other duties and obligations. This section will describe Osages' history with federal responsibility and how we have envisioned it at various points in time.

Deep relations of responsibility are something that many Native communities fostered before the colonial process and are often evident in Indigenous epistemologies, treaties with colonial nations, and ongoing approaches to sovereignty.[7] Scholars Heidi Kiiwetinepinesiik Stark and Kekek Jason Stark of the Turtle Mountain Band of Chippewas demonstrate that Anishinaabe peoples built treaty relationships with European settlers in the tradition of earlier social relationships, such as those with nonhumans. These relationships were predicated on mutual respect, shared responsibilities, and continued renewal.[8] Similarly, Iroquois understood the treaty relationship as a "Covenant Chain," which Robert Williams of the Lumbee Tribe of North Carolina describes as a metaphor for "two once-alien groups connected in an interdependent relationship of peace, solidarity, and trust."[9] While many, if not all, treaties were signed under extreme duress through outright fraud and manipulation, the act of signing still signaled not only Indigenous agency but an insistence on federal obligations going forward.[10] The failures of the federal government to meet its treaty obligations over the years does not mean that these responsibilities have ceased to exist. On the contrary, the weight of this responsibility only deepens with neglect.

Like other Indigenous communities, Osages have long built our social fabric around the notion of responsibility. As Osage elder Eddy Red Eagle Jr. relates, this can be seen in our clan names and how they often represent the kinds of obligations we have to each other. "Those attributes shape you and bring character to Osages. It defines how we are meant to work together for the strength of the family, clan, and tribe."[11] Observing the universe as an interrelated system, Osages sought to model our own structures on such relations of responsibility.

Osages and other Native peoples never lived in isolation but relied on trade networks and regular exchange. US scholar Kathleen DuVal writes of precolonial Native peoples, "North Americans came to believe that power resulted from extensive connections. A wide network of diplomatic exchange brought in powerful goods and knowledge and could potentially raise allied armies in time of war."[12] DuVal goes on to describe the stereotype of isolated Native communities as "grossly inaccurate. To be isolated was always to court disaster."[13] As DuVal points out, this stereotype attempts to deny the social and political nature of Indigenous peoples and paints Native peoples as isolated nomads wandering the wilderness in need of civilization. In fact, it was through networks of connection and support that Indigenous peoples not only survived but built thriving communities.[14]

When Osages found French and later Spanish colonizers trespassing on our land in the late seventeenth and eighteenth centuries, we chose to use these traders to expand our networks and territorial control. In fact, as DuVal goes on to write, "The Osages proved far more successful than either France or Spain at building a mid-continental empire. Throughout the eighteenth century, they expanded their native ground and became the region's primary economic and military power."[15] Connections to European traders are what enabled Osages to maintain internal control over our own affairs and practices, including the language. By building relations of responsibility with outsiders, Osages thrived politically and socially.

Just one year after the United States dubiously claimed jurisdiction of Osage lands through the Louisiana Purchase from the French, Osage leaders actively sought once again to build a relationship of obligation, insisting on meeting directly with President Thomas Jefferson. Osage leaders visited Jefferson in 1804, convincing him to open a government trading post where goods would be sold at fair prices and a blacksmith could be housed to provide desired goods. Jefferson was deeply affected by Osage strength during this encounter. After meeting the delegation, he wrote, "The truth is they are the great nation South of the Missouri, their possession extending from thence to the Red River, as the Sioux are great North of that river. With these two nations we must stand well, because in their quarter we are miserably weak."[16] In this exchange, Osage leaders worked directly with Jefferson to establish a strong relationship.

Unlike in their relationships with European colonists, where Osages clearly had the upper hand in terms of numbers and territorial control, Osages were in a much weaker position by the nineteenth century. A large influx of settlers invaded Osage land in the late eighteenth century, particularly the Cherokees, who were themselves displaced by American settlers.[17] These different waves of settlers disrupted and undermined existing systems of Osage governance and territorial control. Osage leaders believed, however, that by building relationships of responsibility with the US government, they would be able to regain control over their territory, and they thus reluctantly began entering treaties with the United States.[18]

In an effort to "stand well" with the Osage Nation, the federal government built trading posts, forts, and treaty-based relationships. The 1808 Treaty of Fort Clark, the first made with Osage leaders, is a powerful example of both the potential and limitations of the treaty as a tool for building relations of responsibility. Osage leaders were summoned to a newly built fort and presented with the terms of the treaty. This was not the kind of negotiated agreement they were accustomed to, and many Osage leaders did not sign it or move from the ceded lands following the treaty. The treaty did have the language of "protection," which future treaties picked up on and which ultimately formed the foundation of the trust relationship. It read, "The United States receives the Great and Little Osage nations into their friendship and under their protection; and the said nations, on their part, declare that they will consider themselves under the protection of no other power whatsoever."[19] This language was designed to distance Osage leadership from their strong relationships with European powers, but it also acknowledged some of what Osage leaders desired: improved trade relations and additional protection from enemy sovereigns, Native and non-Native.

Having the United States recognize Osage authority and pledge resources for support was a vital strategy that ensured Osage survival in the context of multiple colonizations. These treaties clearly recognized the complete authority of Osages over our land and those who came into Osage territory, and offered resources to ensure others also recognized that authority. This was a key relationship Osages needed to foster, especially within existing understandings of social relationships with outsiders. The language of protection, while certainly pejorative in intention, was likely understood by many Osages at the time and since as fostering federal responsibility.

The federal government has, however, repeatedly failed to live up to its promises of protection. The treaty moment was the beginning of the massive erosion of Osage land and authority, as treaties diminished Osages' landholdings while solidifying the United States' jurisdiction. From 1808 until 1839, seven treaties stripped Osage control over 75 percent of our land base.[20] Each treaty used the language of protection as a justification for why the Osage Nation needed to cede additional territory, arguing this was the only way that the "desired protection" could be maintained. The 1825 treaty, known simply as the Treaty with the Osage, reads, "In order to more effectually extend to said tribes, that protection of the government so much desired by them, it is agreed as follows: ARTICLE 1. The Great and Little Osage tribes or nations do hereby cede and relinquish to the United States all their right, title, interest and claims to lands."[21] As these treaties tied promises of future protection with the loss of land, they signaled their failure to live up to their promises of protection and ultimately twisted the notion of responsibility itself.[22] Despite the US government's many failures to follow through on its promises, Osage leaders had little choice but to continue advocating for a strong vision of what this trust relationship would entail.

The federal courts have been another space in which the US government has twisted the trust relationship, positioning itself as the guardian and American Indian nations as wards.[23] The specific terminology of a "trust responsibility" and "wards" dates to Chief Justice John Marshall's opinions in the 1820s and 1830s, where he argued that Native nations were "domestic dependent" nations, not subject to state laws but instead beholden to federal oversight.[24] As Delaware Tribe of Indians scholar Joanne Barker writes about Marshall's decision in *Johnson's Lessee v. McIntosh* of 1823, "SCOTUS rewrote treaty history."[25] At this crucial moment in American colonization, by rewriting the history of the territory, the US government attempted to diminish the clear Native authorities and their own responsibilities that treaties had enshrined.

Marshall tried to make Native nations "domestic and dependent" through the deployment of colonial stereotypes. In the unanimous decision of *Johnson v. McIntosh*, Marshall justified European conquest of the land by saying, "The Tribes of Indians inhabiting this country were fierce savages whose occupation was war, and whose subsistence was drawn chiefly from the forest. To leave them in possession of their country, was to leave the country a wilderness."[26] By denying the networks of connection Native peoples built and the complex societies they had before colonization, Marshall was attempting to eliminate Native nations' jurisdiction and authority over the territory. From this decision was also born the notion of plenary authority, which claimed to grant the federal government the right to make unilateral decisions related to Native nations. Most dangerously, the trust relationship's promises of protection, which have at times been acted on and at other times been ignored, work alongside claims to plenary authority to position the United States as the supreme authority over the territory. Native nations have not, however, given up on the vision of federal responsibility as a tool to support our best interests and even self-government.

From the eighteenth century until the present, Indigenous officials have used treaties, laws, court decisions, policies, and even the BIA itself to grow our land bases and strengthen the reach of our sovereignty.[27] As Lumbee Tribe of North Carolina scholar David E. Wilkins and Creek Nation descendant scholar K. Tsianina Lomawaima argue, Native nations continue to push for a "reciprocal vision of trust," which involves the "intertwining of moral, political and legal obligations," whereby "tribal and federal rights, properties, and sovereignty are equally entitled to deep and profound respect."[28] The US Supreme Court itself has acknowledged these ongoing responsibilities, such as when the Court in 1942 determined that the federal government had "a moral obligation of the highest responsibility and trust" to Native nations.[29] Demanding that the trust relationship fulfill these intertwined "moral, political and legal obligations" is a vital move that has ensured the continued existence of Native nations.

Self-governance, while sometimes understood through notions of autonomy or separation, comes out of treaty promises and other federal responsibilities to ensure Indigenous sovereignty. Tribal leaders, including Osages, have advocated and lobbied for a fundamentally different kind of trust relationship. Native activism of the 1960s and 1970s, particularly the Indian occupation of Alcatraz Island from 1969 to 1971 and the takeover of the BIA Central Office building in Washington, D.C., in November 1972, provided a catalyst. Congress responded to these pressures by passing the Indian Self-Determination and Education Assistance Act (Public Law 93-638) in 1975.[30] The idea behind self-governance, which is sometimes referred to as compacting but which has also been accomplished through 638 contracts and multiple-year funding agreements, was to transfer program oversight and funds from the BIA to the nations themselves.[31]

This policy once again positioned Indigenous self-governance at the core of federal responsibilities, attempting to move the BIA away from its entrenched paternalism. This movement was facilitated by Native people taking over many of the roles and responsibilities within the BIA. Choctaw Nation scholar Valerie Lambert writes that Native peoples have shifted the BIA toward Native understandings of the trust responsibility. For example, she writes about the impacts of leaders such as Menominee Indian Tribe of Wisconsin scholar and civil servant Ada Deer. "Deer was coauthor of an AIPRC [American Indian Policy Review Commission] pronouncement that was circulated widely and now provides a framework for BIA workers as they carry out their work. The assertion is that the federal trust responsibility includes an obligation to protect tribal sovereignty and to provide those services 'required to protect and enhance Indian lands, resources, and self-government.'"[32] These seismic shifts enabled Native nations to have control over how programs, ranging from healthcare to minerals leasing, would be enacted, as well as how federal funds would be used. Rather than accepting the more paternalistic relationship that gave the BIA authority over all the programs, services, functions, and activities of each nation, interested American Indian nations negotiated with the BIA to establish the roles and responsibilities each government would have in running various programs, reframing the trust as more of a partnership.[33]

Given the lingering fears instilled during the 1950s termination era, many Native nations had been concerned that this shift in the trust relationship was just the latest attempt by the federal government to terminate their relations with Native nations. The self-governance legislation attempted to address these concerns directly by including language about the continuation of the trust responsibility in the legislation itself. Additional changes were made through subsequent legislation in 1994 and 2000, further streamlining the process. By 2014, almost forty years after implementation of the Indian Self-Determination and Education Assistance Act, however, only about 50 percent of Native nations had entered into some form of self-governance.[34] As the next section will demonstrate, much of this lingering hesitation has to do with the many failures that have marked the trust relationship and the colonial policies that have been created in its name.

"There Is Something in That Land That Will Take Care of the Osage People"

While Indigenous communities across the globe often act as defenders of the lands and waters they call home, pitting themselves against destructive energy development efforts, Osages have had a fundamentally different relationship with extractive energy. As this section will chronicle, this difference can be seen in our oral history of how we came to our current reservation, the ways in which we have directly benefited from this industry, and Osage insistence today that our minerals continue to be something we must determine how best to utilize. The legacy of our mineral estate, however, is also the thing that has most complicated our efforts of self-governance and has spurred settler violence and graft. This section will detail the history of these dual legacies.

Ultimately, moving forward with Osage self-governance means recognizing the violence that has marked our history with extractive industries, and the trust relationship that has so often facilitated such atrocities as the Osage Reign of Terror.

In 1870, after conflicts with white settlers on the former Osage reservation in Kansas, Osage leaders began considering a move to Indian Territory.[35] Several leaders went to look at the proposed land, which was then part of the Cherokee reservation but had been part of the territory Osages had ceded two generations before. When the leaders returned, one by the name of ⅄ΛDAʞΛ gave a speech that urged Osages to move to this place, saying, "There is something in that land that will take care of the Osage people in the future. Our children will never starve."[36] Based on this advice, the Osage Nation purchased the current Osage reservation in fee simple from the Cherokee Nation.[37] In 1872, the US Congress established the purchased lands as the Osage reservation.[38]

Twenty-four years after the reservation was established, settlers discovered oil on Osage land, fulfilling ⅄ΛDAʞΛ prophecy in the minds of many Osages. In this moment, however, the US government used its role as trustee to support the interests of white businesses rather than Osage interests. Oil production on Osage land began at the end of the nineteenth century, with a blanket lease to the entire reservation going to Kansas railroad magnate Henry Foster and his brother Edwin in 1896. The Osage agent H. B. Freeman, from the Office of Indian Affairs in the US War Department, negotiated the deal with Foster. Only after the fact was it put to a vote by the National Council, the legislative body of the 1881 Constitution of the Osage Nation. The initial lease passed by the narrow margin of seven to six, but National Council annulled the contract a year later. William Pollock, Freeman's successor as Osage agent, overrode the National Council seven months later, reinstating the contract.[39] Given the competitive advantage the Osage Nation lost by giving a blanket lease to one company, it is hard to understand the Office of Indian Affairs' motivation here as anything but an example of early corporate lobbying, not unlike what happened later across Indian Country, and what continues to happen across the globe.[40]

Another extreme failure of the US government to live up to its promises of protection came with the allotment era (1887–1934), which broke apart Native nation territory through the allotment of land to individual Native peoples and opened up two-thirds of Native land (138 million acres) to non-Native settlement.[41] The US government could not as easily force the Osage Nation into allotting our lands, like it did with other Native nations, because we had purchased the reservation land and had an oil lease for the entire reservation territory.[42] After failing to convince the Osage Nation's 1881 government to agree to allotment, the BIA illegally abolished our government and appointed its own allotment-friendly Osages to serve as leaders on a new tribal council.[43] Such drastic moves mirrored the ways the BIA had undermined previous Osage governance systems to gain an upper hand at the end of the nineteenth century and are clear evidence of the failures of federal relations of responsibility to serve Osage Nation interests.

Still, Osage leaders did not give up on the idea of federal responsibility, instead using it to maintain as much authority as they could. Even when the Osage Nation was forced to allot, leaders negotiated for the subsurface—including rights to oil, natural gas, and other minerals—to be kept under the communal ownership of the Osage Tribe and put in trust with the US government. James Bigheart, Osage chief from 1875 until 1906, understood the importance of retaining collective ownership over as much as possible and negotiated to keep the mineral estate from being allotted and to only allot the surface lands to Osages listed on the membership rolls, unlike other allotment processes that opened most of the land to settlement.

Even with, and perhaps because of, the extreme failures of federal responsibility before, during, and after the creation of our mineral estate, Osage leaders have remained committed to holding the government accountable to its trust commitments, including the protection and direct management of the mineral estate. Because of this insistence, we have had to navigate deeply complicated relationships and outcomes. Established in 1906 through an act of the US Congress, the Osage Mineral Estate Trust created a 1.47-million-acre reservation, generational wealth with the privileges wealth affords, and a tool to fight off termination, but it also inadvertently introduced extreme violence, reliance on extractive industry, and an impediment to other Osage self-governance efforts.

The 1906 act established a clear precedent for what federal responsibility would look like in the Osage context. The United States would control leasing of reservation lands for minerals exploration, requiring that any lease with the Osage Nation be approved by the United States to be valid. Further, the United States, through the Department of the Interior, would manage the lease relationship with oil companies and others. The federal government would receive all oil royalty payments, invest the funds, and pay out the funds to those with a share in the mineral estate. Indicative of the federal government's lack of interest in maintaining this relationship long term, the congressional act included a provision that it would end after twenty-five years.[44]

While the US government has overseen the extraction of minerals and the dispersal of funds from our minerals trust, Osages have had to continually insist on the federal government's responsibility to our interests. In 1917, the tribal council complained in a hearing before the US Congress that BIA superintendent George Wright was "more greatly concerned about and is more favorable to the interests of big oil companies and men of large financial means and political influence than he is to the interests of the Osage people."[45] The tribal council went on to argue that the agency was spending Osage annuitant money needlessly and without their consent. Elected US officials were time and again more beholden to corporate interests that funded their election campaigns than they were to the trust relationship.[46]

The quarterly payments from the estate did afford Osages a lifestyle beyond that of anyone else during that period, with Osages being dubbed "the richest per capita on earth."[47] After the discovery of oil in 1897, the market for Osage oil grew dramatically, bringing the Osages much wealth. At its peak in 1925, each share earned $13,200 per quarter, which would be equivalent to almost $1 million a year in 2023. Osages used these funds in a whole host of ways, much as wealthy non-Osages of the period did. They bought houses and cars, hired white drivers and domestic help, sent their children to top-ranked schools, and traveled widely.[48] In some cases, Osages also used these funds to ensure that they could develop and continue cultural practices and lifeways. Osage weddings, funerals, dances, meals, ceremonies, and other events became larger and more extravagant. The wealth also ensured that Osages did not have to work and could devote more time to these activities.[49]

Such wealth was quite exceptional in rural Oklahoma, however, and challenged stereotypes of the poor Indian in need of white civilization, motivating in the local white population widespread concern, gossip, greed, outrage, graft, and violence.[50] Many people came onto the Osage reservation as legal guardians, merchants, suitors, swindlers, and even murderers to access this wealth.[51] After local and federal authorities failed to intervene, the Osage Tribe paid the newly minted Federal Bureau of Investigation to investigate the murders of sixty Osages, which ended in several convictions.[52] Such a move reinforced the importance of federal responsibility, as it was the only law enforcement agency able to make prosecutions in this era.

The federal government should, however, not be viewed simplistically as the hero of this story. Osage systems of justice had been undermined by the illegal dismantling of our 1881 government, which the BIA replaced with a tribal council form of government that had no system of justice. Furthermore, deeming Osages "incompetent" to manage our money, the federal government had created the system of legal guardians, who were perfectly positioned to profit from Osages in legal and illegal ways.[53] The Osage Nation–financed federal intervention did not halt the loss of millions of dollars to price-gouging shop owners and BIA-approved legal guardians. As US scholar Alexandra Harmon states, these settlers "could skim money from their charges' account with an ease too tempting for many to resist."[54] In this context, instead of protecting lives or monies, such reliance on the United States facilitated massive devastation.

Despite the many limitations the trust relationship has created, Osages have strategically deployed it as a tool to stop various federal policies of elimination. While originally slated to expire after twenty-five years, the tribal council was able to extend the mineral estate until 1958 by insisting on our need for this continued relationship. Finally, the tribal council in 1978 was able to convince the US government to change the language concerning the duration of the mineral estate from "until otherwise provided by an Act of Congress" to "in perpetuity."[55] Such constant threats are no doubt part of why protecting trust assets has become such a core Osage commitment.

While Osages generally have had our own unique legislation, we have also had to navigate the "pendulum swings" of federal Indian policy.[56] In 1953, the Osage Tribe, along with over one hundred other American Indian nations, including the Menominee and the Klamath Tribes, faced termination through House Concurrent Resolution 108, because we were believed to be successfully "assimilated" into American society. The federal government had long been trying to "get out of the Indian business," but the period of termination was its most transparent attempt.[57] In 1953, as on many occasions throughout the twentieth century, the Osage Tribal Council responded to the threats of termination by sending representatives to Washington. During this trip, Osages trained as lawyers were able to negotiate for continued recognition by promising to pay their own operating costs through Osage Mineral Estate proceeds. This process created a stronger attachment to the trust relationship, which Osage leaders saw as ensuring the continuation of the Nation.[58]

The system of government enforced through the 1906 Osage Allotment Act also drastically limited citizenship, meaning that the government was not accountable to most Osage descendants. Under the Osage Tribal Council created through the 1906 act, the only people who had a vote or could run for office were males over the age of eighteen, although these rights were later extended to women. Through an amendment in the 1950s, which was negotiated with Osage leadership under the threat of Osage termination, voting in the Osage Tribe became tied to one's share of a headright in the Osage Mineral Estate, passed down from someone on the 1906 roll. This meant that most Osage descendants were unable to vote because their family members had not willed the headright to them or were still living. By 2004, only four thousand of the roughly sixteen thousand descendants were eligible to vote in Osage elections, based solely on their inheritance of a share.

The Osage Mineral Estate Trust spread discord within families. My grandfather George Orville Dennison was born eighteen months before the July 1, 1907, cutoff date. As a result, he received three 160-acre parcels of land within the Osage reservation, a 1/2, 230th share of all monies produced from the mineral estate, and a vote in Osage elections when he turned twenty-one.[59] His two brothers, who were born after the 1907 cutoff date, received nothing and had no voice in the government. This led my great-grandmother to distribute my grandfather's money among the three boys until my grandfather married, when his wife put an end to the redistribution. These mineral estate proceeds divided my family, leading my great-grandmother to favor the brothers' children at gift-giving occasions. This in turn estranged my father, who as a young boy did not understand the disparity, from the larger family.

Mineral estate proceeds also divided the Osage Nation, creating additional challenges for our self-governance efforts. Starting around the 1960s, as more and more descendants were disenfranchised from Osage political life, they began fighting for equal voting rights through organizations such as the Osage Nation Organization. My grandfather and even my non-Osage grandmother often voiced their disapproval of nonshareholder Osages who wanted to reform Osage government, believing that "they are just trying to get our money."[60] This was a common refrain among many Osage shareholders, who believed that federal control was more likely to protect their financial interests than Osage control.[61] Differential access to this wealth acted as a wedge between family members and undermined relationships with the Nation, especially for those were ineligible to vote or run for office.

BIA failures to fulfill its trust responsibility continued throughout the twentieth century. The BIA has very little congressional oversight, and efforts at internal and external reform have been stymied by its unwieldy structure and an aversion to change. Internal conflicts, entrenched bureaucratic structures, deeply embedded paternalism, and fears of job loss all undermined the facilitation of self-governance agreements early on.[62] The BIA was even worse at its designated job of managing trust assets, with devastating results. As historian Roxanne Dunbar-Ortiz writes, "The US Department of the Interior, as trustee of Indigenous assets, had lost, squandered, stolen, and otherwise wasted hundreds of millions of dollars dating back to the forced land allotment beginning in the late 1880s."[63] This mismanagement led to a class action law-suit, representing nearly a half million Native individuals, and a $3.4 billion settlement in 2009, which, while the largest settlement the US government has ever entered into, was only a tiny fraction of the $137 billion documented mismanagement put forward in the plaintiffs' case.[64]

In 2011 the Osage Nation was also partially successful in its efforts to hold the federal government responsible for its many failures as its trustee. The US government finally negotiated a settlement agreement with annuitants after twelve years of US Court of Federal Claims trust accounting and trust man-agement lawsuits, a US District Court for the District of Columbia trust accounting case, and extensive discovery, motions, and rulings. On October 14, 2011, the US government paid $380 million to compensate for the mis-management of tribal trust funds that occurred between 1972 and 2000.[65] This was an important win that clearly demonstrated the importance of the trust relationship as a useful tool for holding the federal government accountable. As this represented only a small fraction of the monies that had been misman-aged, however, it is hard to see lawsuits as a solid strategy going forward.

The history of the Osage Mineral Estate Trust is a powerful case study for understanding why, despite all the devastation, Osages and other Native peoples are refusing to let the federal government off the hook. Indigenous scholars are doing an exemplary job of critiquing all of these settler state structures and focusing on Indigenous practices that offer refusals of or alter-natives to these structures.[66] As Navajo Nation scholar Andrew Curley writes of such scholarly critiques, "These narratives . . . have difficulty capturing how indigenous peoples work through colonial structures for survival. . . . Although these frameworks free indigenous scholarship from colonial limita-tions, they also miss important areas of social, political, and cultural life within Native communities that work contrary to ideals of resurgence."[67] As have the many different ways Navajo engage with coal production, the Osage Mineral Estate has created tensions and divergent approaches to the trust re-lationship, self-governance, and a reliance on extractive industries. As Curley and Navajo Nation scholar Majerle Lister write elsewhere, Indigenous na-tions have often turned to extractive industries because of the dire situations created by limiting Indigenous self-governance.[68] To understand Native na-tions' embrace of extractive industries and a toxic trust relationship with the federal government, we must understand the strategic decisions Native na-tion leaders are making to ensure the future of our nations.

Given that colonial processes have created messy governing systems, inad-equate processes of accountability, and diminished infrastructure, it should not be surprising that the process of finding solutions to the Osage Mineral Estate will be deeply fraught and difficult. Osage leaders have passed down an understanding of the trust relationship as ensuring protection and support, and our current leaders remain committed to forcing the US government to accept its responsibilities. They are ultimately trying to move these commitments forward in ways that open possibilities for our future rather than foreclose them.

"I Remain Committed to Keeping the Government Separate from the Minerals"

One of the most frequently articulated and stickiest concerns surrounding minerals self-governance in the Osage context is that it raises complex jurisdictional issues. Given the ways colonial systems have skewed Osage governance by attempting to turn the Osage Nation into a minerals corporation, it is not surprising that even as the Osage Nation was able to reform around the 2006 constitution, there would be difficulties left to sort out. Osages have fought to keep the trust relationship intact for so long that shifting it in any way is viewed with great concern.

As this section will discuss, most Osage voters in 2006 had approved a constitution that moved the minerals council, formally the sole governing body of Osages, to the status of an independent minerals-focused board within the reconstituted Osage Nation government. Crucially, the officials of the minerals council and the Nation are now elected by different, but partially overlapping, constituencies.[69] In order for the mineral estate to become self-governing, these officials are going to have to find ways of working together and headright holders are going to have to put some level of trust in the larger Osage Nation, some of whose leaders do not hold a headright. With the colonial history detailed in the previous section, especially settlers' repeated attempts to take Osage lands, monies, and resources, it should not be surprising that Osage headright holders are deeply distrustful.[70]

Back at the 2016 OSA meeting, Chief Standing Bear dealt with this issue of national involvement head-on, arguing that it was essential to solving the issues the mineral estate was facing. As an attorney who had long worked across Indian Country spearheading self-governance movements, he was a frequent advocate for Native people solving their own problems. Chief Standing Bear was well positioned to make this case because he himself was a headright holder and someone who had helped to form the OSA. He responded to Foreman's list of concerns by agreeing that the BIA was not being a good partner in minerals management, but insisted that there were many things that the Osage Nation could do to immediately mitigate the situation. He offered as a model the Southern Ute, who had created limited liability companies (LLCs) to develop their own minerals. He wanted the minerals council to work with Osage Nation Energy, an LLC established by the Nation, to do similar kinds of work. He also suggested working with the newly created Osage Nation Ranch to establish a burying beetle refuge that could sell environmental offset credits to producers wanting to drill in the Osage, which would address one of the more costly environmental impediments producers were currently facing.[71] In this meeting, as in many other settings, he was full of suggestions for how Osages might navigate challenges through their own resourcefulness.

At the end of his speech, Chief Standing Bear turned directly to the issue of self-governance, suggesting it was the only way forward and that the fears associated with Osage national involvement were unfounded. "I know compacting is a no-no word around here and that there are concerns about the Nation being involved in the minerals, but there are laws in place that ensure we cannot access that money or take over management from the Osage Minerals Council. There is only one way to fix all of these issues and that is to take it over, but the minerals council would have to take the lead on this. Don't complain about it, take it over. We have to take over the minerals because the BIA are not our friends."[72] Chief Standing Bear thus acknowledged the deep tension in the room, reiterating that the money distributed to the headright holders, as well as the authority of the Osage Minerals Council, was protected by both Osage and US law. By suggesting "compacting," Standing Bear was arguing for creating a self-determination contract through the Indian Self-Determination and Education Assistance Act of 1975, which would allow the transfer of most of the operations of minerals management from the BIA to the Osage Nation. By positioning self-governance agreements as the only way of fixing the many problems the mineral estate was facing, Standing Bear was envisioning a new kind of relationship with the federal government, one in which it was responsible for ensuring Osage Nation self-governance.

Not everyone in the room was convinced, however. While some clapped, others looked very concerned. One Osage congresswoman responded above the noise of the room, "I remain committed to keeping the government separate from the minerals." In making this simple statement, she was reiterating that she would not approve any self-governance agreements, which required Osage Nation congressional approval, or any of the other efforts by the Nation to develop the minerals. As a non–headright holder who had not yet, but likely would, inherit a headright with the passing of her parents, she, like many Osages, had been raised to understand the mineral estate as something she should not be involved in until it was "her time." The colonially created headright system had long served to alienate non-headright-holding Osages, keeping them disengaged from Osage governance during the twentieth century. Now, under the 2006 constitution, this colonial wedge continued to act, limiting self-governance capacities around the mineral estate. Her concerns were widespread enough that the Osage Congress had not created its own environmental laws in its ten years of existence due to the controversies it created.[73]

At the core of these tensions over keeping the minerals separated from the Nation was a concern about who it was that the US trust relationship protected and in what contexts. While according to the 1906 act the Osage Nation (formally the Osage Tribe) is legally the trustee of the Osage Mineral Estate, the Osage Nation could not redistribute payments or otherwise diminish the mineral estate.[74] What was considered diminishment, however, was a point of great contention. Other Native nations deal with a similar conundrum concerning trust land, though their experiences play out a little differently. As former assistant secretary for Indian affairs Kevin Washburn asks, "Can the United States simultaneously have a robust and respectful government-to-government relationship with tribes and yet come between tribes and its own members when those members own interests in individual trust land?"[75] The primary tension for Washburn here is whether the federal trust obligation is to Native nations or to their citizens. Defining the ultimate trustee is at the core of Osage debates about federal responsibility.

Tensions over the connection between the Osage Minerals Council, which was elected by headright holders, and the Osage Nation Congress, which was elected by registered descendants of the 1906 Osage allotment roll (only about a fourth of whom held headrights), can be traced back to the minerals trust. Throughout the twentieth century there were many failed attempts at government reform, whereby Osages fought against this colonially imposed, though at times Osage Tribal Council–embraced, disenfranchisement.[76] These efforts failed in part because they were done through the federal court system, rather than through the US Congress, which was required to amend the 1906 act. Reform efforts were also stymied by headright holders who were afraid that the point of the reform was to redistribute the headright interests, not just the votes. This prevailing attitude of "they are just trying to get our money" made it hard for any reform process to take place. Other issues facing the Nation, such as the lack of economic development or checks and balances under the Osage Tribal Council government, were left unresolved in

the face of the overwhelming concern about not disturbing the trust relationship with individuals.[77] In this way, the system not only drastically limited
citizenship but created a government that was, at least until the twenty-first
century, almost entirely devoted to minerals leasing and operating just a few
other federal grants, with little money available for governmental operations.
Put simply, the focus on protecting trust assets has long limited the Osage
Nation's capacity for self-governance.

These limitations and tensions between the Nation and the minerals
council were on display under the 1994 Osage Constitution. The constitution
was created out of a reform effort mandated by a federal court and later over-
turned by a higher court. In trying to navigate the tension between the headright holders and non–headright holders, the constitution created a new
national council to serve all Osage descendants and left the minerals council
in place to manage the mineral estate. This governing document made the
mistake of not clearly delineating the duties of the respective councils, and
many departments, businesses, and individuals were uncertain which council
they served or whom to consult when issues arose. Because the Osage Tribal
Council had managed affairs for so long, the challenges of changing to a new
structure only further complicated these interactions. Another problem was
that the buildings, equipment, federal funds, and other possessions had ambiguous ownership, with the result that both sides made claims to them. The
tribal council also argued that the national council was meddling in its affairs
through the creation of laws that could potentially affect the mineral estate.

During the 2004–6 reform effort, the writers of the 2006 constitution
dealt with the colonial legacy of the Osage Minerals Council by placing it as
an elected board within the new constitutional government, but some headright holders remained alarmed about this incorporation.[78] Most of the early
Osage Minerals Council officials elected under the 2006 constitution fought
their body's incorporation within the larger Osage Nation. Neither federal
nor Osage courts, however, agreed that this incorporation represented a diminishment of their headrights, which continued to be protected by both
federal and Osage laws. While headright holders had long felt that these two
entities needed to be as separate as possible, maintaining this separation
meant that the Osage Nation was entirely reliant on the federal government
for environmental laws and minerals oversight. It also meant that it was reliant on corporations and individual producers, generally non-Osage, for economic development opportunities.

Colonial interventions into Osage governance, under the rubric of federal
responsibility, continue to limit Osage leaders' actions. Even after ten years of

operating within the 2006 constitutional structure, the minerals council still had not accepted its placement inside the Osage Nation. On September 9, 2016, the Osage Nation Supreme Court rejected the minerals council's argument that it was not subject to the constitution and laws of the Nation, including the ethics law, which it had been refusing to comply with.[79] The minerals council then voted a year later to sue the Osage Nation over ownership of the mineral estate. Two months later it rescinded this resolution, acknowledging that it was a government entity within the Osage Nation.[80] Even with this acknowledgment, however, tensions arise any time the larger Osage Nation government might be required to act on behalf of the mineral estate. Moving beyond this colonially created tension over authority is one of the most important projects for the Osage Nation as we envision and enact self-governance over the minerals.

"My Mother Taught Me How to Defend Our Trust"

Headright holders were also deeply concerned that self-governance would affect Osages' ability to hold the federal government accountable whenever things went awry. For generations, defending the trust has meant ensuring that our relationship with the federal government remains unchanged, but this has led to very awkward processes and structures not supporting Osage interests. Accountability has long been a core tenet of Osage relations of responsibility with the federal government, but it is also an area of diminishing returns. As this section will demonstrate, not only does such a focus on accountability mean we are only recapturing a small fraction of our losses, but it is also focusing the federal government's efforts on avoiding liability rather than enacting its responsibilities.

Talee Redcorn, a long-term member of the Osage Minerals Council, was the next to speak during the February 2016 OSA meeting. He argued that the minerals council was moving things forward, if not through the kinds of self-determination strategies outlined by the chief. Instead, he focused on their efforts of holding the BIA accountable through complaint letters and litigation. He explained that "the strongest thing the Osage can say is that we are not being treated appropriately and the US government must respond. I grew up on trust land and I chose to live on it now because I love our people. My mother taught me how to defend our trust."[81] In this instance, as well as many of the other minerals council discussions at this time, the priority of defending the assets was seen as the paramount function of the trust relationship. Redcorn went on to describe the minerals council as a 100 percent per-cap organization, with only $1 million per year going to administrative costs, most of which was devoted to litigation.[82] Here and elsewhere, defending the trust by holding the federal government responsible for its mismanagement meant not investing in self-governance efforts. Redcorn understood federal responsibility to protect Osage assets as something inherited from his ancestors who fought hard to maintain this relationship. Unfortunately, the US government has continually failed to live up to its promises of asset protection, as best evidenced in the 2011 mismanagement lawsuit.

The settlement from the lawsuit has done little to ensure responsible relations. The relationship between the Osage Minerals Council and the regional BIA office, especially under the leadership of Phillips, was deeply strained. In fact, the multiple concerns raised during the 2016 OSA meeting, especially that of cumbersome and costly environmental reviews and Freedom of Information Act (FOIA) requests, were likely the fallout of the success of the lawsuit and a 2014 evaluation report by the inspector general that followed, entitled *BIA Needs Sweeping Changes to Manage the Osage Nation's Energy Resources.* Number 14 of its thirty-three recommendations, for example, was to "develop and implement oversight procedures to ensure compliance with the NEPA [National Environmental Protection Act] for all Osage Nation oil and gas activities."[83] Empowered by this mandate, Phillips ignored minerals councilors' arguments that they were still under the last negotiated rules, which dated back to 1979. Although the federal government was still developing the relevant environmental impact statement and negotiated rules in consultation with the minerals council, Phillips insisted on completely halting drilling and other permits while she created her own extensive environmental assessment process.[84]

Phillips's actions are a classic example of the ways that a focus on accountability can backfire, especially in adversarial situations, working to center administrator energy on avoiding liability. European scholars Cris Shore and Susan Wright term this phenomenon "coercive accountability," where new bureaucratic technologies, especially new assessment measures, work to obscure fault, shifting the blame for organizational issues from the administrators to "the process" or those they are supposed to be serving.[85] The 2014 evaluation report's larger focus was actually on the BIA's trust responsibility to "obtain maximum royalty payments on behalf of the headright holders."[86] This mandate was clearly not one that Phillips felt compelled to follow, as it was completely at odds not just with the cumbersome environmental review process but also with the halt in processing drilling permits Phillips had issued. Furthermore, the report called for hiring the necessary permanent staff to address the NEPA requirements, something Phillips seemed unwilling or unable to do. It was ultimately quite clear that suing for accountability had not fostered the kind of responsibility that Osages were seeking.

Environmental assessments were not the only area in which this focus on avoiding liability was playing out. As discussed at the beginning of the 2016 OSA meeting, Phillips was now also insisting that all well data be accessed through FOIA requests.[87] This change, much like the changes in environmental assessments, perplexed Osage headright holders at the time, but were also likely driven by concerns over BIA liability for mismanagement. The same 2014 evaluation report stated that the minerals council "is exerting significant influence over the Agency, which inhibits the Agency's ability to manage the tribe's oil and gas program."[88] By limiting access to well data, the BIA was reasserting its own authority over the mineral estate. Furthermore, the evaluation report discussed how the lease files, which include the well data, were not digitized and were being checked out without a backup or even proper record, bringing a great deal of liability to the BIA every time this information was distributed.[89] In addition to hurting drilling, this almost impossible FOIA process meant that the minerals council did not have the information it needed to identify and plug orphaned wells.[90] This was a particularly absurd situation, as the minerals council's effort to plug orphaned wells was financed by a federal grant.[91] The focus on liability was thus not only diminishing royalty payments but also creating more environmental and safety hazards. Such contradictions further demonstrate that Phillips was not motivated by concern for the landowners or the land, as she would not turn these materials over even with a FOIA request, except in an extremely redacted, and thus unusable, form.

While the goal of the 2011 lawsuit had been to hold the BIA accountable for its mismanagement, the impact was ultimately that the BIA had become hyperfocused on protecting identified areas of liability. This focus overshadowed its real duties of fulfilling its trust responsibilities, either obtaining the maximum royalty payments or protecting the land. The case of the Osage Nation Mineral Estate demonstrates the extreme limitations of the federal trust relationship as a tool of asset protection. With these limitations, more and more Osages are having to shift expectations of federal accountability, responsibility, and protections, given the reality that federal officials are not acting in the best interests of Osages.

Osage leaders have had some success, however, in using federal lawsuits against corporations that illegally exploit the mineral estate. In forcing the US government to hold these corporations accountable, the trust maintains its power and importance. This potency is exemplified in an ongoing case, which at the time of this writing was in the Tenth Circuit Court of Appeals, against Osage Wind, LLC; Enel Kansas, LLC; and Enel Green Power North America, Inc. The United States and the Osage Minerals Council sued these companies over illegal mining that occurred when a wind farm was built on the Osage reservation. In 2017 the Tenth Circuit Court held that, in building their eighty-four wind turbines, these companies failed to get leases for mining from the minerals council and the secretary of the interior as is required under the trust. Six years later, this case was still caught up in the court system.[92] In describing his commitment to this case and other lawsuits, minerals council chairman Waller said, "My last move as an Osage will always be attacking those who hurt my people. . . . This trust enables every battle I wage."[93] For Waller and other Osage leaders, the trust is what allows them to work toward a reconciliation of what we are owed, even while knowing that it will only ever be a fraction of what is due.

"At Some Point We Need to Stand Up for Our Sovereignty"

By September 2020 the relationship between the Osage Minerals Council and the BIA was reaching a breaking point. The failures of the current system were finally demonstrating to most Osage leaders and shareholders that the federal government was not a responsible manager of the mineral estate. This section will look closely at that shift and the many challenges ahead as Osages seek to enact self-governance over minerals. Osages are ultimately shifting our understanding of what the federal relationship is good for, re-enshrining Osage self-governance as a key tool. Figuring out how to best enact self-governance over minerals is part of what it means for us to move the Osage Nation into the future.

By 2020, new problems were layered on top of and exacerbating the existing issues of BIA management. The September 2020 quarterly payment was down to its lowest point since 1973, almost half of what it had been just a year before, and a fraction of what it was in its highest year of 2012. Despite biannual meetings with the director of the BIA and other senior leadership, the minerals council was unable to resolve most of its issues and additional tensions continued to arise. Phillips was still Osage superintendent, despite the minerals council and the Osage Nation Congress both passing resolutions of "no confidence" in 2017 that specifically asked for her removal. Not only was Phillips refusing to regularly share information with the minerals council, but offices throughout the Nation were unable to get the information they needed to do their work.[94] In addition to the issues already discussed, Phillips was now shutting down wells for nonproduction, against the wishes of the minerals council and despite the extenuating circumstances of the global pandemic. Additionally, it now appeared that the BIA had been holding payment checks longer than the forty-eight hours required by law without paying the promised interest on these amounts.[95]

In addition to these factors demonstrating the limits of direct BIA control, there were also changes in federal policy that promised to further facilitate minerals self-governance. In December 2019 the Department of the Interior released additional clarifications surrounding its 2005 Tribal Energy Resource Agreement (TERA) process. As the *Osage News* described in a community meeting announcement, a TERA "allows a tribe to review, approve and manage leases, business agreements and rights of way for energy development on tribal land without having to go through the Secretary of Interior every step of the way."[96] This negotiated process would allow Native nations to take over certain functions from the federal government.

During the community meeting hosted on Zoom on September 3, 2020, Wilson Pipestem, the minerals council's lawyer, explained the major pros and cons of the TERA process. He described how a TERA would allow the Osage Nation to create laws around environmental protection, deciding for itself what standards to use, rather than using the standards that were applied to all federal lands. Self-governance could also allow for the creation of more efficient processes, as the federal system was known for its many layers of oversight, which slowed and complicated even the most basic processes. Going into a great deal of depth on federal and Osage Nation laws, Wilson made the case that the minerals council would oversee these processes and should not fear Osage Nation involvement because federal and Osage laws protected the mineral estate.

Pipestem went on to explain that one of the major cons of the process was the inability to later withdraw from a bad deal should the minerals council negotiate one, and that a TERA would prohibit the Nation from suing the federal government for mismanagement. As one of the lawyers involved in the 2011 settlement, Pipestem explained how exceptionally hard it was to prove mismanagement and what a small fraction of mismanaged funds were returned even when it was possible to prove. Pipestem's primary concern around the process was that it was not yet clear what kind of funding would be possible, as it might be financially impossible to take over these programs if the federal government was not willing to pass along its current operating funds, a core negotiated feature of these self-governance agreements.

What was perhaps most surprising about this community meeting was that for the first time the idea of minerals self-governance seemed to be gaining real traction, with no one throughout the meeting, including during the question-and-answer period, expressing any concerns about it disrupting the status of the trust. In fact, Talee Redcorn, who had long argued for the need to maintain the trust during his extended term as a minerals councilman, made a case during this meeting that self-governance had become a necessity. To the list of pros Pipestem had offered, for example, Redcorn chimed in and said that self-governance would also solve the FOIA issues, which were hindering Osage access to needed information.

In a phone conversation with Redcorn following the meeting, he explained to me what had shifted for him in recent years. "I am now convinced the BIA does not care. We won three lawsuits and the BIA is only making it more difficult. At some point we need to stand up for our sovereignty. They are only looking out for themselves."[97] As Redcorn spoke with me that Labor Day, he no longer saw the federal government as the entity that would protect his land, assets, and way of life. He saw it as more concerned with preventing future lawsuits than proactively acting in his best interest. He instead hoped that the Osage Nation could itself act as a protector.

In this conversation, however, it was also clear that there were still concrete tensions that needed to be addressed, especially over how authority would be shared between the Osage Minerals Council and the larger Osage Nation. He said, "The Nation thinks they own the village and maybe even my house; that is not a productive stance. The Nation must recognize and protect."[98] The village Redcorn spoke of here was land that, like the headrights, was held in trust for the "Osage Tribe of Indians" (now referred to as the Osage Nation), and some Osage citizens saw themselves as the ultimate beneficiaries of it. He did not see the headrights or the trust land he lived on as belonging to the Nation, but to members of that Nation like himself. This tension takes us back to discussions of the nature of the trust relationship itself, and Washburn's question of whether protecting self-governance or individual assets was the most fundamental aspect of the trust relationship. For Redcorn and some other Osage headright holders, protection of these assets was their core motivation.

As with the mineral estate, however, it was very clear that relying on the federal government to protect and promote the villages was not working. Federal policies and neglect had devastated these communities. From his front yard, where he had taken a break from changing the oil in his truck to answer my phone call, Redcorn looked around the Pawhuska village he called home, saying, "I look at all the houses out there and they are all empty because of drugs. We need to generate jobs. If we are going to be a people, we need employment, education, sports."[99] In the context of the Pawhuska Indian village, much like the mineral estate itself, relying on the federal government has had a stagnating and even deteriorating impact.

Successfully enacting self-governance means planning and preparing carefully. Through 2021 the Osage Minerals Council continued to research the self-governance options available to it, including the TERA, a compact contract, and a combination of the two. The council worked with the Osage Nation Congress, the Office of the Chiefs, and consultants to do "a market analysis, technical analysis, financial analysis, economic analysis, and environmental analysis."[100] While this extensive research clearly demonstrated financial as well as other benefits of rethinking the relationships within the minerals trust, lingering concerns remain about working with the larger Osage Nation, whether these changes would diminish or strengthen the trust relationship, the funding this new management system would require, the limited capacity of the current minerals council, and whether the BIA or the State of Oklahoma would attempt to sabotage Osage efforts.[101]

Within the constraints of the self-governance options available, the Osage Nation would not be taking over minerals management entirely. Certain aspects, such as the distribution of the royalty checks from minerals, are considered inherent federal functions and will stay under BIA management.[102] Other aspects, including some environmental constraints, would remain in place due to federal laws. In a phone conversation in October 2021, Osage Minerals Council chairman Waller argued that "self-governance allows us to have options as a Nation, not that we have to do it all ourselves. We must stop fighting federal laws and just pick out the pieces we can handle. Our systems must be ready to handle everything we take on. Our Nation needs to be able to handle everything that will come at us."[103] Osage leaders see the limitations of the BIA as the manager of our minerals and are working slowly to plan and enact self-governance.

The Osage Nation must also carefully navigate the many fraught relationships the Osage Mineral Estate Trust has generated, especially with our environment. As Curley and Lister write, "For generations, Indigenous peoples were able to survive on their lands through strategic engagement with extractive industries and capitalism. The legacies of these practices scar the landscape. They helped us survive on the land but also destroyed much of it in the process."[104] Osage soil, water, plants, animals, and bodies have all been polluted through an extractive industry that externalizes its costs, including the lasting health impacts for those living on the reservation. There is no doubt that the Osage Mineral Estate has been one of the primary tools by which Osages have survived, both economically and politically, but we must make sure we are also looking at the costs of this lifeline as we go forward. Waller acknowledged this challenge, saying, "I am looking way out of the box. I am looking at carbon capture. I am going to plug more wells than I drilled and I know I am helping the climate. You can't spend money if the earth is on fire."[105] Changing the distribution of power from the federal government and corporations to Native nations must be at the core of any environmental movement in Indian Country, but it alone will not address the long-term costs of extractive industries.[106]

Of course, the impact of the Osage Mineral Estate on our ways of relating is not limited to the environment; it affects all aspects of our lives, especially the institutions we govern ourselves with. Washburn argues: "Routine tribal operation of federal programs has also had salubrious effects on tribal governments. Through running federal programs, tribes have not only become much more sophisticated in providing services, but also have improved tribal capacities for responsible administration, such as budgeting, enforcing internal controls, and undergoing audits."[107] Such an assertion drastically overstates the positive impacts of the trust relationship to date while also hiding the extensive damage this relationship has done to the functioning of Native nation government. It does, however, point to one of the important consequences of federal systems of recognition. To run these federal programs, Native nations have had to create state-like systems, which contain much of the bureaucratic baggage that has stymied the BIA and other bureaucratic institutions. The next chapter will describe the challenges of nation building in such bureaucratic spaces.

The trust relationship between the federal government and Native nations is a deeply fraught space. In the Osage context, it has facilitated the erosion of our lands, a shifting and limiting of our government and citizenship, the murder and theft of our lives and assets, a deep reliance on federal paternalism, an underdevelopment of our own self-governance capacities, and extreme mismanagement of our assets. From the beginning of this relationship, however, Osage leaders have held the federal government to its promise of protection. Osage and other Native leaders are now demonstrating that the strength of this trust relationship is tied to its ability to foster Native self-governance. As the Osage Mineral Estate case demonstrates, focusing the trust on federal accountability rather than on developing self-governance can have disastrous effects. Self-governance, however, is also a deeply challenging process, which must be approached with great care and planning, as the following chapter will explore in more depth. The Osage Nation, like many Native nations, has continually utilized our trust relationship with the federal government to ensure that we have a future. To continue our ongoing process of moving the Osage Nation into the future, however, Osages are recognizing the violence that the federal government has done in its role as our trustee and seeking our own solutions to the many problems we face.

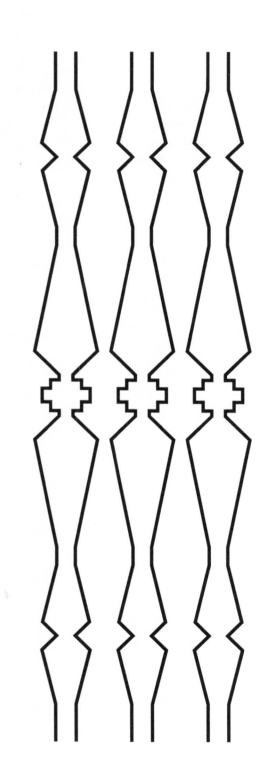

CHAPTER THREE

Health

"It Is No Longer What IHS Says Goes"

Two days into their July 2015 Special Session, the Osage Nation Congress was ready to vote on compacting the Indian Health Service (IHS) facility located on their campus in Pawhuska, Oklahoma.[1] This would mean that the Osage Nation would enter into a self-governance agreement with the IHS, which outlined the amount of funds the IHS would provide each year and what materials they would pass on to the Nation. Inheriting the existing clinic building and all equipment from the IHS, the Osage Nation would take on all the duties of operating the clinic.

Congressman R. J. Walker spoke first, describing the clinic as a key piece of the Osage Nation's campus (the area in Pawhuska that held most of the government's buildings, operations, and services). He was very excited about what would be possible with the clinic under Osage control, including programs tailored to Osage needs, much more robust staffing, new equipment, and eventually a new building. Such changes were desperately needed, as the IHS had long neglected the now dilapidated Pawhuska facility, which only had two full-time physicians and outdated equipment. He concluded by saying, "This is our healthcare and our responsibility."[2]

The new congresswoman Angela Pratt picked up on these themes, saying that she was in support, but that this was something the Congress needed to stay on top of to ease constituent concerns.[3] Many Osages worried that the Osage Nation was not equipped to run such an unwieldy healthcare bureaucracy. Joe Conner, an Osage from Fairfax, Oklahoma, ran Paradox Consulting, a company that had conducted feasibility studies for tribes wanting to compact their health clinics. He had recently written an op-ed in the *Osage News* describing two things necessary for ensuring the success of compacting IHS facilities: economic and management feasibility. "Will the dollars the tribe gets from the Indian Health Service and dollars and collections from insured Indian patients be enough to maintain the level of service patients now receive? ... Does the Osage Nation have the expertise to operate a healthcare system like that of the Indian Health Service?"[4] Osage congressional research demonstrated that by adding insured Indian patient funds, especially of Osage employees, to the funds from the IHS, the Nation would actually increase the revenue available for healthcare. And given that many of the clinic employees had said they were willing to stay on, it seemed as if the Nation did have the expertise needed.

Congresswoman Shannon Edwards responded to Pratt's concerns by saying that they should not operate from a place of fear, and that she herself was not afraid, as this project had been in the works for at least ten years. Congressman Kugee Supernaw also supported compacting, but offered the caution that unlike the economic development opportunities the Nation was running, there was more than money on the line with this clinic—health and lives would also be affected. Given the high stakes of operating a clinic, this was something that required extensive planning and preparation.[5]

Congressman Ron Shaw then stood to speak on the legislation he had sponsored. Shaw had thirty-five years of medical experience, which included service as the former medical director of the Citizen Potawatomi Nation's Health Services. He described some of the history behind this effort and his vision for what this clinic could become.

> When I was on the Osage Health Advisory board, we toured the nice new facility the Choctaw had built in McAlister. We asked, "Why can't we have this?" The IHS has provided us a service and their employees have worked hard for us, but we are prepared to take this to the next level. . . . My goal is to be the premier healthcare provider in the area, including Tulsa. You won't recognize this in a few years. . . . It is no longer what IHS says goes. What they decide we must live with. We are the decision makers now. After today it will be the Osage Nation's decision. We will truly be in control of our health destiny here on the reservation.[6]

More than anything else, it was this ability of Osages to finally be in control of our own healthcare that motivated the important move.

The vote that followed was in unanimous support of compacting the clinic. In these Osage Nation Congress discussions during 2015, it was clear that while some Osages remained concerned about whether the IHS clinic was something the Osage Nation could run successfully, Osage leaders felt like the Nation was ready to take on this massive project. They envisioned the former IHS health clinic as a space they could transform, creating not only higher standards of care but a new order that would finally meet Osage health needs. They envisioned not only a fancy new building or updated equipment but the creation of a national healthcare system.

Despite the assurances offered by the Osage Nation Congress, there were many logistical reasons to fear the compacting process. Even with its many years of experience facilitating transitions to self-governance, the IHS did not have any concrete process in place. In fact, the shift from IHS to Osage control seemed more designed to sabotage than support Osage healthcare efforts. Two days before turning over the facility, all IHS files were removed from the clinic, leaving no records of patient healthcare or employee certification. On the day that the Osage Nation took control, the clinic no longer had any contracts for essentials like banking or billing.[7] What they did leave behind was a scarcely functional and long-neglected facility filled with outdated and broken equipment.

This chapter argues that creating an infrastructure that can better meet the health needs of the Osage people is a central project of Osage nation building in the twenty-first century that moves the Osage Nation into the future. Such a move is requiring Osage officials to create more ordered relations among the many healthcare programs that serve Osages, and other American Indians, on the Osage reservation. The story of trying to turn the dilapidated Pawhuska Indian Health Center into a premier Native health facility is a powerful case study for understanding the challenges and possibilities in using colonial structures, especially bureaucracy, to facilitate Indigenous health. Many Native nations have taken over neglected federal programs and attempted to use these structures to build networks of care for their citizens.[8] What these communities inherit in this transition, however, creates many obstacles to such care.

With the state of governmental programs such as the IHS, it is almost impossible to imagine Native nations not wanting to take over these programs, but in doing so, these nations are being forced into a new set of relations. This chapter begins with a brief discussion of Osage conceptions of "order," and how this vital concept is at the core of Osage engagements with bureaucracy, particularly in our healthcare. This will be followed by an interrogation of the history of colonial health efforts, including a discussion of how Native peoples have repeatedly tried to intervene in these spaces of colonial disorder, neglect, assimilation, and elimination. I will then turn to the twenty-first-century IHS transition and clinic accreditation processes for the newly minted Wahzhazhe Health Center, where Osages attempted to bring order to a neglected space and cumbersome healthcare bureaucracy. While increased billing provided improved equipment, facilities, and even services, challenges remain in building relations of order into bureaucracies, especially those

108 *Chapter Three*

burdened with national and industry standards, policies, and procedures. In 2022 the Osage Nation finally passed a bill that allowed the health programs enough independence to design systems and structures to meet their own needs, but the challenges of creating a space of care within a large bureaucracy remain daunting.

"Follow These Ways and We Will Show You How to Live"

Turning the long-neglected IHS facility into a medical facility that could provide care has led Osage officials to again seek relations of order in an intentional and thoughtful system of organization. Here and in other Osage contexts, "order" does not signal authoritarian relationships but rather a set of intentional and thoughtful relations. In moments of disruption, Osages have repeatedly looked to the models around us to find a new order that will better serve our needs.[9] This section will describe various examples of what these relations of order have looked like in Osage practices, and how they are a fundamental part of moving to a new country. I will also connect these attempts to create order with other academic discussions of bureaucracy, demonstrating bureaucracy's limitations and possibilities as an organizational form.

As this book has discussed, the search for order has been a fundamental driver of Osage structures from our origin story to our twenty-first-century government reform. In our origin story, the four groups that later became Osages came together and moved away from "earth-ugliness" to a new country where we created a new order.[10] Our clan structure served as a fundamental guide for this order, identifying everyone's role in the family and community. Oral histories of the Osage Nation describe the sociopolitical structure of the Nation as consisting of multiple groups, including the ᏒᎪᏉᎪ (Earth People) and the ᎬᏂᏗᎣ (Sky People). Within these groups there were multiple clans representing the spectrum of life on earth. The clan system created a network of relationships, called ᏉᎪᏒᎣ, that ensured that everyone depended on each other and that all had to act together as one group toward the goal of ensuring a future for generations to come.[11] We looked to each of these different elements, whether the "gentle sky" or the "brown horse," to guide how that individual needed to behave and engage with family and community.

Each had their own role to play and even a specific location within the geographical layout of the houses in each village. Describing this structure, Osage elder Eddy Red Eagle Jr. said, "Order solidified itself in the clans. Follow these ways and we will show you how to live. The only way they could do that was to separate out those duties and put specific knowledge in different clans. When issues developed, different people had a responsibility to contribute."[12] Order in this context meant understanding your specific role, working as a unified group, and playing your part for the good of the whole.

Much like the cosmos, with its many shifting "cycles of birth, growth, maturity, and death," Osage order was not static but necessarily changed over time.[13] Some examples of these changes in Osage structure during the nineteenth century are a substantial growth in the number of clans from fourteen to twenty-four, as well as the development of new ceremonial practices. These changes accommodated expansions Osages had in population and territory during this period, ensuring that order was maintained as the Nation grew.[14] Osages' many practices, whether they be ꓵꞆꝋꞖꞣꞥ, weddings, funerals, namings, Native American Church ceremonies, or community meals, are constantly being adapted to meet our needs.[15] Like other examples of order, ꓵꞆꝋꞖꞣꞥ are a set of practices adopted from those around us in a period when we were navigating extensive change. When Osages were forced to leave our Kansas territory and move to the reservation, we left behind our complex holistic governmental and spiritual system and practices, which were no longer working in the colonial context. The Kaw Nation and Ponca Tribe, neighbors and relatives of the Osage, gifted the ceremony by bringing a drum to each of our newly established villages in the Oklahoma reservation. Leaders modified these adopted practices so they served Osage needs.

ꓵꞆꝋꞖꞣꞥ have a meticulous order designed to promote unity. Although the ceremony differs slightly from village to village, each village (referred to now as "districts") has a similar committee headed by a drumkeeper, a position of honor passed among males from different families within the district, who is charged with leading the committee and the district's activities. Additional positions include a head committeeman, the spokesperson for the drumkeeper and the committee; whipmen, who keep order throughout the ceremony; singers, both male and female, who are led by a head singer; cooks—one of the most valued positions within the committee—who are responsible for preparing meals for the host committee and visiting committees and led by a head cook; drum warmers, who tend to the drum before and after the dance; advisers, both male and female, who advise the drumkeeper on conducting the dance; and waterboys, the younger males of the district, who provide water to the dancers and singers under the arbor. The longevity of this ceremony is often attributed to each person's commitment to fulfilling their role and acting in the interests of the community rather than their own personal interests.

The order created in ᏁᏘᎣᏓᏏᎥ is something that Osages point to as an example of how we work together best as a people; when we have clear roles and are working toward a common good. Discussing the challenges facing the Osage Nation in 2012, Vann Bighorse, then director of the Osage Cultural Center, expressed the opinion that we "needed to learn from the Osage ᏁᏘᎣᏓᏏᎥ dances, when everything (especially political fighting) was put aside for those three weeks in June and everyone from the drumkeeper to the cooks focused on making the whole thing run smoothly. Each person had a set role and one didn't interfere with the roles of others."[16] Accepted roles are vital to the success of these annual dances and clearly manifest Osage notions of order.

During the writing of the preamble of the constitution, Osage government reform commissioners discussed the importance of order to Osages historically.[17] Reform commissioner Charles Red Corn argued, "We need to get that thought in there that the ancients were real organized."[18] The program coordinator Hepsi Barnett agreed, suggesting the language include, "Throughout the passage of history, [Osages] always looked for order."[19] The group ultimately decided on this sentence: "Acknowledging our ancient tribal order as the foundation of our present government, first reformed in the 1881 Constitution of the Osage Nation, we continue our legacy by again reorganizing our government."[20] The legacy they are referring to here is not just constitutional government but the ongoing search for order through reorganization.

This Osage conception of order has also influenced Osage Nation Supreme Court decisions over separation of powers between the Congress and executive branch. In its 2017 decision *Standing Bear v. Pratt*, the court cited ethnologist Francis La Flesche talking about how the clan system reflected one of the Osages' earliest known examples of order with clear roles designed to support the common good. "Basic knowledge was shared by the twenty-four clan priesthoods, [yet] each clan also had exclusive control over parts of this knowledge."[21] The Justices used this quote as an early example of how separation of powers assigned roles and responsibilities, as well as separation of functions. Looking to these accounts of our history, the court found that having defined roles and responsibilities was an important living value that the parties had a constitutional duty to uphold.[22]

In the process of compacting the IHS's Pawhuska clinic, Osages were once again seeking to create a new order, this time through bureaucracy. The *Merriam-Webster* dictionary has several definitions of *bureaucracy*, two of which are relevant here. The first is "a body of nonelected government officials."[23] Part of the motivation for having nonelected employees making health decisions, at least in the context of the Osage Nation, was that elected officials don't necessarily have the knowledge or skills to run such specialized programs. The second definition of *bureaucracy* is a "government character-ized by specialization of functions, adherence to fixed rules, and a hierarchy of authority."[24] Most of these core elements can be seen in other Osage con-ceptions of order. Certainly, each person having their own specific role and following the expected protocols fits neatly within our understanding of what has made our structures successful.

While these abstract definitions of bureaucracy demonstrate why Osages might choose to embrace such a form, they do not represent what such usage looks like in practice, nor do they indicate whether it helps us create order. US scholar Monique Nuijten has described bureaucracy as a "hope-generating machine," naming how it can work to convince bureaucrats that the structures they are part of can fix problems in governance, particularly when concerned with equality.[25] Many scholars have named the ways bureaucracies rarely live up to their promises of order and are actually quite arbitrary and capricious in nature.[26] Others have documented the ways that bureaucracies work to main-tain power inequality and create space for colonial values of indifference and individualism to take shape in communities across the globe.[27]

Ethnographic scholarship has also challenged popular understandings of bureaucracy as a tool of domination, painting a more nuanced and compli-cated picture. This scholarship argues that many bureaucratic practices work unevenly and toward diverse goals. Moving away from moral critiques and easy dismissals of bureaucracy, recent scholarship, particularly in India, has revealed how power is negotiated in bureaucratic contexts. At stake in these situations is whose "utopian desires and pragmatic concerns" prevail, demon-strating how bureaucracies are a powerful window into debates about what exactly is the public good.[28]

In the context of Indigenous studies, bureaucracy has generally been ig-nored, despite its growing place in our Native nations. When it is discussed, it is dismissed as an inorganic governing structure imposed by colonial powers and a culturally inappropriate process.[29] One exception to this is Cherokee Nation scholar Clint Carroll, who addresses it head-on, writing, "The current structure of the Cherokee Nation government, based as it is on rationality, citizen equality, and bureaucratic order, inhibits the influ-ence of 'traditional' sources of authority. Nevertheless, more central to my objectives herein is how indigenous communities have developed ways to deal with this dilemma."[30] In his scholarship Carroll demonstrates how the inherited bureaucracy of federal land management, with its complicated "checker boarded" jurisdictions, overwhelms the Cherokee Nation's Natural Resources Department, limiting the work it can do. Carroll's ethnographic focus, however, allows him to observe the creative ways that Cherokee utilize and navigate bureaucracies to meet the needs of their communities.

Building on Carroll's work, this chapter seeks to understand how Osages are dealing with systems of bureaucracy in the context of our healthcare system. In addition to naming the colonial legacies and challenges inherent within this bureaucracy, this chapter describes how Osages are working toward an order for our healthcare, so that it might meet our needs. This is a fraught process filled with choices not of our making, but also a space of continued possibility. In looking at the Osage Nation's search for order through bureaucracy, this chapter demonstrates another way in which Osages are seeking vital relations to move the Osage Nation into the future.

"Invoke Its Protection and Care"

As in the colonial histories this book has shared of Osage language and self-governance, colonial actors and practices have created and continue to create devastating health conditions for Indigenous communities. This section will focus on the ways colonial actors have disrupted Indigenous health practices, fostered disease and illness in Indigenous communities, failed to deliver on promises of care, and brought widespread sickness to Osage people. The goal in telling this story is not to perpetuate the dying Indian myth but to chronicle some of the colonial consequences Osages must navigate as we make decisions for ourselves about what our healthcare will entail.

During the nineteenth century and likely before, Osages' health practices were woven into our spiritual and ceremonial practices. Physical, mental, and spiritual health were intertwined and received daily devotion.[31] In addition and sometimes as part of these regular "rituals," Osages utilized sweat lodges and extensive medicinal plants that have documented, if often undermined, healing capacities.[32] Heat, especially when combined with prayer, removes toxins from the body, supports relaxation, improves joint mobility, reduces pain, increases immunity, and fosters mental clarity.[33] Some examples of medicinal plants utilized by Osages include buffalo gourd, culver's root, dewberry, goat's rue, purple poppy mallow, Seneca snakeroot, smooth sumac, wild indigo, willow, and yarrow.[34] While colonial forces have worked to promote Western biomedical knowledge at the expense of Indigenous health practices, these practices are part of a larger resurgence in Osage and other Indigenous communities.[35]

In addition to these practices, Osages studied the world around us and understood illness, including infectious disease transmission. When there were signs of disease, Osages would disperse in small groups to avoid widespread contagion.[36] Osages were thus able to avoid early pandemics of influenza, cholera, smallpox, and other colonial diseases by literally moving to a new country. For example, nineteenth-century US scholar James Owen Dorsey recorded the sayings of town criers, who ran from village to village sharing news. "Wát se -ně añkí hase tápi au! Nǔⁿ pa eǐ taⁿ hǔ wákøiⁿ tsé taakgá, étaⁿ" ("Let us flee from the disease called Waste-ne! A great many will soon die if they do not fear to face it, therefore it is good to flee"), one is recorded as saying.[37] Here again we see how the process of moving meant observing the world and making changes, in this case literal moves, to ensure that the Osage people had a future.

As each subsequent treaty moved us onto increasingly smaller parcels of land, it became harder to flee infection. During the 1830s, Osage homelands in what is now Kansas, Arkansas, Missouri, and Oklahoma began filling with settlers and refugees from the east, primarily consisting of Cherokees forcefully removed from what had become the state of Georgia. This tragic violence devastated the Cherokee community by uprooting them from their homelands and killing thousands (at least one-fourth of those who made the trip). Given their weakened immunity from the stress of this rupture and the duress of the forced march of 2,200 miles, it is not surprising that they were suffering from a surge of diseases when they arrived on Osage homelands.[38]

Around 1832 treaties began to include funding and staffing for health services within Native communities.[39] The 1865 Treaty with the Osage, for example, included stipulations for a physician and stated that "the Osages acknowledge their dependence on the Government of the United States, and invoke its protection and care."[40] Such articulations of "dependence" and "protection" served federal interests at the time by positioning Native nations as internal to, rather than external from, the United States. Simultaneously, however, this language also created what Native peoples understood as a set of relational responsibilities, which they have fought hard to enforce, as the previous chapter discussed in detail. These obligations have been confirmed and further defined in Supreme Court decisions, congressional legislation, executive orders, and various policies. Since these treaties, different federal agencies have been charged with running health programs for Native peoples, including the War Department, the Department of the Interior, and eventually the Public Health Service, which created a new division that became known at the Indian Health Service (IHS) in 1955.[41]

The federal government's health efforts were part of larger assimilation policies, which attempted to eliminate Native nations' claims to territory by severing the ties Native peoples had to their ways of life, communities, and governance structures. Historians typically consider the assimilation era of US policy as lasting from 1880 to 1920, although assimilationist ideologies were already circulating before 1880 and many policies and institutions have lasted well beyond the 1920s, including the hospitals and clinics. Boarding schools; forced adoption; sterilization; a focus on small-scale farming; the outlawing and discouragement of a wide spectrum of Native practices, especially those related to healthcare; and the destruction of connections to traditional foods were all tools used to disrupt the health of Native families, communities, and nations.[42] The 1887 Dawes Act and subsequent allotment efforts were a central feature of this period, opening up ninety million acres of land to white settlement and transferring the vast majority of Native nation territory to private ownership.[43]

Alongside schools, the federal government used Western medical practitioners and their institutions as key tools in its effort to assimilate and thus eliminate Osage and other Native peoples' ways of life. As they did with boarding schools, discussed in the previous chapter, Osages met this effort with their own efforts to assimilate these individuals and institutions to meet our own needs. This contested process is at the core of what moving the Osage Nation into the future has entailed. The first permanent hospital was erected on Osage territory in 1885, adjacent to the school building.[44] In his annual report to the commissioner of Indian affairs the year before, nearby Indian agent P. B. Hunt described the need for a hospital to disrupt the continued influence of local medical practices. He argued that "every Indian brought from the camp to the hospital would be thrown directly under the civilizing and Christianizing influences."[45] In claiming to provide health interventions, federal agents not only covered over the infectious and lifestyle diseases they were inflicting on Native peoples, but they attempted to undermine the systems of care that had long supported our peoples.

During the early twentieth century, assimilationist projects worked to discredit Native practices and associate white medical approaches and general lifestyle choices with health and well-being. US scholar Brianna Theobald tells the story of these colonial health efforts through the lens of Native childbirth and the Crow Indian Hospital. She describes the many official policies and unofficial practices federal employees used to move childbirth into the hospital starting in the 1910s, including the 1912–18 Save the Babies campaign.[46] This campaign attempted to discredit Indigenous practices of childbirth and infancy, utilizing Euro-American women as field matrons who would visit the houses of pregnant women to impart lessons that "blended Euro-American gender ideology, family norms, and Westernized medical care."[47] While this example and similar missionary-style efforts were framed as fulfilling a moral obligation to save Natives from sickness and death, they were built from and reinforced colonial ideologies of Indigenous inferiority. Ignoring and even hiding the devastating impact of colonialism on Native peoples, assimilation-based health policies positioned Natives as inherently dirty and ignorant, while hospitals were considered safe spaces where best practices would be enacted. Such efforts were underway long before antibiotics led hospitals to improve maternal and infant healthcare outcomes starting around the 1950s.[48]

Despite these racist initiatives, however, Native peoples have attempted to create our own relationships with these clinics, seeking to gain control over our own healthcare even in these deeply colonized clinics. As trusted community members took positions in these hospitals and on advisory boards around the mid-twentieth century, policies were created to meet community needs, especially around visitation. Such efforts led to many Native peoples developing what Theobald terms the "hospital habit."[49] Native peoples labored to indigenize these spaces through constant negotiation, but tensions remained over not only how much authority Native peoples would have over these spaces but how much funding they would receive from the US Congress.[50] Writing about the impact of congressional budget shifts during and after World War II on Navajo health choices, US scholar Wade Davies argues, "Traditional healing had been steadfast through the years, but Western medicine at mid-century proved undependable. The more American Indian people demanded Bureau of Indian Affairs medical care, the more reliant they were on Congressional appropriations, and the more affected they were by broad changes at the national and global levels."[51] While the New Deal ushered in a surge of funding for federal health initiatives that increased Native usage, World War II cutbacks solidified consistent neglect in funding Indian health efforts.

Given the clearly racist and assimilationist nature of its programs, as well as the failures to adequately fund facilities, staff, and equipment, it is not surprising that Native peoples continued to feel disrespected in these spaces even as they became increasingly reliant on them. The violence of these spaces was particularly stark in the 1970s when between 25 and 45 percent of Native American women of reproductive age were sterilized, many forcefully or without appropriate consent.[52] As US scholar Jane Lawrence writes,

Native women have described extensive healthcare malfeasance concerning sterilization, including "failure to provide women with necessary information regarding sterilization; use of coercion to get signatures on the consent forms, improper consent forms; and lack of an appropriate waiting period (at least seventy-two hours) between the signing of a consent form and the surgical procedure."[53] As part of her evidence, Lawrence includes statistics that are a composite of Ponca, Omaha, and Osage birth records showing a drastic decline in the average number of children from 2.73 in 1970 to 1.51 in 1980.[54] Such widespread sterilization had a devastating impact on Native nations. Not only did it cause those individual women excessive harm, but it also frequently disrupted their relationships with their husbands, families, and communities, in addition to denying a generation of Native people the ability to build a future for our peoples.

The horrific nature of widespread sterilization galvanized Native women and nations to demand fundamental change. The Women of All Red Nations established in Rapid City, South Dakota, in 1974, for example, organized Native women across the nation and took these issues to the international stage, arguing for sovereignty over their bodies. Speaking at the Conference of Discrimination against Indigenous Peoples in Geneva, Switzerland, in September 1977, Marie Sanchez (Northern Cheyenne) said, "The Indian women of the Western Hemisphere are the target of the genocide that is still ongoing, that is still the policy of the United States of America. We are undergoing a modern form called sterilization."[55] Naming sterilization as a clear manifestation of ongoing genocide was a vital step in demanding self-determination and ultimately respect. This activism was occurring simultaneously with the larger Red Power and tribal sovereignty movements of the 1960s and 1970s, which sought increased Native nation control over federal programs. Well beyond healthcare, the many ways the federal government failed to uphold its treaty promises created a strong impetus for self-determination, and this advocacy resulted in new congressional legislation and policy.[56]

While the Indian Self-Determination and Education Assistance Act (Public Law 93-638) created an opening for self-governance over programs administered by the federal government, not all nations immediately sought to run these programs themselves, especially IHS clinics. Some Native peoples, including many Osages, argued that self-governance was the latest strategy of termination, and that the federal government was just using neoliberal strategies to diminish its treaty and moral obligations.[57] Native leaders, for example, described the policy of self-governance as "'termination by appropriation' because the tribes would be on the hook for program operations during an era of shrinking resources."[58] Others pointed out that there was not enough funding available to operate the clinics at the necessary level and that Native nations were being set up to fail.[59] In a similar vein, other Native leaders argued for increased IHS funding so that the federal government could fulfill its obligations.[60] These concerns continue to surface, especially as courts are increasingly unwilling to hold the federal government accountable for lapses in the trust responsibility when tribes are operating under self-determination.[61] In the twenty-first century, however, a younger set of Native voters and leaders have come into power who think of self-governance as a vital step for rebuilding respect with Native nations and peoples, especially in the face of consistent colonial neglect and malfeasance.[62]

Furthermore, self-governance was particularly slow in the context of the IHS because its administrators have been hesitant to hand over authority. US scholar Fletcher McClellan describes the early implementation challenges of Public Law 93-638 by saying, "Contracting between federal agencies and tribal organizations required significant change in the attitudes and behavior of agencies who were heretofore reluctant to relinquish program control to tribal governments."[63] The latitude built into the law allowed the IHS and Bureau of Indian Affairs to deny or significantly scale back self-determination based on a lack of funding.[64] In the context of the IHS, the decision-making process was also overly cumbersome, requiring approvals at both the local agency and central office levels.[65] Former assistant secretary for Indian affairs Kevin Washburn describes this continued hesitancy in the IHS in the twenty-first century as resulting from a more inculcated savior complex that many healthcare professionals have.[66] Change has come slowly as newer, often Native, employees take on positions at the IHS. These employees see the improvements that have resulted from Native nation control and are helping to facilitate this transfer of authority.[67]

Finally, the Osage Nation did not have the bureaucratic infrastructure to run the clinic itself until the twenty-first century as a result of the extreme limitations placed on Osage governance by the 1906 act, where the governing body was primarily intended to oversee minerals extraction. Osages were hardly alone in having to navigate such colonially imposed limitations. Almost all previous federal policies—whether allotment or the New Deal, which replaced Native nation governments with cookie-cutter tribal councils—worked to limit the capacity of Native nation governments.[68] Without the robust checks and balances that were built into many earlier Native nation governments, it is far harder to successfully manage a healthcare facility. With the passage of the 2006 Osage Nation Constitution, the Osage people again formed a governing structure that was much better equipped for large-scale management and fostering relations of order.

Osage Nation officials were primarily motivated to compact the clinic because of the limited services and poor conditions offered at the facility, most of which stemmed from underfunding by at least 30 percent.[69] Compared with the $7,784 that the US government spent on the average Medicare beneficiary in the early twenty-first century, the IHS only spent $2,130 per capita. Even the healthcare for federal prisoners had significantly more money devoted to it per capita, at $3,242.[70] In the Pawhuska IHS facility, this limited funding meant that there were often only one or two doctors in the clinic, and turnover was frequent. The building and equipment were literally falling apart. Over the years, the IHS had invested almost no money in maintenance, and most of the equipment in the Pawhuska clinic had already served in two other facilities. The x-ray machine was designed for use on animals, and the wiring in the building did not support existing, much less updated, equipment.[71] Compacting meant that the Osage Nation could develop third-party billing of insurance companies and Medicare to generate additional revenue. It also meant that the Osage Nation could gain far more authority over the running of the clinic. Under the IHS, the clinic was a field office of the Pawnee Indian health clinic, and thus the facilities manager had minimal decision-making power or responsibility. Almost all decisions had to go through a large bureaucratic network, slowing everything from treatment to hiring. In taking over this space, Osages hoped they could build a network of care, which the federal government had failed to do.

The need to intervene in this failed colonial healthcare system was made even more urgent given the health crises of many Osages and other Native peoples living in the Pawhuska area. This community, as in other Indigenous communities, has a broad spectrum of health consequences, which are directly linked to historical and ongoing colonial policies and trauma.[72] Even after self-determination became the official federal policy, Indigenous health practices, foodways, and community support networks continue to be under attack and IHS clinics are not making the necessary health interventions, especially in preventative care. American Indian and Alaska Native peoples have some of the worst health outcomes of any population in the United States, with a life expectancy of 2.3 years less than their white counterparts.[73] American Indian populations have 80 percent lifetime prevalence of psychological and emotional issues, often directly or indirectly connected to generational trauma.[74] Additional research has shown a direct connection between the stress, trauma, and racism experienced by American Indians and various diseases, including cardiometabolic disease.[75] In 2013 the Pawhuska Indian Health Center reported that "this patient population faces disproportionately high rates of chronic conditions, such as high blood pressure (also called hypertension), heart disease, and diabetes."[76] A central part of moving the Osage Nation into the future is the disruption of this colonially created health crisis.

By 2015, when the Osage Nation compacted, a small majority of IHS facilities were being operated through self-governance agreements. According to the IHS website, "The IHS and Tribes have negotiated 90 self-governance compacts that are funded through 115 funding agreements with over 350 (or 60 percent) of the 567 federally recognized Tribes. This program constitutes approximately $1.8 billion (or nearly 40 percent) of the IHS budget."[77] While there are many markers of success for these programs, including increased funding to these facilities, the growing number of participants is perhaps the largest marker of success. In 2015, Osage Nation leadership decided that a key piece of fostering a healthy future for the Osage people was taking over the operations of the Pawhuska Indian Health Center. Creating a network of care out of this disorder remains an exceptional challenge.

"I Need You All to Hear Some of What We Are Up Against"

The challenges that faced the Osage Nation as we compacted the clinic were far greater and more complicated than anyone in the government realized in 2015. Not only had the IHS deeply neglected the facility and equipment of the building, but the transition process seemed designed to sabotage patient care. The Osage Nation also had to create a structure within its government operations to oversee and manage not just the clinic itself but all the various grant-funded health programs so that they could work together toward the end of meeting the extensive health needs of the Osage people. This section will detail the many challenges that faced the Osage Nation immediately following the compacting process and explain the reasons why bureaucracy came to be understood as a solution to the challenges the Nation was facing. This case is a powerful example of how bureaucracy works as a "hope-generating machine" in the Osage context.[78]

Just a month after Congress had authorized compacting the health clinic, it was already clear to Chief Geoffrey Standing Bear that there were going to be major challenges with taking over the IHS clinic. On August 17, 2015, Standing Bear, Assistant Chief Raymond Red Corn, and several staff members discussed at length the challenges the Nation was facing during their regular Monday-morning staff meeting. When I arrived, they were already sitting around the conference table in a small nondescript room of the Pawhuska Business Development Center, where the executive branch had its temporary office while their building was being remodeled. The center was managed by Tri Country Tech, a twenty-thousand-square-foot public education institution serving northeast Oklahoma with five industrial bays, ten office spaces, two classrooms, and one conference room that the Nation frequently utilized, especially for boards that did not have their own dedicated offices or employees who were waiting for their office space to be remodeled.

Turning more specifically to the issues of the clinic, Standing Bear explained that the ability of the clinic to buy pharmaceuticals and charge insurance companies, including Medicare, would not transfer, and that "our elders are scared to death."[79] This statement, while meant figuratively, hung in the air, underscoring the life-and-death issues at stake, especially for some older Osages who relied on medications and care they received from this facility. Given that the clinic was already in operation, Osage leadership had assumed that it could pick up where the IHS left off and build out from there, but it was becoming very clear what an uphill battle it would be to take over the clinic. All contracts had to be renegotiated, even for banking. Many of these contracts, especially for billing, required accreditation or special exceptions to be operative. Accreditation required not only identifying the right organization and going through at least a nine-month approval process but also the creation of entirely new policies and procedures to fit within the new organization's models and stipulations. It was going to require the development of an immense amount of specified knowledge and dedicated time on the part of Osage leaders to pull off this transition.

Most problematically, the IHS had no transition process in place, and there was no clear information on how to go about getting exceptions until accreditation could be secured. Naming this impediment, Standing Bear said, "The problem is that the IHS people won't talk to us, which is crucial for getting things done. We can't make the transition on our own, we need IHS help." Red Corn agreed: "We were told that these things would be grandfathered in, but we are now seeing that is not how it works. We need to stop relying on anyone giving us bad information." Standing Bear agreed: "There is so much we need to do that no one has told us about."[80] This lack of communication and misleading information were large stumbling blocks. They hindered the Osage Nation's ability to plan for the transition and limited the Nation's understanding of what the transition even entailed.

In taking over the clinic from IHS, the Osage Nation inherited an unwieldy healthcare bureaucracy, with all the requirements and hindrances such entities contain, without the ongoing relationships to banks, insurance, billing, or accreditation needed. While compacting opened the possibility of vastly improving the services offered and the quality of the facility, it also brought the entire infrastructure of the Nation into a new set of relations. It was already clear that the nation's HR, accounting, and other indirect services were going to be overwhelmed by the new, vastly more complicated, unique, and highly time-sensitive needs of the clinic. Furthermore, it was deeply challenging to figure out the management structure, especially the role that elected Osage leadership would play in the management of the health programs. What was clear was that a new order had to be established.

The 2006 Osage Constitution's primary tool for creating order was the development of a robust bureaucracy. The 2006 constitution created the bureaucracy through a structure of boards to oversee programs and businesses, moving them out from under the direct management of the elected officials into spaces where the individuals running them would have more specialization and develop unique rules and regulations to manage them. These boards were tasked with overseeing operations of various Osage Nation entities, especially business enterprises. Article VII—Executive, Section 14, of the 2006 Osage Nation Constitution reads, "There shall be established, by Osage law, a Tribal Enterprise Board(s) in the Executive Branch, and the Principal Chief shall appoint qualified professionals to oversee operations of Osage Nation business enterprises, by and with the advice and consent of the Osage Nation Congress. The Osage Nation Congress shall reserve the right to review any action taken by the Board, and may approve the Annual Plan of Operation for the coming year. No Osage Nation elected official may be appointed to such Board."[81] The writers of the constitution included this bureaucracy because of the many constituent concerns expressed throughout the 2004–6 Osage government reform process about elected officials who had been running the Nation's businesses, not only because they lacked the relevant experience but because of the potential for corruption given the lack of oversight.[82] These are classic concerns that frequently motivate the development of bureaucracies. Given Osages' long-standing search for order, such an embrace should not be surprising.

With the passage of the constitution, the Osage Nation's bureaucracy has grown exponentially, but with limited success. Board members were often quite knowledgeable, but they almost always had other full-time jobs, meaning they were limited in terms of what they could be expected to take on. While the board model worked well to create a separation of powers from elected officials, the workload, especially getting initiatives off the ground, was immense.

Unlike career bureaucrats, they could only focus some of their energies on the efforts. Furthermore, the exact nature of the relationship with the executive branch and Osage Congress was often fraught, especially for nonenterprise boards that did not have clear enough guidelines for how beholden they were to the mandates of elected officials. Finally, especially in the case of business enterprises, the board structure did not stop corruption and significant financial losses for the Nation.[83]

One recent example shows some of the challenges, but also Osage officials' ongoing embrace of bureaucracy to try and create order. In early February 2023 the Osage Nation Congress held a hearing on the excessive spending of the CEO of the Osage Nation Casinos, Byron Bighorse. From January 2019 until December 2021, Bighorse spent $400,000 on food, alcohol, children's golf clubs, travel, clothing, and car detailing. During the third day of the hearing, congressional officials questioned current and recent Gaming Enterprise Board members about their bylaws and practices. Responding to a question from Congresswoman Jodie Revard about the board's supervision of the CEO, former board member Mark Simms said that while the board followed federal and Osage regulations, there was nothing that would have prevented this spending. "We watch all of the policies and procedures. We go through MICS [Minimum Internal Control Standards], TICS [Tribal Internal Control Standards] and SICS [System of Internal Controls]. As far as looking at each expense of the CEO, we have never done it in these nine years—and this has been one of our downfalls and is why we're here. We don't have any policy to say this isn't right. There's nothing in the policies that says what's 'excessive.' In reality, the CEO has had carte blanche."[84] Following this discussion, congressional members asked about the changes that had been made and whether they would be enough to stop this spending. Congress also questioned the board about why they gave Bighorse a $600,000 separation package to resign while he was being investigated. This example demonstrates that none of these core bureaucratic elements, whether separation of management from elected officials, specialization of functions, adherence to fixed rules, or hierarchies of authority, prevented excessive spending. However, it was clear throughout this hearing that it was not the bureaucracy that was being questioned, but the individuals involved and whether additional rules needed to be put in place. The promise of a better bureaucracy continued to motivate Osage officials.

It was this same hope for order that motivated Osage leaders to use bureaucracy to address the healthcare crisis the Nation had inherited from the IHS. The Osage Nation Health Authority was enacted by the Osage Nation Congress in 2011, and its board was charged with "planning, direction, coordinating, delivering, and improving health services" in the Nation, but the scope of this initial charge was limited to the few grant-funded health initiatives the Nation ran.[85] In this original law (ONCA 11-116), the health authority was envisioned more as an advisory board, but as compacting came into focus the Nation gave the board more independence and duties, so that it more closely resembled the enterprise boards. In September 2014 a new law (ONCA 14-63) made the board responsible for a clear set of duties, including credentialing staff, implementing compacting, and developing an annual budget.[86] In August 2015 it was still not clear how the Osage Nation Health Division leader, clinic director, executive branch, Osage Congress, and Health Authority Board were going to interact or who was going to take on which responsibilities. Additionally, all the nation's health programs needed to be reorganized to better work together. Relations between these entities were imagined and reimagined many times during the early years of operating the clinic, as Osage leaders sought order through bureaucracy.

As the transfer date drew closer, the health board was struggling under the weight of compacting, especially in the face of the poor communication from the IHS. In addition to the actual negotiations over what specific services they would take over initially, they also needed to plan for the transition period. While the Osage Nation had authorized money for them to hire a consultant, it was now becoming clear that the consultant needed additional training and did not have the information she needed to plan and facilitate the transition. Reflecting on the challenges of securing the needed medication and billing contracts, Standing Bear pointed out, "Health Authority has the ability to do this on their own, but I am hearing they aren't doing it. We might have to look into separation."[87] Considering the stakes of this program, and the board's lack of capacity under the current arrangement of being partially in and partially outside the Osage Nation, Chief Standing Bear recognized early on that additional modifications to the governance structure were needed. However, he saw these challenges as motivating, rather than bringing into question, the Nation's usage of bureaucracy.

An Osage Health Authority meeting on February 18, 2016, in Pawhuska demonstrated not only the many challenges that were created in inheriting the IHS bureaucracy but the challenges ahead in creating order for our healthcare through an embrace of this bureaucracy. As I entered the Pawhuska Business Development Center's medium-sized classroom, I quickly realized that there were not enough seats for everyone in attendance.[88] As I helped to unstack and place chairs around the room, I saw that this Osage Health Authority Board meeting was overflowing with upper-level Osage Nation administrators and officials. This was especially striking because the meeting was held after business hours. Three months into compacting the clinic, the many challenges of the transition were piling up. Almost all eight program directors within the health division of the Osage Nation were present, as was the health division director, three Osage Congress members, one candidate for Congress, the chief and his two most senior staff, three doctors, multiple people from the accounting department, and the director of the Office of Self-Governance, Planning, and Grant Management.[89]

This meeting presented an important opportunity to share the challenges of operating the unwieldy healthcare bureaucracy inherited from the IHS. The solutions offered were focused on building additional layers of bureaucracy into the Nation, rather than disparaging bureaucracy. The meeting began with a financial report from the Osage Nation Treasurer's Office in which the comptroller for the Nation described the challenges of bringing the Wahzhazhe Health Center, as the Pawhuska clinic had been renamed, into the accounting systems of the Nation. Many of the standard forms and protocols, such as re-quiring all transactions to go through the accounting office, were creating bottlenecks. Specific standards needed to be developed for the center. Vari-ous inventories and summary reports still needed to be set up. Mike Moore, the current chairman of the Health Authority Board, who was also the presi-dent and COO of Jane Phillips Medical Center in the neighboring town of Bartlesville, argued that if accounting could be done by Wahzhazhe Health Center staff rather than through the Nation, it would happen much more quickly and could be designed to best fit their special needs. Manon Till-man, the Osage Nation's division leader for health and wellness and de facto lead for the Wahzhazhe Health Center, agreed but said that until billing con-tracts were secured and insurance companies could be billed, they could not afford to hire additional staff. They were thus stuck in a nasty cycle of not having the money needed to hire staff that would allow them to make more money.[90]

The incongruities of bringing the Wahzhazhe Health Center within the accounting department of the Nation were just some of the challenges facing the Nation that many of those involved believed could be solved through bu-reaucracy. After several reports from Candy Thomas, the director of the Of-fice of Self-Governance, Planning, and Grant Management, in which she described her behind-the-scenes work to build partnerships and ensure fund-ing compliance, the meeting turned to a health center update from Tillman. Tillman first discussed the challenges of staffing, saying that they had only been able to secure a temporary dentist because the dentist would need to be an Osage employee, rather than a federal employee as with the compacted positions. This meant there were not the same incentives in terms of loan reduction or years-of-service bonuses. Also, given the remote location of the Wahzhazhe Health Center and the poor state of the equipment, it was hard to draw health providers into the position. By further separating the hiring from the Nation, and developing their own specialized policies, Tillman hoped these problems could be addressed.[91]

Paula Stabler, an Osage who had agreed to take on directing the health center on an interim basis when the IHS facility director had left abruptly during the transition, ominously began her report, "I need you all to hear some of what we are up against."[92] She then detailed the challenges of developing their revenue streams, primarily through billing insurance companies and Medicare. This was a complicated issue with many different moving pieces. Most billing was going to have to wait for accreditation. One contractor was willing to work with them, but everything had to be submitted by paper. For the dental contractor, there were new codes that needed to be used, which required training, but they were being told that their staff was not yet eligible for training. They now had over three hundred claims that had piled up, but they were continuing to seek alternative solutions. These are all classic examples of the challenges that bureaucracies create.[93]

Of course, the challenges of bureaucracy were not the only disorder the IHS passed on to the Osage Nation with the health clinic. Stabler then went on to describe the electric wiring as so outdated and poorly designed that when the radiologist tried using the new equipment, it shocked him and ruined several other pieces of equipment. When the dental equipment was used, the entire office lost power. The switches and wiring all needed to be converted. The scheduling system the IHS used was highly decentralized and often created conflicts and delays. Stabler had just come from a meeting with the local postmaster, who was concerned by the number of checks the Wahzhazhe Health Center was now being sent. Stabler explained to the postmaster and the room that the Nation's bank did not have any online banking services, which meant payments needed to be sent via the postal service.

Tillman interjected amid this stream of concerns that, while there was so much unanticipated work and time invested with the transition, "this clinic staff is doing an amazing job. We have been seeing patients without a hitch. We are now analyzing ourselves and making improvements. . . . Visits are up 30 percent and all the doctors have full plates."[94] Tillman wanted to be sure to point out that, while the challenges the IHS transition created for the Osage Nation were immense, the staff of the clinic, including Stabler, were going above and beyond to address these issues and move forward in the best possible way.

Following Tillman's praise, several Osage congresspeople spoke up, asking questions about the long list of challenges inherited from the IHS, especially the wiring and billing issues. Stabler did assure them that they were handling these problems, that the center was on track with its budget plans, and that she was being very careful not to spend more money than they had despite the preponderance of needs. From this discussion the Osage Nation Congress was convinced to contribute $500,000 to pay for some of the immediate needs, and the executive branch agreed to prioritize the center's needs going forward. In these ways, the Health Authority Board meeting served an important role, allowing the various leaders to understand the challenges and work together toward some immediate solutions. It was also a space where, despite the many problems it created, bureaucracy continued to generate hope among Osage officials.

"I Have Seen a Lot of Committed People Knocking Themselves Out"

As accreditation drew closer, it was becoming increasingly clear that one of the biggest challenges was how the Wahzhazhe Health Center was going to be incorporated into the Osage Nation's governing structure. In addition to the poor infrastructure, the massive health bureaucracy created large strains on the Nation's infrastructure and leadership. To solve these problems, Osage leaders turned to the further bureaucratization of Osage healthcare. This section looks at the discussions that occurred during the accreditation process as a window into the kinds of problems the healthcare bureaucracy created for the Nation and how Osage leaders were attempting to move the health clinic to a new country.

Creating a clear leadership structure was a core aspect of seeking order in this context. After months of meetings, including weekly staff meetings that Standing Bear and other senior executive staff regularly attended to help ensure problems were being addressed, Tillman and Stabler brought in a mock surveyor who could help the Wahzhazhe Health Center prepare for the accreditation survey that was six weeks away.[95] The staff began with a presentation that addressed issues of government structure. The mock surveyor pointed out that more clarity was needed on the issue of the governing board and how the health center fit within the governing structure of the Nation. Even as they started the tour, this issue was still on the mock surveyor's mind, and he expressed concern that there were too many different leadership systems at play with the Wahzhazhe Health Center and that a clarity of management was vital for their success.

Despite all the work from Tillman, Stabler and the Wahzhazhe Health Center staff since the transition from the IHS, there was still a great deal left to do before the building would be up to the standards required for accreditation. Stabler, Tillman, the compliance and performance officer Laura Sawney, and one of the doctors joined the tour, jotting down notes about additional improvements they should be making. As they walked, the mock surveyor pointed out a series of deficiencies, including the quality of construction, exposed wood, clutter, damaged ceiling tiles, anything still imprinted with IHS, electronics too close to sinks, and poor lighting. The group was going to have to work overtime to make the suggested changes in time for the official survey in six weeks.

Long-term data collection is a hallmark feature of bureaucracies, and something Osage health leaders saw as a key tool for creating better services. Returning to the conference room, the group discussed the quality improvement (QI) projects that were a central part of the Accreditation Association for Ambulatory Health Care (AAAHC) accreditation but were a challenge without the long-term data the IHS had stripped from the health center. The mock surveyor explained that for a QI you need to show that you have picked an identifiable issue, studied the problem, created a solution for the problem, and done a patient survey. The group discussed one of the current QI projects: overhauling diabetes treatment. The doctor explained that their question was whether scheduling all the patients' appointments in one visit would increase patient attendance. The group then discussed all the steps involved in the QI process as described in the AAAHC materials, including the need to collect data for at least a year.

This conversation, like so many during this period, quickly returned to the challenges the IHS transition created, in this case by not letting the Wahzhazhe Health Center keep easy access to previous patient records or files. Throughout the compacting negotiations, the Osage Nation had attempted to gain access to the patient files, but the IHS repeatedly denied these requests. Reflecting on this constraint, Stabler later said, "It was like the IHS was looking for any dirty trick and that was the dirtiest trick they could pull. They didn't want us to succeed."[96] Whether or not such IHS policies were intended to sabotage Osage efforts, the impact on the Nation's ability to provide care was very real. After the transition Tillman was persistent, making repeated calls to the IHS until someone finally agreed to open the system back up on one computer. It took a center employee many months to transfer this material into the new system, complicating not just accreditation but also patient treatment.[97]

The QI process was not the only place where the lack of easy access to IHS records was creating challenges with the accreditation process. The mock survey group spent a significant amount of time on the HR files and the need to demonstrate that everyone was properly credentialed. Stabler explained, "I had great employment files, but IHS took them and now HR has the new ones."[98] As in so many other aspects of the Wahzhazhe Health Center, Stabler was hindered by the lack of control she had. Not only had the IHS stripped all human resource files from her, but the new files were now housed in the HR department of the Osage Nation, limiting her ability to access them. The mock surveyor responded by saying, "It might be easier for you to have the HR files here. You need to know the situation for all employees. You need to be able to easily get your hands on these materials. AAAHC needs to be assured that it can access them while they are here. It is best to have them all in one location."[99] Stabler and the others agreed that staffing HR themselves would make the most sense, but they were unsure of how that would fit within Osage Nation policy.

The Nation had long centralized services such as accounting and HR, and it was not prepared or equipped for the exceptions the Wahzhazhe Health Center required. This issue became even more pronounced when the center attempted to recruit doctors. The typical practices concerning hiring in the medical profession were widely divergent from the policies and procedures of the Nation, including Osage preference laws. Expanding the bureaucracy— making it so that the health clinic staff, and not the Nation, were the ones in control of these files and processes—came to seem like an obvious solution to the challenges the clinic was facing early on.

The Wahzhazhe Health Center also overwhelmed many of the indirect services the Nation provided, including procurement, accounting, and maintenance. Describing these challenges, Stabler said, "The whole Nation was shocked that this was not just another federal program. The controller didn't want to split apart the accounts and I was regularly told that we had too many orders and contracts. . . . Our accountants had other accounts and could not keep up. We could not get a balance on anything. I had to know I could make payroll!"[100] While the Nation had developed a robust set of indirect services for their various federal and tribal programs, the scope of the Wahzhazhe Health Center was well beyond anything else the Nation operated. Additionally, funding did not happen in the same way because not everything that got billed out was returned, especially at first, and the time frame was unpredictable. The current order could not support the clinic.

Figuring out these relationships between the Nation and the health center was one of the largest challenges faced in its implementation. After a short break, the mock survey group was joined by the treasurer and controller for the Nation. The mock surveyor emphasized that the Wahzhazhe Health Center needed to have control over all its finances, in part because every grant would have its own budget requirements. Stabler used this opportunity to press the treasurer about some changes that she felt were needed. "What we need is someone on your side that is handling all things related to the clinic. . . . We need someone here to work with us on day-to-day accounting. We are making a list of things needed to keep us in compliance. . . . At one point the accountant told us to just keep spending until they told me to stop. They couldn't tell us where we stand on the staffing budget."[101] Responding to these concerns, the mock surveyor suggested that they all needed to turn these challenges into QI projects and address them that way. "This should make it less political and personal."[102] Stabler agreed, saying that people often responded to her like she was asking for special privileges or exceptions, when in fact the health center was a fundamentally different kind of program.

When the day of the AAAHC survey arrived, Stabler, Tillman, and the center's staff had all worked overtime to get as many of the pieces into place as they could. After attending an education staff meeting with Standing Bear, I joined the accreditation meetings already underway. I found the surveyor poring over HR files in the Wahzhazhe Health Center's conference room.[103] As I joined the group, the surveyor was saying that a Safety and Health Achievement Recognition Program certification was missing from the file she was currently looking at. Stabler quickly procured a document fresh from the printer. Looking at the document, the surveyor responded, "You mean to tell me she did this training last night? This is great."[104] Tillman responded that the employee had stayed late and that everyone had been working around the clock to get everything in order. This, once again, led to a discussion of the challenges of having all files taken by the IHS, with the surveyor responding, "The IHS transition is always traumatizing."[105] The surveyor was very supportive and seemed to fully understand the challenges Native nations such as the Osage faced as they attempted to compact IHS clinic facilities. As a Native woman, she had frequently been assigned to work with Native nation health facilities and she had a wealth of knowledge she brought to this two-day intensive conversation.

Throughout the AAAHC surveyor's visit, it was clear that she was committed to working with the Wahzhazhe Health Center staff to not only engage in best practices for patient health and well-being but also help create ordered relationships between the center and the Nation. As in the other conversations, these discussions focused on the need to have key services for accounting, credentialing, IT, and in-house hiring rather than using the services of the Nation, which were not set up or equipped to work with the health center. Of course, this brought up the issues of funding and space, which both created limitations on current growth.

Concluding her two-day visit, the surveyor related to all those assembled what she had found. "I have seen a lot of committed people knocking themselves out to get this place ready for this survey. Patients are provided appropriate privacy and information. . . . You do a good job with the space you have and provide a lot of services."[106] She went on to describe the many challenges the IHS created for the transition, but praised how the staff was quickly creating workarounds and new systems. She noted that while the Nation's administration was eager to help problem-solve, there was still more work to be done to iron out the relationships between the indirect services, the executive branch, the Osage Congress, the Health Authority Board, and the Wahzhazhe Health Center.

From these discussions it became clear that the accreditation site visit had been a resounding success. Accreditation was a turning point for the center, especially in terms of billing insurance companies and thus having funding for improvements and program expansion. As soon as accreditation was successful, the Osage Nation was able to file all the claims to Medicare, Medicaid, and private insurance companies that they had been accumulating over the past nine months. Stabler, always searching for ways to show her respect for her hardworking team, asked the accounting department to let her know when the Wahzhazhe Health Center reached the $1 million mark. Shortly after accreditation, the center had already brought in $1 million, mostly through insurance reimbursements for pharmaceuticals. To celebrate the occasion, Stabler printed out and hung a large banner, made "million-dollar fudge," and thanked all the employees for their hard work. Creating order in these bureaucratic systems is thus also about building relationships and creating spaces where people feel appreciated for their work.[107]

The report generated from this initial accreditation survey also proved useful in motivating Congress to address some of the challenges the Nation faced incorporating a former IHS clinic into the Nation's infrastructure. Ron Shaw sponsored legislation (ONCA 17-119) to address delays with hiring through the Osage Nation's Human Resources Department, as well as issues with the inaccessibility of HR files. This bill changed the duties and responsibilities of the Health Authority Board to "make all personnel decisions re-garding all executive administration and all employees or contractors that provide patient care."[108] This same bill also named the Health Authority Board as a governing board, but it stated that it was "responsible for assisting the Executive Branch in the operation, planning, and budgeting of the Osage Nation health and wellness services."[109] This ambiguous language left continued uncertainty over management of the Wahzhazhe Health Center, especially in areas such as accounting, which continued to be handled through the Nation.

After the first year, Stabler had not only managed to break even, but the center was $600,000 in the black.[110] One of the most pressing needs she identified was a mammography machine. At the time, the center would call around two hundred women who were due for scans and only get twenty-five who would follow through to get theirs done. She had done all the research to get the machine but was told it had to be put on hold when Shaw agreed to resign from Congress and become the center's chief medical officer and CEO. As CEO, Shaw would need to approve all large center purchases. When he came on, he was skeptical of the purchase. He cited recent research that argued mammogram scans were needed less frequently than previously thought and that there were other investments that the clinic needed more.

As in her time as center director, Stabler was persistent. She cited the numbers of Osage women, including her own mother, whom the clinic failed when doctors had not detected their breast cancer. Shaw insisted she was just being sentimental. Even when Stabler moved to Congress, however, she kept working on him, declaring that the center was failing these women. She also explained that most Native women put the health of everyone around them ahead of taking care of their own health, especially when appointments required additional scheduling and travel. Furthermore, she explained, a mammography machine would be a crucial tool to allow doctors to be better diagnosticians, saving the time and money required to have Osages go to referred care. Shaw finally relented and not only purchased the machine but also pushed the doctors to think more in terms of early diagnosis, rather than the more typical IHS focus on treating already-detected problems. In this way Stabler and Shaw were able to raise the level of healthcare in the clinic and address issues that the IHS had a history of missing.

More than a series of site visits or a predetermined checklist, accreditation was about demonstrating an ongoing commitment to creating order. Accreditation marked an important turning point in the transition from IHS to Osage control, allowing for much easier third-party billing and thus improvements to the facility and equipment. By September 2018 it was clear that the center had reached economic feasibility, exceeding its projected operating revenue by $25,000 per month.[111] This meant not only that underfunding was no longer an issue but that the Nation could invest in additional services, programs, and equipment and even begin saving for a new facility. From compacting until 2019, the Wahzhazhe Health Center also grew its staff from 45 to 70 full-time employees, expanded from 1.5 to 5 full-time doctors, and doubled its active patient files.[112] By all indications it was clear that compacting was a robust success that demonstrated the value of Osage self-determination.

"To Establish a Structural and Procedural Framework"

Many of the management feasibility challenges identified throughout the process, however, continued to surface for several years after accreditation, as the Nation struggled to find the right balance between Osage Nation oversight and Health Authority Board control. Incorporating the unwieldy healthcare bureaucracy created by the IHS into the Osage Nation was a complex puzzle that was not solved quickly.

Accounting issues were a continued source of strife between the Nation and the Wahzhazhe Health Center. Shaw left his position in June 2021, stating in his resignation letter, "I have found that I cannot reliably accomplish the task of supervising and being responsible for the financial performance of the Osage Nation Health Services without proper accounting and procurement support. . . . We have a financial officer who has yet to be enabled with access to accounting software or to be enabled with the proper approval authority to expedite financial transactions."[113] As it had when Stabler raised her concerns years earlier, the Osage Nation was still struggling in 2021 to incorporate the larger healthcare bureaucracy into the Nation but was hesitant to fully hand over these functions to the center and the Health Authority Board until a more clear and robust structure could be created.

To address these issues, Chief Standing Bear worked with a team of lawyers, Stabler, and others to draft ONCA 21-31, "to establish a structural and procedural framework for the new Osage Nation Health Care System." This created a new business enterprise that replaced both the Osage Nation Health Services division in the Nation and the Osage Nation Health Authority Board. It gave this entity authority over personnel policies that are different from the Nation's, all healthcare funds (except for transferring compacted federal funds and investigating misappropriations), and managerial and governance functions over all the Nation's healthcare facilities and services. The entity did have to provide the Osage chief and Congress an annual plan and budget, which the Congress would need to approve.

While ONCA 21-31 was not passed when first introduced, it succeeded in April 2022. This new structure meant that the health services of the Osage Nation would finally be treated as more than a program within the Nation. The philosophy behind this new order is to further separate Si-Si A-Pe-Txa (The Health Place), the newly designated name for the Osage Nation Health Authority Board, from the Osage Nation, giving it far more robust management authorities. Such separation demonstrates the ongoing usage of bureaucracy to create order in Osage health. It was not just the Wahzhazhe Health Center that was put under the board but a broad swath of health-related programs, including the "Primary Residential Treatment Centers, the Osage Nation Counseling Center, Prevention, Community Health Representative, Public Health Nursing, Title VI, and any other health care services assigned by the Principal Chief and approved by the board of Si-Si A-Pe-Txa."[114] With this move, Osage Nation leaders further embraced bureaucracy, distancing themselves from daily decision-making authority, as a tool to try to create order for Osage health.

While it is still early in the transition to the Si-Si A-Pe-Txa structure, it appears that the Osage Nation leaders' embrace of bureaucracy is allowing them to meet their goals of being "the premier healthcare provider in the area." In May 2022 the Osage Nation closed on 1.75 acres to build a sixty-five-thousand-square-foot clinic, which could be more than five times the size of the clinic inherited from the IHS. The current plans for the new clinic include securing a $25 million low-interest loan from the US Department of Agriculture, "which will be paid back through the revenue the clinic is able to gain in third party billing. This new space will offer additional services including, physical and occupational therapy to its list of services, along with audiology, pediatrics, podiatry and additional diagnostics such as MRIs."[115] None of this was possible under IHS management, nor without the Osage Nation's embrace of bureaucracy. Furthermore, in a survey filled out by 210 patients in early 2023, respondents had overwhelmingly positive feedback.[116] While bureaucracies continue to create a myriad of challenges in this context as in others, Osage leaders have chosen to embrace bureaucracy's key elements as part of the vital relations necessary in moving the Osage Nation into the future.

CHAPTER FOUR

Land

"It Seems More Existential Necessity"

Arriving back in Oklahoma after teaching a ten-week class over the fall of 2015 at the University of Washington, I found the Osage Nation's assistant chief, Raymond Red Corn, in his newly remodeled office. He was more animated than I had ever seen him, exclaiming that this was a huge moment for the Osage Nation and that he was glad I would be around to see it unfold. Red Corn went on to explain that Ted Turner was selling his forty-three-thousand-acre ranch on the reservation, Bluestem Ranch, and that the Osage Nation might be able to buy back our land.[1] Turner had acquired the reservation land through a series of purchases from other ranchers in 2001 but was now wanting to consolidate his bison ranching operation farther north.[2]

This purchase was exciting because it would reverse the colonial trend of Osage land loss that had begun when we signed our first treaty with the United States in 1808, the Treaty of Fort Clark. Before this period Osage territory included most of what is now Oklahoma, Kansas, Arkansas, and Missouri. It would also be the first time since purchasing the 1,470,000-acre reservation land over a hundred years ago that the Osage Nation could make such a sizable land purchase. Various colonial processes meant that by 2015, the Nation owned less than 7 percent of the land on our reservation, which the State of Oklahoma claimed was Osage County, Oklahoma, but which the Osage Nation continued to argue was reservation land.[3] Due to casino revenues, in the twenty-first century the Osage Nation was finally in a position to reverse these trends and purchase our lands back.[4]

Looking at his computer, where he had pulled up the ranch's parcels on Google Earth, Red Corn excitedly pointed out to me the land's "ugliness," which he hoped would ensure that few other people would be interested.[5] The land was marked by the many imprints of colonialism, especially the destructive powers of long-term ranching, overhunting, overburning, and oil and natural gas extraction, which had happened before Turner purchased the land. While the Bluestem Ranch won an award for its cleanup efforts, there was still much visible damage.[6] The Bureau of Indian Affairs, the federal agency charged with overseeing the oil and gas exploration and production on the reservation, has long failed in its trust duty to monitor production and ensure cleanup.[7]

This land also lacked the kind of infrastructure required for any kind of development. Most of it did not have water, electrical power, or sewage. While there were roads crossing it in meandering paths, few of them were paved or even had gravel, requiring four-wheel-drive vehicles, especially in wet conditions. Extensive fencing crossed the land; however, it was not designed to contain full-grown bison, only the yearlings (younger bison) that had been the Bluestem Ranch's focus. The land also had odd cutouts, where parcels were still owned by other ranchers, sometimes making access between sections impossible without a gate code and permission to cross the owner's land.

Given the "ugliness" of this land—so devastated by the colonial destruction of plants, animals, and minerals, yet not developed for residential, commercial, or industrial use—some might consider this a wasteland.[8] However, for Osage leaders who locate our stories, strength, and sovereignty in this homeland, the importance of owning the land was undeniable. While the satellite image was useful for seeing some aspects of the land, it did not illuminate the larger importance of it to Osages. In trying to name this importance, Red Corn told me, "It seems more existential necessity."[9] Osage leadership saw this land as ensuring our continued existence. They hoped that, in purchasing this land, we could reverse the impacts of colonialism on our territory, bodies, and communities.

The Osage Nation is hardly unique among Indigenous peoples in our long-term commitment to our land. As settler-colonial societies are predicated on disrupting Indigenous connections to our lands and waters, it is little wonder that land is so often at the core of Indigenous identity and who we are planning to be into the future.[10] So many of our ways of creating health are tied to the land, including what we eat, what practices have sustained us as cohesive polities in the past, and the impact of nature on mental health.[11] In her chapter "Land as Life," Tonawanda Seneca Nation scholar Mishuana Goeman points out that "maintaining a relationship to the land is at the heart of indigenous peoples' struggles."[12] Contributing to Goeman's and other Indigenous scholars' theories of land's worth as existing outside its property value, Osage leaders pursued our land base as an existential necessity.

Later the same January day in 2016, Red Corn invited me to join him, Speaker of the Osage Congress Maria Whitehorn, the current ranch manager, and several other ranching specialists on a tour of the Bluestem property being auctioned. We spent the afternoon driving around the forty-three thousand acres of land, asking questions of the ranch manager in a separate car via phone (when we had a signal) and touring one of the bison working pens on foot. As we drove, we were all taken in by the sight of bison yearlings wandering the rolling hills, the golden bluestem grass waving in the afternoon winter sun, and scores of eagles circling above us. This land had a pull that was about far more than increased jurisdiction or economic development. What we felt on this land was a sense of awe that is hard to name but was unmistakably moving.

Colonialism's impacts on our relationships with this land threatened not only our sense of ourselves as a Nation but also our connections, especially to a healthy lifestyle. The purchase of these forty-three thousand acres of ranch land in the center of the reservation required Osage leadership to commit to a shared vision of the Nation, one that understood the land as valuable for more than its economic development potential. Osage Nation officials justified the high costs of reconnecting with this land through the rhetoric of nationhood— that is, territory, power, boldness of action, sovereignty, and independence. More than these common conceptions of nationhood, though, officials envisioned this land as part of a larger move to a new country, where we could build relations with plants and animals that colonial forces had long been trying to sever. Specifically, Osage leaders hoped it would mean that Osage children and elders would have local access to fresh and nutritious foods.[13]

This chapter looks at Osage debates over the value of this land and the Nation's commitment to purchasing it despite the high price we would be forced to pay and its deteriorated condition. This effort to buy back our land was certainly an effort of recovery in two senses of the word: it would enable the Nation to "regain possession of something stolen," and it would help Osages to "return to a normal state of health, mind, and strength."[14] Still, as with Osage language, self-governance, and health, this was not a turning back but a movement forward. Also, as with the language, this land was not lost, because we knew where to find it. Colonial processes had worked to sever our relationship to this land, but this was a relationship that the Nation was committed to building in the twenty-first century, even at great cost. Purchasing the land not only would provide surface title to it but would open more possibilities for an Osage future. Such a move, however, required the development of many layered relations.

This chapter will begin with a discussion of layering, in both Osage and Indigenous studies contexts. This is not the layering of geological stratification, with distinct stratigraphy, but a more fluid conception of layering between all aspects of life, both those overdetermined by colonialism and those whose potential was long ago envisioned by our ancestors. Following this theoretical framing, the chapter turns to discussion of some of the consequences of Osages' removal from our lands. I then go on to describe the twenty-first-century debates over the purchase of the land among executive and congressional officials, including a description of the differing visions for the future of the Nation. I conclude with a discussion of how federal funds earmarked to address the global pandemic in 2020 were able to be quickly purposed to further Osage relationships to the land through the creation of a meat-processing plant, a hydroponic garden, and a bison preserve. This chapter thus demonstrates how Osages are utilizing the strategy of layering to move the Osage Nation into the future.

"Density, Not Difference"

Connecting with the land has required Osage Nation officials to build layered relations. As this section will discuss, the concept of layering comes from an Osage aesthetic, seen most clearly in our clothing, that values layers as a fundamental part of beauty. Layering has powerful similarities to the ways Black and Indigenous studies scholarship has been utilizing the concept of density as an alternative to difference.[15] Dena'ina scholar Jessica Bissett Perea uses density "to critique how 'difference' or 'diversity' tends to homogenize Native American and Indigenous Peoples and to instead signal a recognition of the inextricably intertwined realities of Indigeneity and coloniality."[16] Density is an appreciation of the deeply layered nature of contemporary Indigenous experiences. In the Osage context this involves Osages leaders' decision to utilize, rather than reject, capitalism as a tool for building relations with our land. Rather than only focusing on experiences that are fundamentally different from those in settler society, an eye for layering widens our analytical lens to include a broader set of strategies Indigenous people are deploying to navigate the contemporary world.

Land is core to many Indigenous movements across the globe today.[17] Cherokee Nation scholar Courtney Lewis insightfully points out that Natives tend to see the land bases of our nations as both representations and extensions of our people.[18] In these contexts, land is important not only because it is what colonial systems have most directly targeted, but it is from this land that we can build the political, social, physical, and spiritual relationships that our people need to heal. Another Cherokee Nation scholar, Clint Carroll, cites a Cherokee elder to make the point that controlling resources and enacting cultural practices on the land are ultimately about their responsibility "to honor the spirit of this land."[19] Similarly, in the Osage context, building relationships with the land is not just about the land itself but about building relationships with the various plants and animals that will thrive on this land.

"Landback" is a growing movement, particularly in the United States and Canada, that calls for "returning land to the stewardship of Indigenous peoples."[20] This movement crucially understands landback as more than transferring land ownership. It challenges colonial capitalism's structures, especially those that have been created to serve corporate and federal interests at the expense of Native peoples. Landback movement leaders insist that Indigenous peoples should be granted full and informed consent, not just consultation rights, in their historical territories.[21] This move is a vital one, as too often Native nations engage in government-to-government consultation processes with federal agencies only to be treated as one of many stakeholders whose values are in the minority and can thus easily be ignored. Corporations are particularly good at mobilizing state resources to deny Native nations' sovereignty.[22]

There are several limitations to such movements, however. First, they rely on non-Native willingness to repatriate these lands, which seems both unlikely and fraught. Furthermore, landback movements frequently combine this call for returning lands with a deep critique of capitalism and an insistence that returning lands to Indigenous peoples will "mitigate the impacts of climate change."[23] This movement thus too often falls into the trap of justifying land transfer through the assumption that Native peoples exist outside capitalism and will utilize this land in a fundamentally different way. Such a move maps neatly onto older tropes of the ecological Indian, which have long been critiqued for their positioning of Indigenous peoples as part of nature, rather than deserving of full rights, especially over our lands.[24]

Many Indigenous peoples are not wholly rejecting capitalism or even extractive industries but instead using these as tools for ensuring our future. Speaking directly to these issues of Native relationships to the land and difference, Navajo Nation scholars Andrew Curley and Majerle Lister write, "Critics of tribal governments as inappropriate expressions of Indigenous practices often gesture toward the land, Indigenous relationships with the land, and resurgent cultural practices. However, extractive industries have helped assuage some of the longstanding impacts of genocide, violent displacement, and forced assimilation. For generations, Indigenous peoples were able to survive on their lands through strategic engagement with extractive industries and capitalism."[25] Native nations today must fight for the ability to make these decisions for ourselves, as much on our own terms and toward our own ends as possible. Landback and other environmental movements seem to foreclose the possibility of Native nations using land strategically as we see fit to meet our own needs. There is a real danger of predicating the return of land on the virtue attributed to Native difference. Sometimes, in the search for a fundamentally different path forward for all peoples, the very tools by which Native peoples have been able to fight off the worst aspects of ongoing colonialism are invalidated. By insisting that Indigenous peoples save modernity from itself, landback movements risk contributing to Native elimination. In other words, romantic images of past Indigenous peoples are often positioned as the only real Indians. Challenging these structures of oppression requires work on many different levels.

The search for an outside to colonialism can thus actually contribute to the colonizing trends that limit the options available to Indigenous peoples. Métis Nation scholar Chris Andersen argues that we should focus on "density, not difference," saying that Indigenous knowledge comes from our many varied experiences, not just the things that mark us as unique.[26] Density can be seen when we bring together the lessons Indigenous peoples are learning as we navigate ongoing colonialism, strategically enact a wide variety of practices, pull our values forward through time, and envision stronger futures. Osage Nation discussions of land provide a powerful window into the density of contemporary Native experiences and tools, building relations with our lands that neither fully embrace nor completely reject capitalism or stewardship. Instead, the Osage Nation's purchase of land navigates both capitalism and colonialism to build relations with the land and embrace the strength such a move offers. Building on Andersen's and other scholars' usage of density, this chapter looks at the many relations Osage officials have had to forge to navigate and facilitate this land purchase.[27]

While density provides a useful analytical frame for this work, in this chapter I have chosen layering to describe this phenomenon. First, density sometimes connotes stupidity, which is a connection I want to avoid, even subliminally. More importantly, the concept of density did not resonate with the Osages I talked with. In my experiences Osages have never utilized the term. In a discussion I had with Osage graphic designer Jessica Harjo about creating the cover and chapter heading designs for this book, she asked me to say more about density. In explaining the term, she quickly latched onto the idea of layering, as both graphically easy to represent and something that resonates with her Osage experiences. We discussed the ways that the beautiful and detailed woven belt was worn under Osage shirts, how Osages showed respect by covering our clothing with shawls or blankets, even in the summer, and how Osage ribbon work was created through a process of layering.[28]

Osage ribbon work, born out of eighteenth-century trade with the French, is a particularly well-suited metaphor for understanding Osage approaches to layering. Using the raw material and tools obtained through the colonial process, Osage artists began by tearing silk into strips and then cutting, folding, and sewing them back together to form something both beautiful and uniquely Osage.[29] Ribbon work is most commonly defined as "ribbon strips of contrasting colors that are layered on a textile or leather foundation and which form designs based on the cutting, folding under, and sewing of the ribbon layers."[30] While it is hard to trace precisely, it is thought that ribbon work first dates to the late eighteenth century. It likely began among the southern Great Lakes tribes, from where it spread to Prairie Indians such as the Osage during the removal period.[31] In this way, ribbon work is an example of the ways Native peoples navigated colonialism by forming new relations with materials, practices, and peoples.[32]

In the past I have used ribbon work and layering as metaphors of colonial entanglements.[33] In this context, I want to emphasize the many layered relationships, some of which are deeply mired in past and ongoing colonialism, that this unique and beautiful artform comes out of. It does not come out of a pure or static past, but is an artifact of Indigenous peoples' creative navigation of many different relations. Importantly, these layered relations are not all equal or neutral, but are mired in various power dynamics, which are at times obvious and other times more insidious. Here the many different relations act on and through each other. Like with what Anderson and others point out with density, our power comes from the way we build these layers on top of each other, both those experiences of difference and those more mired in colonial entanglements. It is the relationality between all these layers that makes them powerful.

A central part of what this layering demonstrates is that external relationships are central to, rather than at odds with, self-determination. It is only through the creation of a broad array of relationships that Native nations can enact sovereignty today.[34] US scholar Jessica Cattelino refutes definitions of sovereignty as operating in a zero-sum contest of power. Instead, she describes sovereignty as "interdependent," meaning that, in the Seminole context in which Cattelino works, US sovereignty functions relationally rather than autonomously.[35] While it is important to understand all sovereignty as interdependent, it is also clear that there are uneven power dynamics at stake in negotiations between Indigenous peoples and settler states. These relationships are deeply affected by the structures of power they operate within.

Native nations today can't operate in a realm of fundamental difference but must navigate a layered network of relationships. Osage leaders were willing to deepen relationships with outside agencies because they understood the land as a fundamental piece of the future of the Nation.

For the Osage Nation to buy our land back, it was going to have to form and strengthen many internal and external relationships. First, the Osage Nation's executive branch, Congress, Gaming Enterprise Board, and LLC (an independent company formed by the Osage Nation) were going to have to collaboratively plan how much money to offer for the land, what the goals for use of the land were going to be, who was going to manage the land, and how the programs would be enacted. These entities had frequently been at odds with each other, not only because the 2006 Osage Constitution had structured them through a system of checks and balances but because of the colonial legacies of distrust that continued to affect their many engagements.[36]

Building relations to land meant not only building internal relationships but also that all of these entities had to work together to navigate external relationships with the US federal government, the settlers who wanted to sell their land back to the Osage, other settlers who wanted to do everything in their power to stop the Osage from amassing more land, and external entities such as banks that were needed to bring this land back to the Osage Nation. For the Osage and other Native nations, there are many hard decisions that must be made over which external relationships should be forged. Careful attention had to be paid to the consequences these relationships created, including debt and a reliance on gaming. Finally, relations to the land itself are also layered. While purchasing the land creates associations with capitalism and the state, relations with plants and animals are also core components of the relations we were enacting through the land.

Ultimately, this chapter is intended to add additional layers to our understandings of Indigenous nationhood and capitalism. Rather than providing some sort of fundamentally different engagement with these structures, Osage actions complicate and offer a more strategic story. In this context I see these engagements as relations, some of which are certainly entanglements we have little choice but to navigate, but that Osages have intentionally fostered and positioned to try and meet our own needs. This experience demonstrates how Osage leaders are navigating a host of relationships to recover a land-based future for the Osage Nation despite the ongoing impact of settler colonialism and its many disruptions. This chapter describes the motivations behind and strategies for creating layered relations that are necessitated by land purchases and land-based Native nation government initiatives.

"Cultivating a Space for Wellness"

While Osages have made many moves, our land has always been at the center of our understanding of who we are and who we strive to be. This land-based knowledge is embedded in our clan system, where we learned from the natural world around us to understand the role we need to play in our family and community. It was also embedded in our pre-colonial practices, where the day was centered on land-based engagements, such as prayers that took place at sunrise, sun high, and sunset. And of course, nutrition and healing would not be possible without deep relationships with and knowledge of the land. After describing some of these relationships as they were recorded in our ᘺᘉᘕᘊ ᔕᘉᘕᘉᘕ (origin stories), this section will describe how colonial forces have attempted to disrupt them, but they continue to be here for us to build on.

My clan, ᎬᘉᏃᗝ ᔕᎠᏕᎠᘉᏪᘕ (Gentle Sky), has our own version of moving to the Osage Nation, which an elder of our clan, ᖅᘉᏃᘉ ᘉᏪᘉᗅᘉ, offered to Omaha Tribe scholar Francis La Flesche in 1914. Told as a ᘺᘉᏪᘉ ᔕᘉᏪᘉᘕ, it documents how we chose our territory and built the relationships we needed to thrive on earth. This story importantly ties together many of the themes throughout this book, locating them in our connection to the land. In this story, leaders of the clan sent a messenger to find a place that we might become a nation. He descended from the stars in three different locations, but each time it was night and all he saw was darkness. During the fourth trip, the leaders decided they would accompany the messenger. In this location it was finally light, and the group encountered trees, water, plants, animals, and people. Each of these encounters taught them about the things they needed to become a Nation, offered them names, and showed them the way to live long and healthy lives. Ultimately, the group came to a beautiful house that was beyond description, where they knew they could find peace.[37]

From this story it is possible to see how Osages built the vital relations necessary to become a thriving Nation by learning from the land and all it sustains. Importantly, the second being they encountered was a bison. Part of the ᘺᘉᏪᘉ ᔕᘉᏪᘉᘕ reads in translation, "For a third time the Buffalo threw himself upon the earth, and the white corn, together with the white squash, he tossed into the air. Then spake, saying 'These plants the little ones shall use as food as they travel the path of life. . . . They shall enable themselves to live to see old age'"[38] In addition to sprouting various kinds of corn and squash, the bison also connected Osages with several medicinal plants. These plants, the bison promised, would enable them to "make their limbs to lengthen in growth" and to live long and healthy lives.[39] In this and other ᘺᘉᏪᘉ ᔕᘉᏪᘉᘕ, it is possible to see the ways that Osages at this time understood our animals, plants, foods, and healthy life as all deeply interwoven and emplaced in our lands.

This ∠ŋʞŋ ꜱŋʞŋɑ is also a powerful demonstration of how we understood and valued our relations to our land. These relationships were honored through the regular recitation of this ∠ŋʞŋ ꜱŋʞŋɑ and by our ceremonial practices throughout each day, and they continue to be honored by our people taking on clan names. These are the practices that have allowed us to thrive as a people. The land was vital because it was where we had the relationships necessary to live long, healthy lives. While we moved within our territory and created new practices to address any chaos that developed, we continued to center these relations to place to ensure our health as individuals and as a Nation.

Colonialism, in all its forms, has disrupted, but not extinguished, these relationships. From 1808 until 1839, seven treaties stripped Osage control over ninety-six million acres of land in what would later become Oklahoma, Kansas, Missouri, and Arkansas, representing 75 percent of the Osage land base; in return, we received only $166,000 in cash, annuities, livestock, and farming supplies.[40] These agreements were frequently made not just under duress but under outright deception. According to US scholar Jeffrey Ostler, the 1808 Osage treaty is a classic example of how the United States came to control the land that under the French had been called Louisiana. The US federal government was eager for this land to host other Native peoples they were dislocating, as well as white settlers who continued to clamor for more land. Given that the Osages were uninterested in giving up land to the United States, Indian agent William Clark resorted to outright deception. Later in life he admitted that he had lied to Osage leaders, making them believe that the treaty would only give Americans hunting privileges in Osage territory. The final document, however, signed fifty thousand square miles of land over to US control.[41]

In addition to facilitating generational wealth for settlers, including through the removal of other Natives to this territory, Osage land directly supported "land-grant/grab" universities. As US scholar Robert Lee and Kiowa Tribe scholar Tristan Ahtone report, the federal government gifted the lands from the 1808 and 1825 Osage treaties directly to the University of Missouri, Columbia. The US government demanded Osage lands "as an alternative to their extermination," giving Osages only $700 for them. The university was able to sell some of the lands for $363,000 and is still sitting on fifteen thousand acres of them.[42] This and other universities then furthered white generational privileges, as they not only served white populations but created a system of knowledge that supported their dominance.

The end of the treaty period brought further Indigenous land theft. As happened with many Native nations, the US government removed Osages from our lands in Kansas to a reservation in Indian Territory in 1872. These were lands we had likely never used for farming, only bison hunting. Wild foods, such as yonkapins, pawpaws, prickly pear cactus, and walnuts, as well as harvested foods such as corn, beans, and squash, were much harder to find or grow on the rocky reservation land than they had been on our former reservation land in what would become Kansas.[43] The twice-annual bison hunt had provided a staple of Osage diets, but during this time bison were driven to near extinction by a combination of economic, cultural, and ecological factors that the formation of the United States had ushered in.[44] As Canadian scholar Danielle Taschereau Mamers notes, "At the close of the eighteenth century, there were between 30 and 60 million bison on the continent. By 1892, the population was reduced to only 456 wild bison."[45] This mass destruction is not only symbolic of the destruction of an ecosystem. It is also a symbol of the intentional destruction of Indigenous lifeways and the reign of market capitalism.

Taking these hunting, gathering, and harvesting activities away from us also created a more sedentary, less healthy lifestyle. In addition to severing the relationships that sustained us, the United States also created new relationships with foods that have literally been killing us. The commodities promised, and occasionally delivered, in treaties were all exceptionally high in sodium, fat, and sugar. With these forced dietary and lifestyle changes, Osages, like many Indigenous peoples, are at higher risk of obesity, high blood pressure, and diabetes, all of which lead to premature death.[46]

This is not just a historical problem, but something Osages continue to navigate. As Choctaw Nation scholar Valarie Blue Bird Jernigan writes, "This reliance continues today through the Food Distribution Program on Indian Reservations, through which the US Department of Agriculture provides canned and packaged foods to around 270 tribes with limited access to SNAP. It constitutes the primary food source for 60% of rural and reservation-based American Indians, but the foods tend to be high in fat and sugar. Fresh vegetables are rarely offered."[47] Whether or not Osages rely on the US Department of Agriculture's Supplemental Nutrition Assistance Program, or SNAP, many of those on the reservation are forced to rely on shelf-stable foods that have the same nutritional issues, because much of the Osage reservation is over an hour from markets offering fresh food and produce, creating what is often referred to as a food desert. The dietary and lifestyle impacts of being removed to a small portion of our land base and having our relationships severed with the plants, animals, and practices that sustained our health have had devastating impacts on our overall well-being.

Indigenous communities, however, are demonstrating that building relationships to land can heal our bodies, minds, and communities.[48] This movement, generally known as Indigenous food sovereignty, has been growing exponentially in recent years. Writing about her nation's food sovereignty effort on the grounds of a former residential school, Indigenous studies scholar Charlotte Coté describes how "the Tseshaht garden transformed a space of pain, trauma, sickness, and death" through "tuukʷasiił, cultivating a space for wellness, healing, and cultural revitalization."[49] By enabling the land to feed the Tseshaht people, this project has transformed a space of suffering into one of care and generosity. Without these connections to the land, it is impossible to disrupt the cycles of sickness that colonialism has forced on our peoples. Through the Osage Nation's land purchase, leadership envisioned a similar process of healing that would enable Osages to build layered relationships with our lands and all the life they sustain.

"Re-establish the Surface Reservation through Land Purchases"

Since the passage of the 2006 constitution, Osage officials have been committed to increasing the land base of the Nation. This section will describe these commitments, as well as some of the motivations behind them, by looking at the Nation's strategic plans, failed legislation, and official priorities. In addition to a desire to build relationships with the land, Osage leaders were driven by a desire to control our territory in a fuller way and, ultimately, to have a place from which to ensure a future for the Osage Nation. Land was seen as a core piece of all the other initiatives the Nation wanted to enact, such as those concerning language, self-governance, and health.

In 2007 Osage chief Jim Gray created a large-scale strategic initiative to identify national needs among the citizens and create goals for the first twenty-five years under the new constitution.[50] One of the top ten priorities identified during the June 2007 community survey was to "purchase land to increase the reservation land base."[51] This was seen as directly contributing to community health, education, and cultural knowledge. Land-based programs that taught Osage approaches to practices such as ranching, farming, gathering, hunting, fishing, and burning were only possible if there was land on which to teach those activities. Such activities would not only contribute to the physical health of Osages by offering much-needed fresh foods and exercise in an area where there were few options available, but they would also aid mental health through better diets, outdoor activities, and cultural connections.[52]

Another motivation of some Osage leaders was to neutralize the threat of non-Osage landowners, who currently had a monopoly on Osage lands. The Osage Nation had continually challenged settler efforts, with the result that jurisdiction on the Osage reservation was deeply contested with few clear answers but many creative solutions. These included cross-deputization of law enforcement, negotiated agreements between municipalities, and cofunding of schools and roads.[53] Still, many Osage jurisdictional efforts, such as creating laws over lands and waters, had been thwarted by non-Osage landowners, who, in 2016, owned 93 percent of the Osage reservation land. While subsurface mineral rights to the entire reservation continued to be held in trust for the Osage Nation by the federal government, the vast majority of the surface reservation lands had been taken by non-Osages. Buying back this land was a key first step in reclaiming control over Osage territory.

One blatant example of these tensions played out in late May 2007 when the Osage Nation Congress began reviewing a natural resource bill, quickly rousing controversy. The bill proposed the creation of an environmental commission that would generate legislation for the Osage Nation and enable higher environmental standards. Groups such as the Osage County Cattlemen's Association saw the bill as an attempt by the Osage Nation to assert control over the entire county, which was coterminous with the reservation. Dick Surber, representing the association, was quoted as saying, "We landowners, both Osage and non-Osage, reject blatant attempts by the executive branch of the Osage tribe to exert jurisdiction over our land, air, and water."[54] Some landowners, such as Surber, denied the fact that they lived on a reservation, even though the reservation had never been disestablished by an act of Congress. This denial is part of a long history of settler colonialism and non-Natives' intense hostility to residing on Osage and other Native lands.[55]

While the environmental bill was quickly tabled, it had already unleashed "vitriolic and deafening objections" throughout Osage County.[56] These apprehensions quickly swelled and affected interactions between the Osage Nation and non-Osage residents, including prompting denial of the authority of the Osage Nation's police officers to issue state tickets, even though cross-deputization had been in place for eleven years. The simplest solution to both issues—that of a food desert and the jurisdictional authority of the Osage Nation—was to own a greater portion of the land.

When Standing Bear was elected as chief in 2014, he came into office with ten goals. Many of these came directly out of the twenty-five-year strategic plan, but his goals were particularly focused on the areas that had not yet been addressed. They included the following:

- Maintain or increase funding for core benefits including education scholarship, the Health Benefit Card, Burial Assistance, and Crisis Assistance.
- Re-establish the surface reservation through land purchases.
- Expand language and retain culture.
- Develop a comprehensive healthcare system.
- Promote healthy communities through wellness initiatives and partnerships.
- Create and develop a premier Osage school system.
- Create safer communities through strong law enforcement.
- Improve government-to-government relations through effective communication.
- Eliminate the manufacture and distribution of illegal substances in our villages.
- Ensure the Osage government is accountable to the Osage people.[57]

While his agenda was extremely ambitious, and its enactment would at times spread his administration thin, the Bluestem Ranch purchase directly facilitated several of Standing Bear's goals. He envisioned increased jurisdictional control, but also healthier communities through the potential to grow and eat fresh food as well as land-based wellness initiatives. Surface land ownership was a key resource for retaining language and culture, as well as for the school system Standing Bear envisioned, as it was a place in which we could build layered relationships with lands, animals, and the practices known to our ancestors.

From these strategic visions and goals, it is very clear that in the twenty-first century Osage leaders had a strong commitment to purchasing back land. These commitments had very little to do with the property value or even the current state of this land and far more to do with the political and wellness effects that they hoped the land would engender. Land was necessary for Osages to have a place apart from the settler state, specifically a place to come together as a people and rebuild relationships of respect. It was a space of possibility, a requirement for grounding who Osages were and who we wanted to be.

"We Need to Play the Indian Card"

The story of the purchase of the forty-three-thousand-acre Bluestem Ranch provides a powerful window into the layered relationships necessary for

Native nations to get our land back. To buy this land, Osage leadership had to develop a host of relationships both internally and externally. Internally, the land purchase required us to come together, commit to a shared project, and agree to various compromises. These internal relationships had long been strained by colonial distrust—that is, the skepticism that is inevitable in the face of the many failures of colonial governance systems. This distrust had to be overcome. Additionally, a shared vision of the Nation had to be agreed on—that is, what was most essential for us as a Nation and how we strategically could get there.[58] Externally, we also had to forge relations with the federal government, the land sellers, and bankers. These were all themselves deeply fraught and layered relations. Osage leadership had to further embed the Nation in various relationships to capitalism, but not toward the ends of economic expansion. To build the necessary relationships with the seller, for example, we had to deploy what some would term "strategic essentialism," a seemingly stereotypical rendering of ourselves. This section will describe how, while they were certainly strategic, as nation building requires, these were representations of relationships we felt to be essential to who we are and were thus not essentialist.[59]

Throughout the fall of 2015, multiple Osages had contacted Chief Standing Bear with rumors that media mogul and conservationist Ted Turner was looking to sell his ranch on the Osage reservation. Then, on the evening of December 23, Mark Freeman IV, an Osage who grazed cattle on Turner's Bluestem Ranch, called Standing Bear to let him know that Turner was in fact going through with the sale. The deadline for initial bidding was only thirty days away. Describing this moment to me, Standing Bear said that "everything slowed down, and I could see everything clearly. . . . We were going to do it. We were going to own it. . . . This was a time for action."[60] After calling Red Corn, who shared his vision and was familiar with auction strategies, Standing Bear reached out to David Lamb, who at the time was a senior vice president relationship manager at the Bank of Oklahoma. Lamb had taken the lead on large loans to both the Cherokee and the Muscogee Creek Nations and thus understood what it meant to loan to Native nations. That night Lamb and Standing Bear began an in-depth conversation about what financing such a loan would entail. Standing Bear and Red Corn worked every day, except New Year's, over the next month to bring this vision into reality.[61]

The day after I toured the ranch with Red Corn, I joined both him and Chief Standing Bear in Pawhuska for a full day of meetings, which had already begun when I arrived at eight o'clock that morning. When I walked into the Osage executive office suite, it was brightly lit by the newly installed recessed lighting, making the refinished black-and-white-checkered floors gleam and the freshly painted light blue walls glow softly. As I walked in, Standing Bear motioned for me to join him in his office, and I sat in one of the wooden-legged guest chairs facing the desk and pulled my iPad onto my lap to take notes as usual. Standing Bear sat behind his large mahogany desk and Red Corn sat comfortably to the side in one of the overstuffed leather couch chairs. Along the walls were several bookshelves filled with legal, historical, and leadership books, signaling Standing Bear's commitment to learn what he could from the many different resources needed for his unique profession, chief of a Native nation.[62]

The chiefs were deeply engaged in one of their many strategy sessions, with Red Corn filling Standing Bear in on yesterday's tour and discussing who would need to be involved in the land purchase and the best way to accomplish it. They talked about calling a special session of Congress and the many questions they would need to be able to address, such as the different values of the land (business, cultural, and speculative). While some members of Congress were already quite excited about the purchase, others were going to need to be convinced by outside experts that this was a good investment and something the Osage Nation could successfully manage. Since the creation of the 2006 constitution, however, the executive and congressional branches of the Nation had been in tension with each other over how exactly to manage the balance of powers.[63] In order to achieve his goal of purchasing back the Osage land base, Standing Bear had to build these relations carefully.

The chiefs also discussed the possible terms of the loan, including how much they could or should borrow against the casinos, how long the loan term would be, and how many banks would be necessary to service the loan. Luckily the Nation had already developed a strong relationship with various banks and the casinos were profitable enough that Standing Bear felt confident; getting the loan was not going to be a major obstacle. They both shared rumors they had heard about who else was interested in buying the land, including the largest ranching family, the Drummonds, who were purportedly willing to pay $75 million. To purchase Bluestem, various organizations within the Nation had to work together with multiple banks to create a loan package that would convince Turner to sell to the Osage Nation, rather than another top bidder.

Funding for the land was complicated by the fact that the land itself would not be used as collateral for the bank loan. It was essential to Osage officials that no matter what happened in the future, this land could not again be taken from the Osage Nation, as it already had been multiple times, once during the treaty period and then again throughout the twentieth century. Owning the land outright was also a stipulation required by the federal government for putting the land into trust. Having the land in trust with the federal government gave the Osage Nation as much jurisdiction as possible, exempting it from most state laws and taxes. It also offered the highest level of protection against foreclosure or land seizure. Similarly to the minerals trust relationship discussed in chapter 2, exerting Native sovereignty over land means deepening relationships with the federal government. To keep local and state authorities out of Native nation decision-making, Native nations have often chosen to strengthen their relationship with the federal government.[64]

Given these priorities, the bank loan would need to be secured another way. The Osage Gaming Enterprise Board would thus also have to be involved, as the regular income from the casinos was the best tool available to the Nation to guarantee the loan. As the gaming enterprise had already been trying to convince the Nation to add hotel towers to the Tulsa casino, the ranch purchase offered useful leverage to push forward its plans, which required the consent of the Osage Congress. In this way, the land purchase would also deepen the Nation's reliance on debt and the whims of the hospitality industry, which gave many Osage officials pause.[65]

At nine o'clock that morning, I moved with the chiefs into the conference room for a meeting with members of the Osage Nation's Tallgrass LLC—who were there to discuss the possibility of running the ranch—and other knowledgeable advisers Standing Bear had assembled. The chiefs took their typical places at each end of the table, with Standing Bear positioned closest to the door to his office. Wainscot paneling took up the lower third of the wall and the ceiling was recessed. These various elements worked together to enhance the room's, and Standing Bear's, stately aura. Sitting in one of the leather executive chairs, Standing Bear was framed by the Osage and US flags, with a picture of prominent eighteenth-century Osage chief Pawhuska (White Hair) behind him.[66] Much like Chief Pawhuska, Standing Bear frequently utilized external relationships and capitalism to attempt to expand Osage authority. Nation building in the twenty-first century involved strategically navigating settler-colonial systems, including the claims of the United States to authority over Osage lands and massive loans with corporate banks that would tie up gaming revenue for years to come. Osage leadership felt strongly that it was only through such negotiated relationships that the Osage Nation had a chance to regain our taken lands, assert jurisdiction over our territory, and ensure a future for the Nation.

Standing Bear jumped right in as everyone took their seats. "The biggest angle I heard yesterday was that we can submit a bid early and that we need to play the Indian card."[67] By "playing the Indian card," Standing Bear meant that while it was important to make a good offer for the land, it was also important to craft a message that would appeal to the heart of conservationist Ted Turner, who had dedicated his life to restoring native wildlife in the United States. Standing Bear's long-term passion for bison restoration, evidenced in part through his time serving as a trustee of the Oklahoma chapter of the Nature Conservancy, as well as the typical environmental tropes about Native peoples, would be important tools for convincing Turner that the Osage Nation would be the best steward of this land going forward. Standing Bear was frequently able to pinpoint such important strategies that would help him and the Nation achieve their desired goals.

Rather than seeing this strategy of "playing the Indian card" as strategic essentialism, it should be understood as both strategic and essential to our nation-building efforts. *Strategic essentialism* is defined as "a political strategy whereby differences (within a group) are temporarily downplayed, and unity assumed for the sake of achieving political goals."[68] The common critique of this approach, especially from feminist scholars, is that it may encourage frozen identities that can be used to further inequality. Even when it is embraced in the short term, these scholars frequently discredit it as a long-term strategy.[69] As Fort Sill Apache Tribe scholar Nancy Mithlo has argued, however, in the context of many Indigenous communities there are metaphysical understandings of our relations, especially to landscapes and nationhood, that are very dangerous to dismiss as essentialist.[70] Discussions of identity as constructed miss the vital relations that are actually at work in Indigenous contexts, where identity is layered and in flux but still grounded in strong connections. Naming the importance of our relationship with bison to Turner was a strategic move that gave us an edge over the bids placed by settlers, but it was also a naming of the vital relations many Osages understand as at the core of moving the Osage Nation into the future.

After some discussion, Standing Bear went on to express his concerns about the loan required to purchase the land, and the dangers of saddling the Nation with such a large debt. "I am concerned about the length of the obligations. I don't control the people that come after me."[71] Standing Bear then told a story about a 2015 trip he had taken to Washington, D.C., where he and several other Native nation leaders had been able to have a personal audience with President Barack Obama. When it was his turn, Standing Bear asked, "How are you going to ensure that everything you have accomplished during your two terms is not undermined by the next administration?" Obama looked at him carefully and responded, "That is what we are dealing with now."[72] Like the flags behind him, this story is evidence of Standing Bear's and thus the Osage Nation's ongoing relationship with the federal government. As a statesman on speaking terms with the president of the United States, Standing Bear brought up dangers that they both shared. Rather than playing the role of the subservient "domestic dependent" who needed the benevolence of the US government, Standing Bear crafted their conversation around their mutual goals, specifically that the US leadership would reauthorize an Indian health bill beyond Obama's administration, allowing Native nations ongoing access to treaty-promised federal funding for the health clinics they had taken over from the US government. Fostering shared goals and partnership was a key aspect of how Standing Bear approached his relationship to the federal government.

Standing Bear told this story here, however, to emphasize the importance of long-term planning. From this experience Standing Bear concluded, "We are going to have to put structures in place that will last beyond this administration. We are trying to change the structures and have to figure out how to build in methods of success into these new structures."[73] Standing Bear was concerned here not just about the terms of the loan and the increased reliance on casino revenues this loan would create but also about the larger vision he had for this land and the Osage Nation. He wanted to know who was going to run the ranch but, more important, how it and various other projects could be run successfully. Given that his administration had several new programs that they were becoming even more involved in building and overseeing—including the projects described throughout this book, such as compacting (taking over operations) an Indian Health Service clinic and a language immersion school—Standing Bear really hoped that the ranch could be run by a corporate enterprise board created and governed under Osage law. He envisioned such an approach allowing him to appoint experienced cattlemen—preferably Osages—to run the ranch in a way that connected with Osage Nation programming but was not another project his administration had to manage directly.[74]

From Standing Bear's many discussions about the ranch, it was clear that more than anything else he wanted something that was going to work long-term. This meant rebuilding relationships to the land and even to the non-Osage world. During these early planning meetings Standing Bear shared several possible visions for the land that included innovative ways that the Osage Nation ranch could generate income. One dream he described was of a hunting lodge where Osages could come to learn and where non-Osages would pay top dollar to stay, perhaps even hunting bison. By leveraging outside fetishization of Plains Native lifeways and hunting practices to generate revenue, Standing Bear hoped the Nation could create a space for Osage youth to develop connections to Osage land and foodways, environmental science, and cultural practices. Again, this vision was both strategic and essential. In this and other possible visions Osage leadership had for the ranch, the goal was for the Nation to be successful in generating income in an area beyond gaming and to create land-based programs without placing additional financial burdens on the Osage Nation.

The rest of this day, like most of Chief Standing Bear's days, was filled with meetings. The next meeting was with the Bank of Oklahoma, with which the Nation already had a sizable loan enabling much-needed office space on the "campus" (the area of Pawhuska, Oklahoma, where most Osage government offices were located). When the bankers arrived, they were shown into the conference room and offered a seat at the table. They discussed their loan terms, earnest money, rate percentage, fees, legal expenses, refinancing options for an existing loan, the possibility of tax-exempt status, and the fact that any equity or property liens to secure the loan were unnecessary. Despite the long-term debt this would generate, and the added expansion of casino operations it would facilitate, the importance of this land to the future of the Osage Nation more than outweighed the dangers for Osage leadership. Osages' access to gaming revenues, something that came out of both strategic moves Native nations had enacted and our essential status as sovereign entities, opened up possibilities for national growth. These relationships opened the important possibility of expanding the Nation's territory, a possibility that had not existed since at least the nineteenth century. On January 20, 2016, Standing Bear called the Tenth Special Session of the Osage Congress for the 2015–16 year. While the 2006 Osage Nation Constitution had set out a plan for the Congress to have two sessions a year, one in the fall and one in the spring, during this period there were frequently upwards of fifteen special sessions in which the Congress was asked to consider additional legislation. This meant that they were meeting more often than monthly, with very robust agendas spurred by the sweeping changes Standing Bear was implementing across the Nation to bring into being his ambitious goals. During this session there were twelve different pieces of legislation, including a matching grant for language preservation; funding for the Child, Family, and Senior Community Services Division; and several bills related to the ranch purchase. While most Congress members did not feel that they should be meeting so regularly, during this period they were also not willing to cede any of their decision-making power to the executive office, especially over budgeting.[75]

As part of the opening of the session, Speaker of the Congress Maria Whitehorn spoke about Bluestem ranch, saying, "This is a big opportunity, which makes it a big decision. I believe every member supports building our land base. This was our land and it is no longer. It has a place in all our hearts and there is a lot of emotion. But I am going to draw it back to our seats at this table. We serve 18,000 and not all of them are from here, but their roots are here."[76] In this moment there was a strong commitment among elected officials and voters to reinvigorating relations with the reservation by rebuilding the land base.

Not all members of the Osage Congress, however, agreed that this land was a good investment. The following day, Congress held an appropriations meeting, where a committee of congresspeople discussed the land purchase. Shannon Edwards, a three-term elected official born and raised in Oklahoma City, and a practicing attorney for thirty-five years, was the leading skeptic of the land purchase. After agreeing that both the twenty-five-year strategic plan and most of the people she talked with supported land purchases, she went on to argue, "I have always supported buying land, but I can't support this. I need a plan that would show me that this is more than an emotional bill."[77] Throughout her tenure in Congress, Edwards sponsored numerous bills related to land purchases, but she was deeply skeptical of all investments, wanting to make sure that there were no special interests motivating the deal, that due diligence had been done, and that there was a plan in place to ensure there would be a return on the investment. With the Bluestem Ranch purchase, she wanted to see comparable sales, an appraisal, and an environmental report, none of which were generated. Especially given the clear environmental damage to this land and the Nation's struggles with economic development outside of gaming, she was focused on Congress's constitutional duties to fully assess all proposals on economic terms.[78]

For the majority of Osage congresspeople, the land's value couldn't be assessed by a market survey. For them this land was at the center of who the Osage Nation was in the past and needed to be in the future. The future of the Osage Nation felt dependent on outbidding non-Osage landowners and reversing the trend of Osage land theft. John Maker, then in his first term, responded to Edwards by saying, "I support this as an Osage from here and still living here. This isn't emotional, this is business and practical. My elders have long told me that we first must take care of our children and elders and with whatever we have left we get back the lands that have been lost. That was the wisdom."[79] In making the argument that this land purchase was not emotional but rather dictated by the wisdom that had been passed down, Maker was demonstrating that this move was both strategic and essential. In a later conversation with me he explained how he got his strength from the land, especially when he was sick or was helping people heal from loss during a funeral. For Maker, Osage language, culture, and spirituality are held within the land and that was its real value. The Nation had an obligation to this land at all costs.[80]

Edwards, however, worried about the costs. She later explained, "When we heard that almost the entire purchase price was going to be borrowed with gaming revenue as the collateral, I was skeptical. That revenue was the only thing that allowed the government to fully operate and funded services such as scholarships and health benefits offered to all Osages."[81] Putting those funds on the line, especially for land that was, as she described it, "littered with the remnants of oil and gas explorations and governmental dumping of toxins,"[82] did not feel justified to Edwards. She also pointed out that there had been, and would be again, other lands for sale, both inside and outside the Osage reservation, which would be a better investment. Of the twelve Osage congresspeople, however, only Edwards voted against the land purchase, demonstrating that her many concerns about the land were not persuasive to the other congresspeople.[83]

Behind this specific debate lies a larger set of questions about the goals of the Osage Nation. All Native nations entering gaming have had to negotiate how to distribute casino funds, striking their own balance on how wide to cast their relational network of financial support.[84] Is the Nation going to be primarily focused on investing in the reservation territory and supporting those citizens living locally? Success here would be measured by a growth in the territorial base, the creation of geographically restricted programs and services, and the fostering of a healthier local community. Or is the Nation going to be more driven by the distribution of capital and services equally to all citizens? While both projects require economic development, the latter goal is measured far more in terms of economic success. Though most Native nations attempt to balance these interests, it is not easy. At least in the case of the Bluestem Ranch purchase, investing in the territory of the reservation was prioritized above a return on investment or the generation and distribution of income. The land was viewed as essential, and the Nation would enact the necessary strategic relations to regain it.

On January 21, 2016, the Osage Nation submitted its initial bid to Ted Turner. As part of that bid, Standing Bear included a two-page letter that not only was an emotional appeal for the Osages' offer but also laid out his visions for the ranch. The thrust of both of these efforts is perhaps best summarized by the opening sentence, which in part read, "We seek to regain our lost land and to restore it to the use intended by our ancestors."[85] Given that Turner had never sold land before, multiple Osages I spoke with during this time suggested that he really should be repatriating the land, as it was not lost but taken, and Osage leadership went as far as to send him a text message suggesting this option. Turner's commitment to restoration, however, evidently did not extend to Indigenous peoples' territories, as he did not take the Nation up on this proposal. Clearly, this was still very much a business decision for him. Ultimately, the only way the Osages were going to be able to regain this land was by engaging directly in racial-settler capitalism.

Rather than being duped or even forced into capitalism, Osage officials in this moment were continuing a long tradition of utilizing all available tools and building the relationships necessary to find new ways to reassert their authority and to create a future for the Nation. Theories of racial-settler capitalism allow us to see how the devaluation of racialized life and labor works in tandem with colonial territorial dispossession and genocide to create the systems of oppression that exist in the United States and across the globe today.[86] We must be careful, however, in applying these theories uncritically to Indigenous nations, and instead understand the many layers at work within Native nation building. Many Native nations have used gaming as such a tool to care for their communities and rebuild their relations, and the Osage Nation purchase was another example of this strategic work to secure something we found to be essential.[87]

Osages, of course, also know the full potential for abuse that comes with capitalism, as was evidenced during the 1920s Reign of Terror. The lasting impact of this period of capitalist-fueled genocide, however, was not the rejection of the larger system of racial-settler capitalism but rather a deepening sense that strong relationships, especially with the federal government, were essential to our ongoing survival. It was, in fact, Osage oil wealth that was ultimately used to hire the nascent Federal Bureau of Intelligence to investigate and bring to light the murders. It was also Osage oil wealth that enabled Osages to be trained as lawyers and to fight various efforts of termination throughout the twentieth century.

In their twenty-first-century bid for our land, Osage Nation officials were using their capital to ensure the continuation of the Osage people by building our spiritual and educational connections to the land. After pledging in his letter to Ted Turner to keep this land undivided and under Osage Nation ownership, Standing Bear then went on to describe what he meant by our ancestors' intentions: "We seek to preserve, protect, and sustain the land and use it primarily as a home for the bison that are sacred to us. We do understand the need for use of the bison as a provider of wealth, both monetary and spiritual."[88] Given Turner's passion for bison, this focus is not surprising, but for Standing Bear this commitment was also about strengthening relations that colonialism had been attempting to permanently sever. Later in the letter he further explained what this relationship would look like in the future: "We will use the lands to reconnect our children and youth to nature. We can think of no better learning environment for our children than these lands. Land is central to the culture, traditions, and history of the Osage people."[89] These pledges were part of Standing Bear's vision for and motivation behind acquiring the land.

In the end there were three bidders on the ranch, with the other two of them being cash bidders. Cash bidders are often far more appealing because one typically has to await financing on a land appraisal. Given that Osage gaming revenue had been promised, however, this was not going to be an obstacle. Additionally, Osage leaders were told that their letter had been well received, especially the commitment to bison. The Osage Nation's original bid was not accepted, however, and Chief Standing Bear had to go to the upper limit of what Congress had approved to win the bid on January 28, 2016. Through the development of many layered relations, the Osage Nation was ultimately successful in getting back our land.

"The Land Must Be Made Useful for Our Culture, Language, and the People, Not for the Almighty Dollar"

Even after the purchase, however, questions remained about what the ultimate purpose of the land would be and who would be charged with making those decisions. In this section I will use the debates that occurred over the usage and running of the newly purchased ranch land as a window into the challenges of building layered relations, especially in a three-part government like that of the Osage Nation. Of particular focus here are not only the internal relationships between the various parts of the government but also relations with the landscape. Weighing capitalist pressures to expand wealth against the development of vital relations with the lands, plants, and animals that we know sustain us is a core aspect of moving the Osage Nation into the future.

Shortly after signing the papers, Standing Bear got a call from Kelly Corbin, the head of the Osage Congress Office of Fiscal Performance and Review, who was hosting a meeting between a couple of white ranchers he knew personally and Speaker Whitehorn. The ranchers proposed using a large portion of the ranch for wild horses, which could make the Nation (and the ranchers) a lot of money. Standing Bear vehemently rejected this proposal not only on the grounds that wild horses would destroy the land but also because he was deeply skeptical of the ranchers. Standing Bear reacted forcefully to the proposal, telling me later that all those in the room seemed to have already decided that this was the path for the ranch and that they did not understand the real worth of the land. He told me, "This is about our sacred Heritage, as the land must be made useful for our culture, language, and the people, not for the almighty dollar."[90] In this discussion and throughout the first couple of years of owning the ranch, there were ongoing debates about whether the goal was to rebuild relations with the land for their own sake, or whether these relationships were intended to facilitate other, particularly economic, outcomes.

Tensions continued to mount around the ranch, especially as it got entangled in the ongoing power struggles occurring within the Nation. By mid-April, the Oklahoma spring air was at its most intoxicating, pulling new buds from the prairie ground as well as, apparently, hot-air balloons into the reservation skies. My long morning of meetings began with Congress's Health Authority Committee, which was discussing ongoing tensions with the executive branch. I then attended the Education Task Force meeting, which was debating whether to keep the Head Start programs in the Nation, given the federal limitations this program was saddled with. Afterward, I joined Standing Bear and some of his staff for a meeting with a man who had, without consent, been advertising a hot-air balloon festival he was planning to host on Osage lands. Arriving before the start of the meeting, I took up my now-typical seat in the back corner of the room to the left of Standing Bear. I noticed six congressional bills laid out across the conference table awaiting his signature. Following my gaze, Standing Bear explained with exasperation, "I have no idea what to do with those. They are in violation of the Court's order, but they are also essential budgets!"[91]

The tensions in this period, while complex and multifaceted, primarily came down to how financial authority would be distributed between the legislative branch, which the 2006 Osage Nation Constitution charged with appropriating money and setting laws, and the executive branch, which was charged with running the programs. In its fall 2015 legislative session, just before the land purchase opportunity, the Osage Nation Congress enacted a series of appropriation bills for the 2016 fiscal year. The bills included new provisions to which Standing Bear objected based on what he saw as a usurpation of executive branch power. Congress overrode the principal chief's vetoes and the acts became law. Standing Bear then petitioned the Osage Nation Supreme Court to determine whether the legislative branch exceeded its constitutional authority by performing duties reserved for the executive branch. Because Congress's budget decisions included attempts to make operational decisions about programs reserved for the executive branch, the court ruled Congress's laws to be inconsistent with the 2006 constitution.[92]

This court decision, while decisive, did not settle disputes in the Osage Nation over budgetary authority. These ongoing conflicts complicated all decisions in the Nation, including decisions about the newly purchased land. Several Congress members openly rejected the court's ruling and enacted more appropriation bills containing the same or similar provisions struck down as unconstitutional. Despite the fact that the executive and legislative branches had come together for the purchase of the ranch, relations between the branches throughout this period were, as Standing Bear described, "strained, to put it mildly."[93] In the wake of the move by the United States to consolidate all Osage authority into a single council system of government at the beginning of the twentieth century, Osage officials had to relearn how governance might be divided and authority shared.[94]

With the heavy strains on these relationships during this period, it is not surprising that the ranch's operations became a flashpoint. While separation of powers was always an underlying tension in these debates, other figures, such as bison, wild horses, and the land itself, became the key points of contestation. Congress and the executive branch did agree that the best way of managing the ranch was through the creation of a limited liability company (LLC), entitled Bluestem. Native nations typically utilize LLCs to protect their finances from risky business decisions and appoint knowledgeable specialists to manage the daily operations. To manage not only the land but all Osage affairs, officials had to find ways of compromising, understanding what their unique roles were, and working together toward a shared vision.

Before Standing Bear would have time to focus on what to do with the latest legislation, however, he needed to explain what would be legally required before hosting a hot-air balloon festival on Osage lands and then attend the opening meeting of the Bluestem Ranch LLC board. What followed was a curt and quickly aborted balloon festival planning meeting, in which Standing Bear asked pointed questions about liability insurance, attorney fees, fly permits, food vendor permits, and lease terms, ultimately declaring that this was not a feasible project. We then all jumped in our cars and drove to the Pawhuska Business Development Center, where the Bluestem Ranch board's first meeting would take place.

When Chief Standing Bear arrived at the meeting, he handed out copies of Robert's Rules of Order, the 2006 Osage Nation Constitution, the Bluestem

Ranch's articles of organization, and the recent Osage Nation Supreme Court decision to each of the five members of the board. After opening the meeting with a prayer, both chief and assistant chief addressed the group, saying that while the executive branch had no intention of telling the board what to do, they did have important information to pass along at the beginning of the board's journey. Turner was offering to sell the Nation all the grazing animals and equipment currently on the ranch. The board was still awaiting operating funds for the ranch from the Osage Nation Congress, which had yet to make an appropriation, but it was looking like they would be offered an initial budget of $2 million. Additionally, the current employees were interested in staying on, so the board had to decide whether to retain them. The chiefs went on to discuss other immediate needs for a tax number, attorneys, auditors, accountants, liability insurance, and a board employee to set the agenda.

While the board proceeded with interviewing the current ranch manager to decide whether to keep him on after the transition, Standing Bear returned to his office to decide the fate of the legislation awaiting his final signature. In the end, he signed the appropriation legislation into law to keep the government operating, but he also attached a message to the legislature objecting to those provisions previously declared unconstitutional. Congress took no action to remove the challenged provisions and Standing Bear filed another lawsuit. Ultimately, this led to a second court case in 2016–17, *Standing Bear v. Pratt*, where the court stated, "It appears our failure in *Standing Bear v. Whitehorn* was presuming that each party understood and accepted its role."[95] The court found that elected officials ignored the limitations of their roles in the governmental scheme and suggested to both sides that they needed to create structures to work toward the order and unity that had long been core aspects of Osage forms of governance.[96]

Such order and unity were, however, elusive for the Osage Nation during this period, especially around what should happen with the Osage Nation's new ranch land. In June the Bluestem Ranch board met again, this time with five congressional members and no representation from the chief's office. At the meeting the board concluded that they had not felt like any of the offers from Turner (for the bison, equipment, or employees) were sound economic investments. Furthermore, at this meeting members of the board spoke openly of their concerns about creating a bison preserve, saying that they were not in favor because it would not make money. One of the members argued, "I don't want this ranch to become a money pit. . . . We need to figure out what this bison herd can do besides be something to look at."[97] The board was primarily composed of Osages who had made their living as cattle ranchers.

Members of Congress attending this meeting seemed persuaded by the economic decisions being made for the land and focused most of their interest on what they saw as the excessive interventions of Chief Standing Bear.

Upon hearing that the board was not interested in bison, at least beyond the small number of free bison they could receive from the Intertribal Buffalo Council, Standing Bear grew increasingly exasperated, threatening to either appoint a new board or only lease part of the land to the board, reserving another part of the land for a bison preserve. Standing Bear ultimately left the board intact but continued to demand that they enact his vision for the land as a bison preserve, which was promised in the bid package and was part of his own commitments. In response to these demands, the board filed an ethics complaint with the Osage Nation attorney general against Standing Bear, saying that he was overstepping the line that separated Osage leadership from LLC decision-making. While the case was eventually dismissed, Standing Bear's plan of creating a bison preserve was significantly delayed.

After a lengthy transition process, during which Turner moved all his bison, employees, and equipment from the ranch, the Osage Nation was finally in possession of the land. On August 24, 2016, the Osage Nation held a Bluestem Ranch celebration where Standing Bear gave a speech that detailed the process of buying the land and the duty the Osage Nation had to make sure this land was not destroyed. He argued that some proposals for the land, such as introducing seven thousand wild mustang horses, while lucrative, would cause too much damage to it. He went on to describe his vision for the land: "I hope one year from now we see this land being a refuge for our sacred bison, a classroom for our people—especially our young. A place where Osage companies and individuals will conduct profitable cattle operations, and a place for well-regulated hunting and fishing recreation."[98] Securing this land was a key piece of Standing Bear's vision for building Osage relations with the land, plants, and animals. Importantly this vision was not one simply premised on difference, that is as something totally outside capitalist systems, but a more layered and multivalent approach.

In arguing for the importance of this vision, Standing Bear went on to say that while profit was important for providing key aspects of the Osage Nation today, it was not the only value the Osage Nation was committed to. Locating Osage values in our naming practices, he argued,

> Many of us carry the clan names of our people. These names come from the world important to the Wah-Zha-Zhe. Names such as Wah Tse Ka Wa, the Radiant Star, Le Ta Xhoa, the Grey Hawk, Xiu Tha Wi, the Sacred

Eagle Woman, and Tse Tunka, the Buffalo Bull are just a few of our names. Importantly, you will not find among us names such as profit, rent, or return on investment. Those are words fitting for our Osage casinos and they mean much for providing the money to our education scholarships, our health benefits, our traditional dance arbors, police, elder nutrition programs, and land purchases. We must be careful not to stray too far away from the value of something good. Our traditions, our language, our land, all mean something special when put together. That alone has a value which is priceless. I believe we can do great things in saving ourselves from becoming only a remembrance of history. One hundred years from now we will continue to be known as the Wah-Zha-Zhe, and people can say, the Wah-Zha-Zhe have their own culture, they have their own language, and they have their own lands.[99]

In this powerful definition of what has value and what is in fact priceless—land, language, and traditions—Standing Bear clearly articulates the many layered relations that he sees as necessary for the Osage nation in the twenty-first century. To enact this nationhood not only now but for the next one hundred years, the Osage Nation must engage with systems of profit but is ultimately driven by building land-based relations not for the sake of profit itself.

"We Couldn't Hardly Find Any Meat for Our Kids"

Buying the land was just another step in the ongoing process of moving the Osage Nation into the future. This effort requires an ongoing commitment to developing and maintaining many layered relations, which are often in tension with each other. The stakes of this work are exceptionally high, though, as land is a vital piece of the health and welfare of a people. As this concluding section will demonstrate, layering has been and will continue to be a vital tool for ensuring a future for the Osage Nation. By bringing together federal funding, Osage management, and casino profits, the Osage Nation can begin to offset some of the challenges created by ongoing colonialism, especially for our foodways.

By 2021, the Osage Nation Ranch, as the land had been renamed, had been entirely paid off and contained over three thousand cattle and over two hundred bison.[100] The bison preserve was starting small at 3,200 acres but would grow as the ranch was able to secure more fencing. Standing Bear explained to me that his primary goal was to enact "our ancestors' vision of the land that they saw. The same land we see today."[101] Environmental issues on the land have also continued to plague the Nation, as the land needs around $48 million worth of remediation to be placed in trust.[102] Despite these political and ecological challenges, the Osage Nation has remained committed to building layered relations with this land. This has meant buying the land despite its high costs and deteriorated condition. Core to Standing Bear's commitment to not only buying the land but ensuring it was used as a bison preserve was his sense that Osage nationhood was directly tied to the future imagined by those who came before. At the heart of the land was not only the territorial base but the bison that are core to our ⌔∩ᚴ∩ ↵∩ᚴ∩ɑ, names, health, and relations to place.

The challenges of not being in control of the food chain became even clearer in early 2020 when the COVID-19 pandemic hit and began affecting food distribution, especially in food deserts such as the Osage Nation.[103] Casey Johnson, director of operations under Standing Bear, received word in the spring of 2020 that there was no meat available for student lunches at the Wahzhazhe Early Learning Academy sites in Fairfax and Hominy. He told the *Osage News*, "The supply chain had been disrupted. . . . So, we couldn't hardly find any meat for our kids. It was affecting our children, then it was going to start affecting our elders, so that was one of the things that got us to thinking about if meat prices go through the roof, how are we going to take care of all of our folks?"[104] While the Osage Nation had long been a food desert, the real instability of relying on external entities for food was made very clear during the pandemic.

Responding to these concerns, the Osage Nation filed a Coronavirus Aid, Relief, and Economic Security (CARES) Act application through the US Department of the Treasury in 2020. This funding was part of a large-scale effort by the United States to provide fast and direct economic assistance to Americans. The Osage Nation saw applying for federal assistance as key, not only for food security but ultimately for sovereignty. Again, it was through strengthening our relationships, including with the US government, that the Osage Nation felt like it could best care for its people. An Osage Nation employee task force was formed to administer the CARES Act funding awarded to the Nation, which totaled more than $44 million. Osages would later receive over $100 million additional federal funds from the American Rescue Plan Act, which included additional funds earmarked for the bison preserve and food sovereignty efforts. The original CARES Act task force created an implementation plan that allotted around $17 million to address food security, which included a meat-processing plant, a greenhouse, an aquaponics building, farming equipment, bison, cattle and fences, pens, and feed lots for finishing cattle for meat processing.[105] These food security investments will ultimately enable the Osage Nation to have total control of the food chain for both fresh meats and vegetables, thus asserting sovereignty over our foods.

Food sovereignty means more than access to healthy foods. At the heart of this sovereignty for the Osage is building relationships with the bison, cattle, plants, and ultimately land that will once again foster health, both physical and mental, in the Nation. During his 2021 State of the Nation address, Standing Bear featured the ranch and new facilities as part of his administration's core efforts in the last year. He described the importance of prayer before the first bison slaughter. He also talked about the importance of food sovereignty, saying, "This bison is feeding our children and our elderly as we have done for thousands of years."[106] In addition to feeding the Osage people and selling meat to pay the costs of the facility, the Nation has made the hides and other parts available to Osages for important practices such as drum making. Through strategic decisions and relationship building, the Osage Nation is constructing a future by enacting those relations that kept us healthy in the past. Such practices are not only at the core of what it means for Osages to care for each other in the present, but they are also part of what our ancestors gave us to take us into the future.

Conclusion

"Make a Game Out of It"

My father had a philosophy that pushed me through many of my early life struggles and has continued to serve me in life. Whenever I would complain about a frustrating teacher, an impossible test, or not understanding the point of a monotonous assignment, he would respond with, "Make a game out of it." My earliest memories of this almost daily advice were of annoyance, but over time I came to appreciate this approach and how it guided my life. I now understand that by "Make a game out of it," he meant that while the system might not always be designed for me or the materials engaging to me, my job was to figure out how to thrive anyway. Making a game out of things was perhaps most about shifting my attitude. It was about seeing the openings and potential of the spaces I was in, rather than just the structures and their limitations.

My success in making a game out of it was not measured in how well I followed the instructions given but whether I was able to turn the situation into something that worked for me. This was not learning to play the game as given but figuring out how to make the game play for me. Throughout my education this meant advocating for myself with teachers. I convinced a middle school English teacher to let me bring a handheld spell-checking device to class, a headmaster to let me take a different math class with a teacher whom I understood, and college professors to assign photo essays instead of written work. In these days before accommodations and accessibility became standard practice, each of these exceptions required far more work, but they were what allowed me to find my voice and ultimately thrive.

Throughout my time speaking with, observing, and writing about Osage Nation leaders, I have seen this same philosophy at work. Rather than focusing on the oppression of colonial structures, Osage leaders have been looking for loopholes and making possibilities. In this book I have highlighted these efforts by not just naming the many entanglements of colonialism but also the savvy strategies Native leaders are constantly engaged in. As I quickly learned as a child, this kind of world navigation requires building strong relationships with everyone around you, especially those in power. As this book has demonstrated, Osages have embraced rather than refused technology, extractive industry, bureaucracy, and capitalism. This embrace is not because we inherently appreciate these approaches but because they are the tools available to us. In each of these contexts Osage leaders have deployed them toward our own ends.

This book is a call for the academy, and the field of Indigenous studies in particular, to take seriously the day-to-day work our Native nation leaders are engaged in. It is certainly vital that we make space for what Tanana Athabascan scholar Dian Million calls "intense dreaming," in which we envision a world not driven by colonialism, capitalism, or the other structures that oppress us.[1] Such a calling out and thinking beyond is desperately needed in this world filled with anti-Black and anti-Native structures and sentiments. We must use this work to make sure we are not letting ourselves be defined by these structures, even as we navigate them. However, we also need to do so in a way that does not foreclose the creative strategies our nations have used and continue to use.

The Osage philosophy of moving to a new country offers us a model for appreciating the strategic and essential work of Native nation building. At its core, it is a philosophy of bringing forward the essentials of the Osage Nation, including language, self-governance, health, and land. It is also a process of relationship building that utilizes respect, responsibility, order, and layering as core strategies. This is not a movement to reach a set goal but rather a commitment to keep moving to make things better for future generations. Moving is an effort to reformulate toxic relationships, so that they can be utilized to serve our people and our future. Moving also encourages us to stop being surprised by Native nations' use of technologies, extractive industries, bureaucracy, or capitalism. This book contributes to scholarship that demonstrates that Indigenous presence and futurity are not surprising. To be Osage is to be creative with the tools around us—that is, to make a game out of it.

Historically as well as today, Osage leaders have embraced the latest technologies as part of building our nation and ensuring its future. The Osage philosophy of moving to a new country is one of the ways Osages have narrated this embrace of the new and the letting go of older practices, even as we brought certain key aspects of who we are forward. In the context of the twenty-first-century language department, this has included developing classroom curriculum, a writing system, and a host of digital applications and teaching venues. While colonial actors have intentionally and unintentionally utilized these technologies and others in ways that disrupted our relationships with the language, we still see the potential these technologies offer us. As chapter 1 discusses, however, this embrace of technology needs to be guided by and centered in Osage understandings of respect. This is about utilizing these technologies toward our own rather than others' ends.

Similarly, the Osage Nation has chosen to embrace extractive industries, especially drilling for oil and natural gas. While we have not always liked this choice, or even had the ability to say no, the Osage Nation would likely not exist today without the many creative ways we have used this industry to support ourselves and ensure our future as a Nation. As chapter 2 describes, Osage leaders creatively utilized this industry, the relationships it created, and the funding it provided to keep our reservation intact and our Nation from being terminated. As we continue the process of moving the Osage Nation into the future, we must constantly reassess our relations with these extractive industries, especially in terms of how they are affecting our lands, health, and self-governance.

Within our cultural practices, children are most often expected to learn by taking part and doing, not through direct instruction. As Osage Language Department curriculum specialist Dana Daylight explained to me, "Our way is to throw people in and they figure it out."[2] Moving is how we go about this process as a Nation. As we have been figuring out how to best enact the 2006 Osage Constitution, we have tried various bureaucratic strategies. Recognizing the limitations of elected officials managing programs, for example, the 2006 constitution created a structure of boards that allowed for both separation of authority and checks and balances. As chapter 3 demonstrated, the deployment of an Osage Nation bureaucracy, especially in the field of health, has been a rocky and difficult ordeal, but one that demonstrates what we can gain by taking over and running these unwieldy structures ourselves. We do not have to know the precise end we are working toward; we need only be committed to continually figuring out how to make things better.

From the very beginning of our engagements with colonists, Osages have used capitalism toward our own ends. It was through our insistence that trading posts were built, and we quickly figured out how to secure our territorial authority by monopolizing trade. As chapter 4 illustrates, it was only through our engagements with the market economy that we were able to get our land back in the twenty-first century. These purchases were not about expanding our wealth but about ensuring that Osages could develop the essential relations necessary with the land. This land was not an economic investment but an investment in who we are as a people. Through the development of a host of layered relations, including with ranchers, bankers, and the gaming and hospitality industry, the Osage Nation has been using capitalism to ensure that we have the essential things we need to move the Osage Nation into the future.

Unlike some theories of Indigenous relationality that romanticize this work, this book has been dedicated to demonstrating how messy, fraught, but also essential these relationships are. It offers a close look at what else, beyond refusal or capitulation, our nations are regularly engaging in. Ethnography is a particularly useful tool for seeing and appreciating both the strategic and the essential. Throughout my conversations with and observations of Osage leaders, it was impossible to deny the challenges of their work or their commitment to ensuring that the Nation keeps moving forward. Too often Indigenous studies scholarship has missed the opportunity to name or share these fraught choices and many contingencies of Native nation governance. The constant improvisations and vast expanse of knowledge that this work requires should be appreciated, even as we all continue the work of moving our nations into the future.

Appendix

Osage Orthography Guide

Vowels

Λ	a as in f<u>a</u>ther
α	e as in <u>e</u>gg
∩	i as in sk<u>i</u>
O	o as in g<u>o</u>
U	u as in fl<u>u</u>te
λ	u as in b<u>u</u>t

Nasal Vowels

Λ˙	nasal Λ <u>on</u> like h<u>on</u>k
∩˙	nasal ∩ <u>in</u> like s<u>in</u>g
O˙	nasal O

Diphthongs

Λ	i as in b<u>i</u>te
A	Λ+∩˙
⊙	O+∩˙
α	α+∩˙

Consonants

∫	h	R	br as in <u>br</u>ush	Þ	unvoiced B, lax P (not Pʰ)
ι	l	Ƹ	ts as in ha<u>ts</u>	D	unvoiced D, lax T (not Tʰ)
ℳ	m	ħ	th as in <u>th</u>ey	ķ	unvoiced G, lax K (not Kʰ)
∠	n	ઠ	sh as in <u>sh</u>ip		
ς	s	ⱬ	z as in sei<u>z</u>ure		
ч	w	G	ch as in <u>ch</u>at		
7	z	ķ	ky always ĶU		
↑	Voiceless Tense Gutteral	∫	hy always ∫U		
Ψ	Voiced Lax Gutteral				

Þ′	Þ with immediate glottal catch
ķ′	ķ with immediate glottal catch
Ƹ′	Ƹ with immediate glottal catch

Consonant Clusters

ςÞ	ςD	ςƸ	ςķ		Þↄ	Þઠ
ઠÞ	ઠD	ઠƸ	ઠķ	ઠG	Dↄ	
ↄÞ	ↄD	ↄƸ			ķↄ	ķઠ

Page from the Osage Nation language program materials. Courtesy of Braxton Redeagle.

Notes

Introduction

1. An Act to Reaffirm the Inherent Sovereign Rights of the Osage Tribe to Determine Its Membership and Form of Government, Pub. L. No. 108-431, 118 Stat. 2609 (2004).
2. Gene Dennison, personal communication, Pawhuska, OK, on July 2, 2015.
3. Gene Dennison, Osage Nation court appearance, Pawhuska, OK, July 2, 2015.
4. Dennison, Osage Nation court appearance.
5. Gene Dennison, personal communication, Pawhuska, OK, on July 2, 2015.
6. Anonymous employee, personal communication, Pawhuska, OK, on July 2, 2015.
7. Anonymous employee, personal communication, Pawhuska, OK, on July 2, 2015.
8. Anonymous employee, personal communication, Pawhuska, OK, on July 2, 2015.
9. Baldwin, "Whiteness and Futurity"; Dillon, *Walking the Clouds*; Arvin, Tuck, and Morrill, "Decolonizing Feminism"; Tuck and Gaztambide-Fernández, "Curriculum, Replacement"; Recollet, "Gesturing Indigenous Futurities"; Goodyear-Ka'ōpua, "Indigenous Oceanic Futures"; Laura Harjo, *Spiral to the Stars*.
10. Duarte and Belarde-Lewis, "Imagining," 687.
11. Yazzie, "US Imperialism."
12. Wolfe, "Settler Colonialism."
13. Trask, "Settlers of Color."
14. Tuck and Gaztambide-Fernández, "Curriculum, Replacement."
15. Shoemaker, "Typology of Colonialism."
16. Theobald, *Reproduction on the Reservation*, 3.
17. Carroll, *Roots of Our Renewal*; Cattelino, *High Stakes*; Doerfler, *Those Who Belong*; Kauanui, *Paradoxes of Hawaiian Sovereignty*; Lambert, *Choctaw Nation*; McCarthy, *In Divided Unity*.
18. Kauanui, "'Structure, Not an Event,'" 1.
19. Tuck and Gaztambide-Fernández, "Curriculum, Replacement."
20. Goodyear-Ka'ōpua, "Indigenous Oceanic Futures," 86.
21. Anderson, *Imagined Communities*; Lambert, *Choctaw Nation*; Simpson, "Paths toward a Mohawk Nation"; Andersen, *"Métis."*
22. Both settlers and Indigenous peoples attach many different meanings to the term *tribe*. The term has taken on significant and specific legal status in US federal law and is thus frequently deployed by Native peoples to assert sovereignty. As with all terms, there are advantages and disadvantages to the term and it is important not to get too caught up in semantics or oversimplify complex debates. Teves, Smith, and Raheja, *Native Studies Keywords*.
23. Apes, "Indian's Looking-Glass"; Vine Deloria Jr., *Behind the Trail*.
24. Andersen, *"Métis,"* 19.
25. Importantly, this does not preclude Native peoples' efforts to strategically use or recraft the meaning of terms like *tribe*.

26. Lambert, *Choctaw Nation*, 10.

27. Weber, *Economy and Society*.

28. Simpson, "Paths toward a Mohawk Nation," 121.

29. Alfred, "Sovereignty"; Bruyneel, *Third Space of Sovereignty*; Moreton-Robinson, *Sovereign Subjects*; Kauanui, *Hawaiian Blood*; Cattelino, *High Stakes*; Byrd, "Indigeneity's Difference"; Simpson, "Sovereignty of Critique."

30. Dennison, "Entangled Sovereignties," 685.

31. Dennison, *Colonial Entanglement*; Dennison, "Stitching Osage Governance."

32. See Nadasdy, *Sovereignty's Entailments*, for a recent example.

33. Tuck and Yang, "R-Words," 243.

34. I will discuss my focus on desire over damage in more detail later in the chapter, but it is drawing on the important work of Tuck and Yang, "R-Words."

35. Simpson, "Paths toward a Mohawk Nation," 118.

36. Tully, *Strange Multiplicity*; Alfred, *Heeding the Voices*; Simpson, "Paths toward a Mohawk Nation"; Lyons, *X-Marks*; Andersen, *"Métis."*

37. For clarity and to best match with contemporary usage, I will use the term Osage, even when referring to the historical group, which reportedly went by ⌐∩oʞ∧ᴄʞ∧ (Children of the Middle Waters). According to Osage historian and writer John Joseph Mathews, we became known as Osages when French traders asked one of the groups they were trading with what their name was. Rather than name the larger people they were part of, they said they were part of the subdivision of the Hunkah, called ⁴∧z∧zɑ. When a French missionary wrote ⁴∧z∧zɑ (also spelled Wahzhazhe today), phonetically it became Osage. Mathews, *Osages*.

38. Treaty with the Osage, 7 Stat. 107, ratified April 28, 1810 (1808).

39. Rollings, *Unaffected by the Gospel*.

40. La Flesche, *Osage and the Invisible World*.

41. Warrior, *People and the Word*.

42. Wilson, *The Underground Reservation*, 34.

43. Logan v. Andrus, 457 F. Supp. 1318, 1324 (N.D. Okla. 1978); Dennison, *Colonial Entanglement*.

44. Fletcher v. United States, 116 F.3d 1315 (10th Cir. 1997).

45. For more on this and all the efforts related to Osage government reform, see Dennison, *Colonial Entanglement*.

46. Warrior, *People and the Word*.

47. An Act to Reaffirm the Inherent Sovereign Rights of the Osage Tribe to Determine Its Membership and Form of Government, Pub. L. No. 108-431, 118 Stat. 2609 (2004).

48. Dennison, *Colonial Entanglement*.

49. Cruikshank, *Social Life of Stories*; King, *Truth about Stories*; Stark, "Stories as Law"; Doerfler, *Centering Anishinaabeg Studies*.

50. Justice, *Why Indigenous Literatures Matter*.

51. Stark, "Stories as Law," 250.

52. Mathews, *Osages*, 53. This appears to be the first published usage of the phrase "moving . . . to a new country." Mathews likely drew this origin story from oral histories and from La Flesche, "Osage Tribe."

53. Mathews, *Osages*, 53.

54. Dorsey, *Osage Traditions*.

55. Dorsey, "Osage Myths," 46.

56. Eddie Red Eagle, personal communication, phone, May 8, 2023.

57. As with ᏞᎣᏗᎣᏃᏁ₭Ꮑ here, whenever I use Osage-language words throughout the book, I write them using the Osage orthography, which the Osage Nation Language Department developed in 2015. Honoring Osage sovereignty means honoring our orthography, as chapter 1 will describe in more detail. Given the importance of honoring Osage Nation representations of the language, there will not be any English pronunciation guides in the text, but the appendix includes an orthography guide. I will only use English spellings when I am directly quoting. Additionally, I will only include a translation once per chapter for each word, intentionally forcing readers to do their own orthography recognition and translation thereafter. In addition to privileging the Osage language in this way, my choices are intentionally designed to upset the ease with which we too often translate abstract concepts from one language to another. By using Osage orthography, I am asking readers to come to terms with the limits of their own knowledge base and understanding. It is vital to recognize that Osage words, especially ones like ᏞᎣᏗᎣᏃᏁ₭Ꮑ, have a robust cultural framework, which this book is only hinting at.

58. La Flesche, *Osage and the Invisible World*.

59. La Flesche, "Osage Tribe," 62–63.

60. Drent and Dennison, "New Country Again."

61. La Flesche, "Osage Tribe."

62. Rollings, *Unaffected by the Gospel*, 176–77.

63. DuVal, *Native Ground*, 103.

64. Rollings, *Unaffected by the Gospel*.

65. Rollings.

66. "Great Osage Mission," 110.

67. Rollings, *Unaffected by the Gospel*.

68. The Missouri Province Archive in the Jesuit Archives in St. Louis is a powerful documentation of this. John Klein, "Osage Nation Finds Jesuit Archives," *Tulsa World*, May 10, 2017, https://tulsaworld.com/homepagelatest/john-klein-osage-nation-finds-jesuit-archives -preserved-osage-history/article_2b1f206a-ee3f-5ae5-a575-ae2845feb807.html.

69. Rollings, *Unaffected by the Gospel*.

70. Gibson to Smioth.

71. Dennison, "Logic of Recognition."

72. Edwards, *Osage Women and Empire*.

73. Tixier, *Tixier's Travels*, 236.

74. Rollings, *Unaffected by the Gospel*.

75. Bailey et al., *Art of the Osage*, 143.

76. Bailey et al., 143.

77. Edwards, *Osage Women and Empire*.

78. Warrior, *People and the Word*, 74.

79. Rachel Adams-Heard, "Transcript 'In Trust' Episode Five: The Association," Bloomberg, September 26, 2022, www.bloomberg.com/news/articles/2022-09-27/transcript-in -trust-podcast-episode-five-the-association.

80. Veronica Pipestem, personal communication, email, March 24, 2023.

81. Drent and Dennison, "New Country Again," 62.

82. Laura Harjo, *Spiral to the Stars*, 32.

83. Diaz, "Oceania in the Plains."

84. Moreton-Robinson, "Relationality," 71.

85. TallBear, "Disrupting Settlement"; Tynan, "What Is Relationality?"

86. Tynan, "What Is Relationality?," 599.

87. Wildcat, "Replacing Exclusive Sovereignty."

88. Wildcat, 180.

89. The only previous academic usage of the term *vital relations* I could find was in a 2013 edited volume entitled *Vital Relations: Modernity and the Persistent Life of Kinship*. While not directly relevant to the arguments of this book, the idea that kinship continues to be a core part of contemporary life is not contradictory to my arguments. See McKinnon, *Vital Relations*.

90. *Cambridge Dictionary*, s.v. "vital," accessed August 21, 2023, https://dictionary.cambridge.org/us/dictionary/english/vital.

91. Million defines and demonstrates the importance of intense dreaming in Million, "Intense Dreaming."

92. Nagar and Shirazi, "Radical Vulnerability."

93. Dennison, *Colonial Entanglement*; Dennison, "Stitching Osage Governance"; Dennison, "Logic of Recognition"; Dennison, "Entangled Sovereignties"; Dennison, "'Affects' of Empire."

94. For examples of how this concept has been used, see Tuck, "ANCSA as X-Mark"; Simpson, *Mohawk Interruptus*; Carroll, *Roots of Our Renewal*; and Brown, *Stoking the Fire*.

95. Lyons, *X-Marks*, 3.

96. For some of the best reporting on this period, see Rachel Adams-Heard, *In Trust*, podcast, Bloomberg, accessed November 24, 2022, www.bloomberg.com/features/2022-in-trust-podcast.

97. Mervyn LeRoy, dir., *The FBI Story* (Warner Bros. Pictures, 1959); McAuliffe, *Bloodland*; Red Corn, *Pipe for February*; Grann, *Killers of the Flower Moon*; McAuliffe, *Deaths of Sybil Bolton*; *Osage Murders*; *Back in Time: Osage Murders—the Reign of Terror* (OETA, 2021); Aaron Morvan, "OETA Debuts New Documentary about Early 1900s Osage Murders," OETA, December 29, 2020, www.oeta.tv/blogs/pressroom/oeta-debuts-new-documentary-about-early-1900s-osage-murders/.

98. Charles and Rah, *Unsettling Truths*.

99. Harmon, *Rich Indians*.

100. Harmon.

101. Shannon Shaw Duty, "Martin Scorsese Meets with Chief Standing Bear about 'Killers of the Flower Moon,'" *Osage News*, July 26, 2019, https://osagenews.org/martin-scorsese-meets-with-chief-standing-bear-about-killers-of-the-flower-moon/.

102. Personal communication, Jim Gray, phone, September 14, 2023.

103. Personal communications, Osage reservation, June and July 2021.

104. Julie O'Keefe, personal communication, Tulsa, OK, July 20, 2021.

105. Anonymous communication, Pawhuska, OK, July 6, 2021.

106. Warrior, Robert, "The Missing Politics of Scorsese's 'Killers of the Flower Moon,'" October 20, 2023, https://newlinesmag.com/essays/the-missing-politics-of-scorseses-killers-of-the-flower-moon/.

107. To name just a few: Weaver, "Challenges of Research"; Smith, *Decolonizing Methodologies*; Shawn Wilson, *Research Is Ceremony*; Kovach, *Indigenous Methodologies*; Tuck and McKenzie, *Place in Research*.

108. Moreton-Robinson, "Relationality," 3.

109. Kovach, *Indigenous Methodologies*.

110. Drent and Dennison, "New Country Again."

111. Similarly, Ho Chunk Nation scholar Renya Ramirez credits a local Native leader whom she interviewed with coming up with the core concept of her book. Ramirez, *Native Hubs*.

112. Sara Ahmed, "Making Feminist Points," *Feministkilljoys* (blog), 2013, https://feminist killjoys.com/2013/09/11/making-feminist-points/.

113. While I know that governance (and citizenship) of these entities has been deeply disrupted by colonialism, such identifications felt important as part of recognizing the inherent sovereignty of Indigenous peoples and their continued agency in making such choices. Additionally, I have chosen to label non-Native scholars by their settler country even though such a label flattens the many complicated ways in which people became settlers and their relationships to place. It is useful, however, to understand the geographic contexts out of which this writing occurred. I apologize to anyone I have misrecognized in this process, especially as not everyone makes their preferred terms transparent and they do sometimes change over time.

114. Simpson, "On Ethnographic Refusal," 78.

115. Tuck and Yang, "R-Words."

116. Smith, *Decolonizing Methodologies*.

117. Smith.

118. Moreton-Robinson, "Relationality," 75.

119. Tuck and Yang, "R-Words," 4.

120. Kenney, "Counting, Accounting, and Accountability."

121. Tiffany Lee, "Language, Identity, and Power," 318.

122. Lambert, *Choctaw Nation*, 3.

123. Brayboy and Deyhle, "Insider-Outsider," 165.

124. Raymond Red Corn, personal communication, email, August 16, 2020.

125. Million, *Therapeutic Nations*, 76.

126. Quoted in Manola Secaira, "What Does Indigenous Reclamation Mean? Three Native Voices Discuss," *Crosscut*, April 25, 2021, https://crosscut.com/focus/2021/04/what -does-indigenous-reclamation-mean-three-native-voices-discuss?

127. "Osage Tribal Member Shares Journey of Addiction and Recovery," Holding Hope Series, Osage Nation, accessed August 21, 2023, www.osagenation-nsn.gov/news-events /news/holding-hope-series-osage-tribal-member-shares-journey-addiction-and-recovery.

128. Benny Polacca, "New Osage Nation Domestic Violence Shelter and PRT Facilities Now Open," *Osage News*, December 12, 2017, https://osagenews.org/new-osage-nation -domestic-violence-shelter-and-prt-facilities-now-open/.

129. Stacey Lookout, director of Primary Residential Treatment, Health Authority board meeting, Pawhuska, OK, July 21, 2022.

130. Jodie Revard, personal communication, Zoom interview, February 17, 2022.

131. An additional bill was passed in 2022 (ONCA 22-86), which allocated another $2,979,736 in American Rescue Plan Act funds due to rising construction costs.

132. Revard, personal communication.

133. Jodie Revard, personal communication, telephone conversation, January 26, 2022.

134. Quoted in Benny Polacca, "ON Congress Passes Resolution Supporting Re-establishment of PRT Sweat Lodge," *Osage News*, April 3, 2017, https://osagenews.org/on-congress-passes-resolution-supporting-re-establishment-of-prt-sweat-lodge/.

135. "Osage Nation Treatment Center Focuses on Culturally Relevant Ways to Lead Drug- and Alcohol-Free Lifestyle," Holding Hope Series, Osage Nation, accessed August 21, 2023, www.osagenation-nsn.gov/news-events/news/holding-hope-series-osage-nation-treatment-center-focuses-culturally-relevant-ways.

136. "Osage Nation Treatment Center."

Chapter One

1. An Act to Reaffirm the Inherent Sovereign Rights of the Osage Tribe to Determine Its Membership and Form of Government, Pub. L. No. 108-431, 118 Stat. 2609 (2004).

2. Wilson Pipestem, personal communication, email, March 17, 2023.

3. The account of this event is reconstructed from memory of my time in Pawhuska, Oklahoma, during the summer of 2004.

4. Herman Mongrain Lookout, personal communication, Zoom, August 5, 2022.

5. These are both leadership roles in vital Osage community practices.

6. Herman Mongrain Lookout, personal communication, Zoom, August 12, 2022.

7. Herman Mongrain Lookout, personal communication, Pawhuska, OK, November 19, 2005.

8. "Osage Nation Constitution," Osage Nation, March 11, 2006, www.osagenation-nsn.gov/sites/default/files/library/ConstitutionOfTheOsageNation.pdf (emphasis added).

9. Vann Bighorse, personal communication, Pawhuska, OK, July 8, 2021.

10. Treuer, *Living Our Language*; Basso, *Wisdom Sits in Places*; Sims, "Native Language Planning"; McCarty, *Place to Be Navajo*; Lomawaima and McCarthy, *"To Remain an Indian"*; Lyons, "There's No Translation"; MacFarlane, "Beyond the Divide"; Hauff, "Beyond Numbers."

11. Herman Mongrain Lookout, personal communication, Zoom, October 21, 2022.

12. La Flesche, *Osage and the Invisible World*; La Flesche, "Osage Tribe"; Mathews, *Osages*; Dorsey, *Osage Traditions*.

13. Lookout, personal communication, October 21, 2022.

14. Brugman and Macaulay, "Characterizing Evidentiality."

15. Quintero, *Osage Grammar*.

16. Haspelmath and Sims, *Understanding Morphology*.

17. Smith, *Decolonizing Methodologies*; Shawn Wilson, *Research Is Ceremony*; Tuck and McKenzie, *Place in Research*; Moreton-Robinson, "Relationality"; Byrd, "What's Normative?"; Tynan, "What Is Relationality?"; McCubbin et al., "Relational Well-Being"; Whyte, "Too Late"; Lyons, "There's No Translation."

18. Minthorn and Chávez, "Indigenous Leadership," 5.

19. MacLean, "Culture and Change." For more discussion of this, see Henne-Ochoa et al., "Pathways Forward."

20. Eddy Red Eagle Jr., personal communication, Pawhuska, OK, July 15, 2016.

21. La Flesche, *Osage and the Invisible World.*

22. Eddy Red Eagle Jr., personal communication, phone, November 17, 2021.

23. Eddy Red Eagle Jr., Dennison/Ritter family naming, Skiatook, OK, December 31, 2014.

24. I appreciate Jodi Revard and others pushing back on my initial, broader usage of ꜝꜞꜢꝋ.

25. Eddy Red Eagle Jr., personal communication, email, November 11, 2021.

26. Kovach, *Indigenous Methodologies*, 178.

27. Eddy Red Eagle Jr., personal communication, phone, November 17, 2021.

28. Treuer, *Living Our Language*; Basso, *Wisdom Sits in Places*; Sims, "Native Language Planning"; McCarty, *Place to Be Navajo*; Lomawaima and McCarthy, *"To Remain an Indian"*; Lyons, "There's No Translation"; MacFarlane, "Beyond the Divide"; Hauff, "Beyond Numbers."

29. Hinton, *Bringing Our Languages Home.*

30. Leonard, "Challenging 'Extinction,'" 141–42.

31. Meek, "Failing American Indian Languages"; Pine and Turin, "Language Revitalization."

32. Wolfe, "Settler Colonialism"; Leonard, "Challenging 'Extinction.'"

33. Herman Mongrain Lookout, personal communication, Zoom, October 21, 2022.

34. Leonard, "Producing Language Reclamation."

35. Henne-Ochoa et al., "Pathways Forward."

36. Henne-Ochoa et al., 488.

37. Leonard, "Producing Language Reclamation," 19.

38. Hauff, "Beyond Numbers," 18–19.

39. See also the introduction for a fuller discussion of moving. Mathews, *Osages*, 53, appears to be the first published usage of the phrase "moving to a new country." He likely drew this origin story from oral histories and from the work of Francis La Flesche, including La Flesche, *Osage and the Invisible World.* Here La Flesche takes stories by four different chiefs to create "The GA-HI'-GE O-K'O^N, RITE OF THE CHIEFS," which La Flesche says is a story "to understand the significance in the tribal development" (59).

40. Hunter, Munkres, and Fariss, *Osage Nation NAGPRA Claim*. For an example of the oral history, see Dorsey, "Notes on Quapaw History."

41. Hunter, Munkres, and Fariss, *Osage Nation NAGPRA Claim*. See also Rankin, "Siouan Tribal Contacts."

42. Rankin, "Siouan Tribal Contacts."

43. I understand technology throughout this chapter as any tools that enable manipulation of the environment, natural or built. Martínez, "Tecno-sovereignty"; Rodríguez-Alegría, "Narratives of Conquest."

44. Henning, "Adaptive Patterning."

45. Bailey, *The Osage and the Invisible World*, 45.

46. Pierce, "Legal History."

47. Rollings, *Unaffected by the Gospel*; Danielle Taschereau Mamers, "Historical Photo of Mountain of Bison Skulls Documents Animals on the Brink of Extinction," *Conversation*, December 2, 2020, https://theconversation.com/historical-photo-of-mountain-of-bison-skulls -documents-animals-on-the-brink-of-extinction-148780.

48. Rollings, *Unaffected by the Gospel.*

49. McCaffery, "We-He-Sa-Ki (Hard Rope)."

50. There is not a lot known about the 1861 constitutional government, beyond the contents of the constitution, which is available in Wilkins, *Documents.* Given the strength of the existing political system, the turmoil of the Civil War, and the sense that this new government would just be a tool of the federal government, Osages seem to have quickly abandoned this government.

51. Beede, "Reports of Agents," 54.

52. Wilkins and Stark, *American Indian Politics.*

53. Beede, "Reports of Agents."

54. Rollings, *Unaffected by the Gospel.*

55. Terry Wilson, *Underground Reservation,* 29.

56. Rollings, *Unaffected by the Gospel.* For additional discussion about the economic role of village chiefs, see La Flesche, *Osage and the Invisible World.*

57. Miles, "Reports of Agents" (1881), 85–87.

58. Terry Wilson, *Underground Reservation.*

59. Warrior, *People and the Word,* 75.

60. Miles, "Reports of Agents" (1884), 82–84.

61. Bailey, "Changes in Osage Social Organization," 158.

62. Miles, "Reports of Agents" (1885), 90.

63. Wolfe, "Settler Colonialism."

64. Swan and Cooley, *Wedding Clothes,* 231.

65. Another powerful example of embracing new cultural traditions as a vehicle to carry the language forward can be seen in the Osage adaptations of the Native American Church. Billy Proctor, personal communication, phone, October 13, 2021. See also Swan, "West Moon—East Moon."

66. Swan, "West Moon—East Moon," 293.

67. Swan, 294.

68. S. E. Ruckman, "Drum Ceremony Unites Osages," *Tulsa World,* June 19, 2005.

69. Ryan RedCorn, Osage advanced language class, Pawhuska, OK, March 20, 2006.

70. This information has been compiled from notes I took during many of Lookout's classes and speeches since 2004. For publicly available versions of this narrative, see "Osage Speaker Herman Mongrain Lookout," Pawhuska, OK, Vimeo video, 8:13, posted by Allison Herrera on July 20, 2016, https://vimeo.com/175605625; and Shannon Shaw Duty, "Six Tribes Come Together with One Purpose: Language Preservation," *Osage News,* July 31, 2019, http://osagenews.org/en/article/2019/07/31/six-tribes-come-together-one-purpose -language-preservation/.

71. Herman Mongrain Lookout, personal communication, Pawhuska, OK, July 6, 2022.

72. The 1906 roll, allotment, and the Osage murders will be discussed in more detail in the following chapter.

73. Harmon, *Rich Indians.*

74. Vimeo video, 8:13, posted by Allison Herrera on July 20, 2016, https://vimeo.com /175605625.

75. Shannon Shaw Duty, "Revitalizing Language for an Osage Generation Eager to Learn," *Osage News,* August 1, 2019, https://osagenews.org/revitalizing-language-for-an-osage

-generation-eager-to-learn/. Additional information has been compiled from notes I have taken during many of Lookout's classes and speeches since 2004.

76. Quoted in Nagle, "Osage Language Curriculum," 7.

77. Herman Mongrain Lookout, personal communication, Zoom, December 16, 2022.

78. Dennison, *Colonial Entanglement.*

79. This discussion comes from a conference paper Atterberry presented at the Native American Alaska Native Children in School Conference in Oklahoma City, OK, on October 3, 2022, as well as personal communication over the phone on August 8, 2022.

80. Dorsey, "Osage Myths."

81. For a broader discussion of boarding schools and how early American Indians embraced writing, see Lyons, "Rhetorical Sovereignty."

82. Veronica Pipestem, personal communication, Tulsa, OK, July 1, 2022.

83. Sullivan, "In Memoriam."

84. Veronica Pipestem, personal communication, email, September 20, 2021.

85. Janis Carpenter, personal communication, Pawhuska, OK, July 15, 2022.

86. Janis Carpenter, personal communication, Pawhuska, OK, June 29, 2022.

87. Janis Carpenter, personal communication, Pawhuska, OK, July 22, 2022.

88. Christopher Cote, personal communication, Pawhuska, OK, July 20, 2021.

89. Veronica Pipestem, personal communication, Skiatook, OK, July 30, 2021; Cote, personal communication, July 20, 2021; Braxton Red Eagle, personal communication, Pawhuska, OK, July 29, 2022.

90. Duty, "Revitalizing Language." Correction to relatives listed made after personal communication with Christopher Cote, on July 20, 2021, Pawhuska, OK.

91. Herman Mongrain Lookout, Osage Tribal Council committee meeting, Pawhuska, OK, September 12, 2005.

92. Herman Mongrain Lookout, personal communication, Pawhuska, OK, July 14, 2005.

93. Lookout, personal communication.

94. Herman Mongrain Lookout, advanced language class, Pawhuska, OK, March 20, 2006.

95. Vine Deloria Jr., *Custer Died*, 82.

96. Pratt, "Advantages of Mingling Indians," 260.

97. For one of the earliest discussions of the complexities of the Native boarding school experience, see Lomawaima, *Called It Prairie Light.*

98. Drent and Dennison, "New Country Again."

99. Albury, "Objectives at the Crossroads," 272.

100. Osage Language Department meeting, Pawhuska, OK, July 14, 2005.

101. Billy Proctor, personal communication, phone, October 13, 2021.

102. Proctor, personal communication.

103. This discussion comes from a personal communication with Herman Mongrain Lookout in Pawhuska, OK, on October 4, 2005, and subsequent similar conversations.

104. Herman Mongrain Lookout, personal communication, Pawhuska, OK, July 14, 2005.

105. Herman Mongrain Lookout, personal communication, Pawhuska, OK, July 15, 2021.

106. Pine and Turin, "Language Revitalization."

107. Pine and Turin.

108. Herman Mongrain Lookout, Osage Tribal Council committee meeting, Pawhuska, OK, October 19, 2005.

109. Drent and Dennison, "New Country Again."

110. Lookout, Osage Tribal Council committee meeting, Pawhuska, OK, October 19, 2005.

111. Vimeo video, 8:13, posted by Allison Herrera on July 20, 2016, https://vimeo.com/175605625.

112. Baird, "Wopanaak Language Reclamation Program"; Shannon Shaw Duty, "Herman 'Mogri' Lookout to Receive Honorary Doctorate Degree from Kansas State University," *Osage News*, September 23, 2021, https://osagenews.org/herman-mogri-lookout-to-receive-honorary-doctorate-degree-from-kansas-state-university/.

113. Drent and Dennison, "New Country Again."

114. Barrett-Mills, "Applications of Indigenous Presence."

115. This discussion comes from a video I recorded during one of the Osage Government Reform Commission's constitution drafting meetings, Pawhuska, OK, January 30, 2006.

116. Osage Government Reform Commission constitution drafting meeting, Pawhuska, OK, January 30, 2006.

117. Language Department, Cultural Department, and Osage Government Reform Commission meeting, Pawhuska, OK, February 27, 2006.

118. Language Department, Cultural Department, and Osage Government Reform Commission meeting.

119. Herman Mongrain Lookout, personal communication, Zoom, March 3, 2023; "About Michael Everson," Evertype, accessed August 22, 2023, www.evertype.com/misc/bio.html.

120. Everson, Lookout, and Pratt, "Proposal to Encode," 1–2.

121. Shannon Shaw Duty, "Osage Orthography Included in Unicode 9.0, Language Department Developing App," *Osage News*, July 1, 2016, https://osagenews.org/osage-orthography-included-in-unicode-9-0-language-department-developing-app/; Geneva HorseChief-Hamilton, "Osage Font and Keyboard Available for IOS and Chrome," *Osage News*, November 21, 2018.

122. Janis Carpenter, personal communication, Pawhuska, OK, July 15, 2021.

123. Moore and Hennessy, "New Technologies."

124. Jessica Rosemary Harjo, "Design Study," 22.

125. Veronica Pipestem, personal communication, Skiatook, OK, July 30, 2021.

126. Christopher Cote, personal communication, Pawhuska, OK, July 20, 2021.

127. Cote, personal communication.

128. Braxton Redeagle, personal communication, Pawhuska, OK, July 15, 2021.

129. Vann Bighorse, personal communication, Pawhuska, OK, July 8, 2021.

130. Lyons, "There's No Translation"; Martínez, "Techno-sovereignty."

131. Braxton Redeagle, personal communication, Pawhuska, OK, July 22, 2022.

132. Shannon Shaw Duty, "Osage Language Immersion School Names First Class of Students," *Osage News*, August 4, 2015, https://osagenews.org/osage-language-immersion-school-names-first-class-of-students/.

133. Patrick Martin, quoted in Shannon Shaw Duty, "Daposka Ahnkodapi Achieves Private School Accreditation from State," *Osage News*, June 7, 2021, https://osagenews.org/daposka-ahnkodapi-achieves-private-school-accreditation-from-state/.

134. The discussion is taken from my notes during a conversation with Patrick Martin on June 28, 2021, at the school in Pawhuska, OK.

135. Patrick Martin, personal communication, email, October 21, 2021.

136. Herman Mongrain Lookout, personal communication, Zoom, October 6, 2021.

137. Eddy Red Eagle, personal communication, phone, November 17, 2021.

Chapter Two

1. Osage Shareholders Association meeting, Pawhuska, OK, February 28, 2016.

2. The Osage Minerals Council is an independent body within the Osage Nation whose members are elected by Osage descendants of the 1906 roll, those with a share of the mineral estate. Dennison, *Colonial Entanglement*.

3. Everett Waller, personal communication, phone, November 1, 2021.

4. Susan Foreman, Osage Shareholders Association meeting, Pawhuska, OK, February 28, 2016; Rosemary Wood, "O-Ki-E Thali (Good Speaking)," *Osage News*, September 27, 2017, https://osagenews.org/o-ki-e-thali-good-speaking/.

5. Foreman, Osage Shareholders Association meeting.

6. Dennison, "'Affects' of Empire."

7. Stark and Stark, "Nenabozho Goes Fishing"; Wilkins and Lomawaima, *Uneven Ground*; Cattelino, *High Stakes*; Simpson, *Mohawk Interruptus*; Dennison, "Entangled Sovereignties."

8. Stark and Stark, "Nenabozho Goes Fishing."

9. Williams, *Linking Arms Together*, 97. See also Wilkins and Lomawaima, *Uneven Ground*, for a discussion of how the Cherokee and other Indigenous nations view the trust relationship.

10. Lyons, *X-Marks*.

11. Eddy Red Eagle, personal communication, telephone, November 20, 2021.

12. DuVal, *Native Ground*, 16.

13. DuVal, 16.

14. DuVal.

15. DuVal, 103.

16. Jefferson to Secretary of the Navy.

17. Roberts, *I've Been Here*.

18. DuVal, *Native Ground*.

19. Kappler, *Indian Treaties*, 268.

20. Pierce, "Legal History."

21. Treaty with the Osage, 7 Stat. 240 (1825).

22. Dennison, "Relational Accountability."

23. Wilkins and Lomawaima, *Uneven Ground*.

24. Worcester v. Georgia, 31 U.S. (6 Pet.) 515 (1832); Cherokee Nation v. Georgia, 30 U.S. (5 Pet.) 1 (1831); Johnson v. M'Intosh, 21 U.S. (8 Wheat.) 543 (1823).

25. Barker, "Corporation and the Tribe," 250.

26. *Johnson v. M'Intosh*, 21 U.S. at 590.

27. Lambert, *Native Agency*.

28. Wilkins and Lomawaima, *Uneven Ground*, 13.

29. Seminole Nation v. United States, 316 U.S. 286 (1942).

30. Butler, "Bureau of Indian Affairs"; Lambert, *Native Agency*.

31. *Compacting* is a common phrase Osages use for entering into self-governance agreements with the US government, which allows Native nations to manage and operate federal programs themselves.

32. Lambert, *Native Agency*, 77, citing American Indian Policy Review Commission, *Final Report*, 130.

33. Strommer and Osborne, "History, Status, and Future"; Washburn, "What the Future Holds"; Lambert, *Native Agency*.

34. Strommer and Osborne, "History, Status, and Future."

35. The history and discussion of the trust that follows were provided by an Otoe lawyer, Osage shareholder, and lawyer for the Osage Minerals Council, Wilson Pipestem. Personal communication, email, January 29, 2022.

36. *Legislative Field Hearing on H.R. 2912, to Reaffirm the Inherent Sovereign Rights of the Osage Tribe to Determine Its Membership and Form of Government Before H. Comm. on Resources*, 108th Cong. 14–15 (2004) (statement of Jim Gray, Principal Chief, Osage Tribe).

37. Act of July 15, 1870, ch. 296, 16 Stat. 362–63 (1879).

38. An Act to Confirm to the Great and Little Osage Indians a Reservation in Indian Territory, Act of June 5, 1872, ch. 10, 17 Stat. 228.

39. Terry Wilson, *Underground Reservation*.

40. Weyler, *Blood of the Land*; Coll, *Private Empire*.

41. Chang, "Enclosures of Land."

42. Terry Wilson, *Underground Reservation*.

43. Logan v. Andrus, 457 F. Supp. 1318, 1324 (1978).

44. Wilson Pipestem, personal communication, email, January 29, 2022.

45. US Congress, Senate Committee on Indian Affairs, *Indian Appropriation Bill Hearings*, 549.

46. Harmon, *Rich Indians*.

47. Harmon, 363.

48. Harmon.

49. Herman Mongrain Lookout, University of Washington class presentation, Zoom, January 17, 2023.

50. Philip Deloria, *Indians in Unexpected Places*; Harmon, *Rich Indians*.

51. Terry Wilson, *Underground Reservation*.

52. Federal Bureau of Investigation. "Osage Indian Murders," 2011. http://foia.fbi.gov/foiaindex/osageind.htm.

53. Rachel Adams-Heard, *In Trust*, podcast, Bloomberg, accessed November 24, 2022, www.bloomberg.com/features/2022-in-trust-podcast.

54. Harmon, *Rich Indians*, 197.

55. An Act to Amend Certain Laws Relating to the Osage Tribe of Oklahoma, and for other purposes, Pub. L. 95-496, 92 STAT. 1660 (1978).

56. For a discussion and critique of federal Indian policy as an "oscillating pendulum," see Fixico, "Federal and State Policies."

57. US Congress. House Concurrent Resolution 108, 83rd Congress. U.S. Government Printing Office (1953), B132.

58. Dennison, "'Affects' of Empire."

59. The 2,230th share of the mineral estate was granted to a white woman for life because of her service to the Osage Nation. There were only 2,229 Osages listed on the roll. For more on the 1906 roll, see Terry Wilson, *Underground Reservation*.

60. My parents shared this line, and the stories it came out of, with me while I was doing my research in 2005 as a way of helping me to understand the generational challenges the mineral estate had created for the Osage Nation.

61. Dennison, *Colonial Entanglement*; Dennison, "'Affects' of Empire"; Dennison, "Relational Accountability."

62. Nickeson, "Structure of the Bureau"; Butler, "Bureau of Indian Affairs"; Champagne, "Organizational Change and Conflict"; McClellan, "Implementation and Policy Reformulation."

63. Dunbar-Ortiz, *Indigenous Peoples' History*, 206.

64. Göcke, "US Class Action Settlement."

65. Jim Myers, "Osage Nation, U.S. Settle Legal Battle," *Tulsa World*, October 22, 2011, www.tulsaworld.com/news/article.aspx?subjectid=335&articleid=20111022_16_A1_WASHIN293151.

66. Simpson, *Mohawk Interruptus*; Simpson, "Indigenous Resurgence"; Coulthard and Simpson, "Grounded Normativity."

67. Curley, "T'áá Hwó Ají t'éego," 74.

68. Curley and Lister, "Already Existing Dystopias."

69. The Osage Minerals Council is elected by people who are descendants of someone listed on the 1906 roll and who have inherited or purchased a headright. The Osage Nation officials are elected by descendants of those on the 1906 roll who have chosen to officially enroll as citizens. There are both descendants who are not shareholders and descendants who have chosen not to be citizens, generally because they are enrolled in another Native nation that does not allow for dual enrollment.

70. For a fuller discussion of distrust in the Osage Mineral Estate, see Dennison, "'Affects' of Empire."

71. Geoffrey Standing Bear, Osage Shareholders Association meeting, Pawhuska, OK, February 28, 2016.

72. Standing Bear.

73. "Cattlemen's Group Voices Concerns over Proposed Osage Environmental Bill," *News Examiner-Enterprise* (Barlesville, OK), May 29, 2007.

74. An Act to Reaffirm the Inherent Sovereign Rights of the Osage Tribe to Determine Its Membership and Form of Government, Pub. L. No. 108-431, 118 Stat. 2609 (2004).

75. Washburn, "What the Future Holds," 225.

76. Drent and Dennison, "New Country Again."

77. Dennison, "'Affects' of Empire."

78. Dennison, *Colonial Entanglement*.

79. C Cynthia Boone, Everett Waller, Kathryn Red Corn, Joseph Cheshewalla, and Stephanie Erwin, Duly Elected Minerals Council Members, v. Osage Nation of Oklahoma, No. SCV-2015-01 (Supreme Court of the Osage Nation September 9, 2016).

80. Shannon Shaw Duty, "Osage Minerals Council Rescinds Resolution to Sue the Osage Nation," *Osage News*, November 17, 2017, https://osagenews.org/osage-minerals -council-rescinds-resolution-to-sue-the-osage-nation/.

81. Talee Redcorn, Osage Shareholders Association meeting, Pawhuska, OK, February 28, 2016.

82. Redcorn.

83. Kendall, *BIA Needs Sweeping Changes*, 15.

84. Wood, "O-Ki-E Thali (Good Speaking)."

85. Shore and Wright, "Whose Accountability?" 100. See also Power, *Audit Society*; Strathern, *Audit Cultures*; and Gupta, *Red Tape*.

86. Kendall, *BIA Needs Sweeping Changes*, 1.

87. Wood, "O-Ki-E Thali (Good Speaking)."

88. Kendall, *BIA Needs Sweeping Changes*, 1.

89. Kendall, 29.

90. Orphaned wells are sites that are out of production and no longer have any party legally or financially responsible for them.

91. Candy Thomas, director of strategic planning and self-governance, personal communication, Pawhuska, OK, August 26, 2020.

92. Allison Herrera, "Déjà Vu? Lawyers on both sides of wind farm case revisit 10th circuit decision," *Osage News*, September 25, 2023, https://osagenews.org/deja-vu-lawyers-on -both-sides-of-wind-farm-case-revisit-10th-circuit-decision/.

93. Everett Waller, personal communication, phone, November 11, 2021.

94. Benny Polacca, "Osage Nation Congress Votes 'No Confidence' in BIA Superintendent Robin Phillips," *Osage News*, April 12, 2017, https://osagenews.org/osage-nation-con gress-votes-no-confidence-in-bia-superintendent-robin-phillips/.

95. Lenzy Krehbiel-Burton, "Minerals Council Chairman Warns of 'Devastating' Shareholder Checks," *Osage News*, September 3, 2000, https://osagenews.org/minerals-council -chairman-warns-of-devastating-shareholder-checks/.

96. Shannon Shaw Duty, "Minerals Council to Hold Community Meetings on Tribal Energy Resource Agreements," *Osage News*, September 2, 2020, https://osagenews.org/minerals -council-to-hold-community-meetings-on-tribal-energy-resource-agreements/.

97. Talee Redcorn, personal communication, phone, September 7, 2020.

98. Talee Redcorn, personal communication, phone, September 7, 2020.

99. Talee Redcorn, personal communication, phone, September 7, 2020.

100. Kennedy Sepulvado, "Minerals Council Discusses TERA Options in Zoom Webinar," *Osage News*, August 31, 2021, https://osagenews.org/minerals-council-discusses-tera -options-in-zoom-webinar/.

101. Everett Waller, personal communication, phone, October 15, 2021.

102. Krehbiel-Burton, "Minerals Council Chairman Warns."

103. Everett Waller, personal communication, phone, October 15, 2021.

104. Curley and Lister, "Already Existing Dystopias," 260.

105. Everett Waller, personal communication, phone, October 15, 2021.

106. Curley, "Failed Green Future."

107. Washburn, "What the Future Holds, " 207.

Chapter Three

1. Osage Nation Congress, Seventh Special Session, Pawhuska, OK, July 15, 2015. For additional coverage of this event, see Shannon Shaw Duty, "Osage Nation Compacting Pawhuska IHS Facility, Services and Staff to Be Added," *Osage News*, July 31, 2015, https://osagenews.org/osage-nation-compacting-pawhuska-ihs-facility-services-and-staff-to-be-added/.

2. R. J. Walker, Osage Nation Congress, Seventh Special Session.

3. Angela Pratt, Osage Nation Congress, Seventh Special Session.

4. Joe Conner, "Can Osage Nation Manage Your Health Care?," *Osage News*, July 7, 2005, https://osagenews.org/can-osage-nation-manage-your-health-care/.

5. Shannon Edwards and Kugee Supernaw, Osage Nation Congress, Seventh Special Session.

6. Ron Shaw, Osage Nation Congress, Seventh Special Session.

7. Benny Polacca, "Congress Passes Bill Removing Health Authority Board Duty to Make Personnel Decisions," *Osage News*, September 10, 2020, https://osagenews.org/congress-passes-bill-removing-health-authority-board-duty-to-make-personnel-decisions/.

8. National Indian Health Board et al., *Tribal Perspectives*; Jorgensen, *Rebuilding Native Nations*; Bylander, "Designing a Health System."

9. See Mathews, *Osages*; Warrior, *People and the Word*; and Drent and Dennison, "New Country Again."

10. Mathews, *Osages*, 53.

11. La Flesche, *Osage and the Invisible World*.

12. Eddy Red Eagle, personal communication, phone, June 15, 2022.

13. La Flesche, *Osage and the Invisible World*, 34.

14. Rollings, *Unaffected by the Gospel*.

15. Drent and Dennison, "New Country Again."

16. Dennison, "Stitching Osage Governance," 124.

17. Drent and Dennison, "New Country Again."

18. Charles Red Corn, Osage Government Reform Commission writing retreat, Pawhuska, OK, January 30, 2006.

19. Hepsi Barnett, Osage Government Reform Commission writing retreat.

20. "Osage Nation Constitution," Osage Nation, March 11, 2006, 1, https://www.osagenation-nsn.gov/sites/default/files/documents/ON_Constitution_03042020.pdf.

21. La Flesche, *Osage and the Invisible World*, 74.

22. Drent and Dennison, "New Country Again."

23. *Merriam-Webster*, s.v. "bureaucracy," accessed February 3, 2023, www.merriam-webster.com/dictionary/bureaucracy.

24. *Merriam-Webster*, s.v. "bureaucracy."

25. Nuijten, *Power, Community*, 152.

26. Herzfeld, *Social Production of Indifference*; Bernstein, "Social Life of Regulation"; Feldman, *Governing Gaza*; Hoag, "Magic of the Populace"; Hetherington, *Guerrilla Auditors*; Hull, *Government of Paper*; Mathur, *Paper Tiger*; Bear and Mathur, "Introduction."

27. Power, *Audit Society*; Shore and Wright, "Coercive Accountability"; Strathern, *Audit Cultures*; Kipnis, "Audit Cultures"; Gupta, *Red Tape*.

28. Bear and Mathur, "Introduction," 19.

29. Vine Deloria Jr. and Lytle, *Nations Within*; Alfred, "Sovereignty"; Coulthard, *Red Skin, White Masks*.

30. Carroll, "Shaping New Homelands, 140."

31. La Flesche, *Traditions of the Osage*.

32. La Flesche, "Osage Tribe."

33. Livingston, "Medical Risks."

34. Osage Nation, "FACT SHEET: Edible Wild Plants Gathered by the Osage," https://osagenation.s3.amazonaws.com/D/D.3.a.EdiblWildPlants-FactSheet.docx.

35. Hollenberg and Muzzin, "Epistemological Challenges"; Joseph, "Walking on Our Lands"; Benny Polacca, "ON Congress Passes Resolution Supporting Re-establishment of PRT Sweat Lodge," *Osage News*, April 3, 2017, https://osagenews.org/on-congress-passes-resolution-supporting-re-establishment-of-prt-sweat-lodge/.

36. DuVal, *Native Ground*.

37. Dorsey, "Osage Myths."

38. Perdue and Green, *Cherokee Nation*.

39. Lawrence, "Indian Health Service."

40. Treaty with the Osage, 14 Stat. 687, September 29, 1865, ratified June 26, 1866.

41. Indian Health Service, *The First 50 Years of the Indian Health Service*, 2005, www.ihs.gov/sites/newsroom/themes/responsive2017/display_objects/documents/GOLD_BOOK_part1.pdf.

42. Wilkins and Stark, *American Indian Politics*.

43. Wilkins and Stark.

44. Miles, "Reports of Agents" (1885).

45. Hunt, "Reports of Agents," 81.

46. Theobald, *Reproduction on the Reservation*.

47. Emmerich, "'Save the Babies!,'" 397.

48. Theobald, *Reproduction on the Reservation*.

49. Theobald, 44.

50. Theobald.

51. Davies, *Healing Ways*, 50.

52. Lawrence, "Indian Health Service"; Torpy, "Native American Women"; Carpio, "Lost Generation"; Ralstin-Lewis, "Continuing Struggle against Genocide"; Theobald, *Reproduction on the Reservation*.

53. Lawrence, "Indian Health Service," 400.

54. During the same period, white women's child productivity only dropped from 2.42 to 2.14. Lawrence, 400.

55. Cobb, *Say We Are Nations*, 178.

56. Butler, "Bureau of Indian Affairs."

57. McClellan, "Implementation and Policy Reformulation," 48; Dennison, *Colonial Entanglement*.

58. Mark Trahant, "The Indian Health Service Paradox," *Kaiser Health News*, September 16, 2009, https://khn.org/news/091709trahant/.

59. McClellan, "Implementation and Policy Reformulation."

60. See, for example, "Testimony to the U.S. Senate Select Committee on Indian Affairs," Washington, DC, July 17, 2008, https://www.indian.senate.gov/sites/default/files /Robert%20Moore%20testimony_0.doc.

61. Washburn, "What the Future Holds."

62. Dennison, *Colonial Entanglement.*

63. McClellan, "Implementation and Policy Reformulation."

64. Strommer and Osborne, "History, Status, and Future."

65. McClellan, "Implementation and Policy Reformulation."

66. Washburn, "What the Future Holds."

67. Champagne, "Organizational Change and Conflict."

68. Champagne.

69. Osage News, "Health Board Explores Contracting / Compacting IHS Clinic." May 19, 2009.

70. Trahant, "Indian Health Service Paradox."

71. Paula Stabler, mock survey meeting, Pawhuska, OK, March 16, 2016.

72. Walters et al., "Bodies Don't."

73. Heron, *Deaths*; Carron, "Health Disparities."

74. Robin et al., "Prevalence and Characteristics."

75. Melissa E. Lewis et al., "Stress and Cardiometabolic Disease."

76. "Success Story: Pawhuska Indian Health Center Achieves Success for Its Population," *Success Story: Pawhuska Indian Health Center Achieves Success for Its Population* (blog), 2013, https://millionhearts.hhs.gov/partners-progress/champions/success-stories/2013 -underserved2.html.

77. "Tribal Self-Governance," fact sheet, Indian Health Service, July 2016, www.ihs.gov /newsroom/factsheets/tribalselfgovernance/.

78. Nuijten, *Power, Community*, 152.

79. Executive Staff meeting, Pawhuska, OK, August 17, 2015.

80. Executive Staff meeting, Pawhuska, OK, August 17, 2015.

81. "Osage Nation Constitution," 13.

82. Dennison, *Colonial Entanglement.*

83. Shannon Shaw Duty, "Osage Nation Files Suit against Former Osage LLC Management and Consultants," *Osage News*, June 3, 2015, https://osagenews.org/osage-nation-files -suit-against-former-osage-llc-management-and-consultants/.

84. Louise Red Corn, "Gaming Enterprise Board Members Questioned on Day 3 of Congressional Hearing," *Osage News*, February 10, 2023, https://osagenews.org/gaming -enterprise-board-members-questioned-on-day-3-of-congressional-hearing/.

85. "Si-Si A-Pe-Txa Board." Osage Nation, accessed May 12, 2021, www.osagenation-nsn .gov/who-we-are/health-authority-board.

86. Ron Shaw, "An Act to Amend the Osage Nation Health Authority Board Act, ONCA 11-116, to Remove the Requirement to Have Policies and Procedures Presented and Approved by the Osage Nation Congress; and to Establish an Alternate Effective Date," Pub. L. No. 14-63 (2014), www.osagenation-nsn.gov/who-we-are/congress-legislative-branch /legislation-search/onca-14-63.

87. Executive Staff meeting, Pawhuska, OK, August 17, 2015.

88. Osage Health Authority meeting, Pawhuska, OK, February 18, 2016.

89. Osage Health Authority meeting.

90. Osage Health Authority meeting.

91. Osage Health Authority meeting.

92. Paula Stabler, Osage Health Authority meeting.

93. Osage Health Authority meeting.

94. Manon Tillman, Osage Health Authority meeting.

95. This discussion is taken from my notes while observing the mock survey on March 16, 2016, in Pawhuska, OK.

96. Paula Stabler, personal communication, Pawhuska, OK, July 20, 2021.

97. Paula Stabler, personal communication, Pawhuska, OK, July 20, 2021.

98. Paula Stabler, mock survey meeting, Pawhuska, OK, March 16, 2016.

99. Mock Surveyor, mock survey meeting, Pawhuska, OK, March 16, 2016.

100. Paula Stabler, personal communication, Zoom, March 23, 2021.

101. Paula Stabler, personal communication, Pawhuska, OK, July 20, 2021.

102. Mock Surveyor, mock survey meeting, Pawhuska, OK, March 16, 2016. Personal communication, Pawhuska, OK, July 20, 2021.

103. This discussion is taken from my notes while observing the AAAHC accreditation survey on April 29 and 30, 2016, in Pawhuska, OK.

104. Surveyor, AAAHC accreditation survey, Pawhuska, OK, April 29, 2016.

105. Surveyor, AAAHC accreditation survey, Pawhuska, OK, April 29, 2016.

106. Surveyor, AAAHC accreditation survey, Pawhuska, OK, April 30, 2016.

107. Paula Stabler, personal communication, Pawhuska, OK, July 20, 2021.

108. Ron Shaw, "An Act to Amend the Osage Nation Health Authority Board Act, 16 ONC 7-102 Through 7-105," Pub. L. No. 17-119 (2017).

109. Shaw.

110. Paula Stabler, personal communication, Pawhuska, OK, July 20, 2021.

111. Benny Polacca, "Wah-Zha-Zhi Health Center Expected to Exceed Projected Revenue This Year," *Osage News*, September 4, 2018, https://osagenews.org/wah-zha-zhi-health-center-expected-to-exceed-projected-revenue-this-year/.

112. "Osage Nation Health Services: Wahzhazhe Health Center," Osage Nation, accessed August 24, 2023, www.osagenation-nsn.gov/what-we-do/wahzhazhe-health-center; Benny Polacca, "Wah-Zha-Zhi Health Clinic Earns Accreditation Status," *Osage News*, July 9, 2019, https://osagenews.org/wah-zha-zhi-health-clinic-earns-accreditation-status/.

113. Shannon Shaw Duty, "Wah-Zha-Zhe Health Center CEO and Osage Nation Treasurer Resign," *Osage News*, April 21, 2021, https://osagenews.org/wah-zha-zhe-health-center-ceo-and-osage-nation-treasurer-resign/.

114. "Si-Si A-Pe-Txa Board of Directors Sworn In," Osage Nation, July 20, 2022, www.osagenation-nsn.gov/news-events/news/si-si-pe-txa-board-directors-sworn.

115. Louise Red Corn, "Strategic Land Purchases Make Way for Sleek, New Medical Clinic," *Osage News*, May 26, 2022, https://osagenews.org/strategic-land-purchases-make-way-for-sleek-new-medical-clinic/.

116. Louise Red Corn, "Patient Surveys Praise Wahzhazhe Health Center as New Leadership Rights Ship," *Osage News*, February 27, 2023, https://osagenews.org/patient-surveys-praise-wahzhazhe-health-center-as-new-leadership-rights-ship/.

Chapter Four

1. Raymond Red Corn, personal communication, Pawhuska, OK, January 4, 2016.

2. "TV Mogul Ted Turner Buys Buffalo Ranch in Osage County," News on 6, November 22, 2001, www.newson6.com/story/5e3680db2f69d76f62095001/tv-mogul-ted-turner -buys-buffalo-ranch-in-osage-county.

3. At the time of publication, the Osage Nation's *McGirt* ruling is still pending, but the reservation case appears very clear given the Creek precedent.

4. Michael Overall, "Osage Nation Finalizes Deal to Buy Ted Turner's Ranch," *Tulsa World*, June 10, 2016.

5. Red Corn, personal communication.

6. "The Private Land Management Award," *Grapevine* 41 (2016): 3.

7. There is a particularly damning 2014 report from the Office of Inspector General for the US Department of the Interior, which outlined some of the things that needed to change to ensure that the Bureau of Indian Affairs was meeting its trust obligations to the Osage land and people. Kendall, *BIA Needs Sweeping Changes*.

8. Fox, *Downwind*; Voyles, *Wastelanding*.

9. Raymond Red Corn, personal communication, email, February 14, 2021.

10. Claxton and Price, "Whose Land Is It?," 116.

11. Coté, *Drum in One Hand*.

12. Goeman, "Land as Life," 71.

13. Red Corn, personal communication, email, February 14, 2021.

14. *Lexico*, s.v. "recover," accessed April 4, 2022, www.lexico.com/en/definition/recover (now defunct).

15. Kelley, "On the Density of Black Being;" Andersen, "Critical Indigenous Studies"; Moreton-Robinson, *White Possessive*; Perea, *Sound Relations*.

16. Perea, *Sound Relations*, 8.

17. Goeman, "Land as Life"; Johnson, *Land Is Our History*.

18. Courtney Lewis, *Sovereign Entrepreneurs*.

19. Carroll, "Shaping New Homelands," 144.

20. Claire Elisa Thompson, "Returning the Land: Indigenous Leaders on the Growing 'Landback' Movement and Their Fight for Climate Justice," *Grist*, November 25, 2020, https://grist.org/fix/indigenous-landback-movement-can-it-help-climate/.

21. "Landback Manifesto," Landback, accessed February 20, 2021, https://landback.org /manifesto/.

22. Estes, *Our History*.

23. Thompson, "Returning the Land."

24. Harris, "Whiteness as Property"; Krech, *Ecological Indian*; Harkin and Lewis, *Native Americans*.

25. Curley and Lister, "Already Existing Dystopias," 259–60.

26. Andersen, "Critical Indigenous Studies," 82.

27. Kelley, *Yo' Mama's Disfunktional!*; Walter and Anderson, "Paradigm of Indigenous Methodologies"; Moreton-Robinson, *White Possessive*; Perea, *Sound Relations*.

28. Jessica Harjo, personal communication, phone, January 20, 2023.

29. Bailey et al., *Art of the Osage*.

30. Bailey et al., 270.

31. Oberholtzer, "Silk Ribbonwork"; Pannabecker, "Cultural Authentication of Ribbon"; Ackerman, "Tradition of Meskwaki Ribbonwork."

32. Powell, "Creating an Osage Future: Art, Resistance, and Self-Representation."

33. Dennison, *Colonial Entanglement*; Dennison, "Stitching Osage Governance"; Dennison, "Entangled Sovereignties."

34. Dennison, "Entangled Sovereignties"; Rifkin, *Speaking for the People*.

35. Cattelino, *High Stakes*, 164.

36. Dennison, "Relational Accountability."

37. This excerpt is adapted from "Ni´-ki Wi-gi-e of the Tsi´-zhu Wa-Shta´-ge Gens" in La Flesche, "Osage Tribe," 274–85.

38. La Flesche, "Osage Tribe," 280. While the text refers to buffalo, a better translation is "bison."

39. La Flesche, 279.

40. Pierce, "Legal History."

41. Ostler, *Surviving Genocide*.

42. Robert Lee and Tristan Ahtone, "Land-Grab Universities: Expropriated Indigenous Land Is the Foundation of the Land-Grant University System," *High Country News*, March 30, 2020, www.hcn.org/issues/52.4/indigenous-affairs-education-land-grab-universities.

43. Osage Nation, "Osage Foods," *Osage Culture Traveling Trunk and Web Project* (blog), accessed March 11, 2021, http://osageculturetravelingtrunk.weebly.com/uploads/4/8/8/7/48872935/osage_foods.pdf.

44. Isenberg, *Destruction of the Bison*.

45. Danielle Taschereau Mamers, "Historical Photo of Mountain of Bison Skulls Documents Animals on the Brink of Extinction," *Conversation*, December 2, 2020, https://theconversation.com/historical-photo-of-mountain-of-bison-skulls-documents-animals-on-the-brink-of-extinction-148780.

46. Jernigan et al., "Community-Based Participatory Research."

47. Valarie Blue Bird Jernigan, "Ending Food Insecurity in Native Communities Means Restoring Land Rights, Handing Back Control," *Conversation*, May 27, 2021, https://theconversation.com/ending-food-insecurity-in-native-communities-means-restoring-land-rights-handing-back-control-158858.

48. Mihesuah, Hoover, and LaDuke, *Indigenous Food Sovereignty*.

49. Coté, *A Drum in One Hand*, 90.

50. The Osage are hardly alone among Native nations in using strategic planning as a way to bring their historical values into contemporary practices. For a discussion in the context of the Navajo Nation, see Hale, "Empowered Sovereignty."

51. Osage Nation, *25-Year Vision*, 40.

52. Mihesuah, Hoover, and LaDuke, *Indigenous Food Sovereignty*; Coté, *Drum in One Hand*.

53. Dennison, "Entangled Sovereignties."

54. Elizabeth Kinney, "Osage County Ranchers Worried Over Wording in Osage Nation Constitution," News Channel 8, accessed August 15, 2007.

55. Biolsi, *Deadliest Enemies*; Wagoner, *"They Treated Us"*; Wolfe, "Settler Colonialism"; Dennison, "Whitewashing Indigenous Oklahoma"; Montoya, "#We Need."

56. "Natural Resource Bill Prompts Protests," *Bigheart (OK) Times*, May 31, 2007.

57. Document provided by Geoffrey Standing Bear. No date.

58. Dennison, "'Affects' of Empire."

59. Mithlo, "No Word for Art?"

60. Geoffrey M. Standing Bear, personal communication, email, February 14, 2021.

61. Standing Bear, personal communication.

62. This following discussion come from notes I took during this Chiefs' meeting, in Pawhuska, OK, on January 5, 2016.

63. Dennison, "Stitching Osage Governance"; Drent and Dennison, "New Country Again."

64. Chiefs' meeting.

65. Chiefs' meeting.

66. Chief Pawhuska was best known for being part of the deadliest battle between Indian and American troops in 1791. He received his name when he attempted to scalp one of the fallen officers during this battle but instead just pulled off his wig. Pawhuska was the most prominent chief of the Osage during this period, in part because of his close relationships with French traders, which helped to establish an Osage empire. DuVal, *Native Ground*.

67. Standing Bear, Tallgrass LLC meeting, Pawhuska, OK, January 5, 2016.

68. Eide, "Strategic Essentialism," 2.

69. Spivak, "Can the Subaltern Speak?"; Spivak, "Subaltern Studies"; Eide, "Strategic Essentialism."

70. Mithlo, "No Word for Art?"

71. Geoffrey M. Standing Bear, planning meeting, Pawhuska, OK, January 5, 2016.

72. Standing Bear, planning meeting.

73. Standing Bear, planning meeting.

74. Planning meeting.

75. Osage Nation Congress, Tenth Special Session, Pawhuska, OK, January 20, 2016.

76. Maria Whitehorn, Osage Nation Congress, Tenth Special Session.

77. Shannon Edwards, Osage Nation Congress, Tenth Special Session.

78. Shannon Edwards, personal communication, email, March 7 and April 11, 2022.

79. John Maker, Osage Nation Congress, Tenth Special Session.

80. John Maker, personal communication, phone, April 15, 2022.

81. Shannon Edwards, personal communication, email, March 7, 2022.

82. Edwards, personal communication.

83. Osage Nation Congress, Tenth Special Session.

84. Cattelino, "Fungibility"; Courtney Lewis, "Western North Carolina."

85. Geoffrey M. Standing Bear, bid letter to Ted Turner, January 21, 2016.

86. Fong, "Racial-Settler Capitalism."

87. Cattelino, *High Stakes*; Cattelino, "Fungibility"; Courtney Lewis, "Western North Carolina."

88. Standing Bear, bid letter to Turner.

89. Standing Bear.

90. Geoffrey Standing Bear, personal communication, email, February 14, 2021.

91. Geoffrey Standing Bear, personal communication, Pawhuska, OK, April 20, 2016.

92. Drent and Dennison, "New Country Again."

93. Standing Bear, personal communication, email, February 14, 2021.

94. For a fuller discussion of this topic, see Drent and Dennison, "New Country Again."

95. Standing Bear v. Pratt, Osage Nation SCO-2016-01.

96. Drent and Dennison, "New Country Again."

97. Shannon Shaw Duty, "Bluestem Ranch Board and Standing Bear at Odds over Bison," *Osage News*, June 15, 2016, https://osagenews.org/bluestem-ranch-board-and -standing-bear-at-odds-over-bison/.

98. Geoffrey Standing Bear, Bluestem Ranch Celebration speech, northwest of Hominy, OK, August 24, 2016.

99. Geoffrey Standing Bear, Bluestem Ranch Celebration speech, August 24, 2016.

100. Benny Polacca, "Osage Nation Pays Off $67M Ranch Loan in Less than Five Years," *Osage News*, July 13, 2021, https://osagenews.org/osage-nation-pays-off-67m-ranch-loan-in -less-than-five-years/; Jessica Brent, "Osage Nation Ranch Doubles Bison Herd," *Osage News*, November 8, 2021, https://osagenews.org/osage-nation-ranch-doubles-bison-herd/.

101. Geoffrey Standing Bear, personal communication, email, February 14, 2021.

102. Shannon Edwards, personal communication, email, March 7, 2022.

103. A food desert is defined by the FDA in terms of residents both being low income (having less of an ability to afford food) and having low access (having to travel a long distance to a large grocery store or food market). Grogg, *Primer on 638 Authority*.

104. Benny Polacca, "Officials Celebrate Opening of Meat Processing Plant," *Osage News*, February 1, 2021, https://osagenews.org/officials-celebrate-opening-of-meat-processing-plant/.

105. Osage Nation CARES Task Force, "Osage Nation CARES Act Implementation Plan," Pawhuska, OK, 2020.

106. Osage Nation, "State of the Nation Address with Principal Chief Geoffrey Standing Bear," March 12, 2021, YouTube video, 22:30, www.youtube.com/watch?v=KUOqQsJo3ds.

Conclusion

1. Million, "Intense Dreaming."

2. Dana Daylight, personal communication, Pawhuska, OK, July 15, 2021.

Bibliography

Ackerman, Brenda. "The Tradition of Meskwaki Ribbonwork: Cultural Meanings, Continuity, and Change." Iowa State University, 2008.

Albury, Nathan John. "Objectives at the Crossroads: Critical Theory and Self-Determination in Indigenous Language Revitalization." *Critical Inquiry in Language Studies* 12, no. 4 (October 2, 2015): 256–82.

Alfred, Gerald R. *Heeding the Voices of Our Ancestors: Kahnawake Mohawk Politics and the Rise of Native Nationalism.* New York: Oxford University Press, 1995.

———. "Sovereignty." In *A Companion to American Indian History*, edited by Phil Deloria and Neal Salisbury, 460–76. New York: Blackwell Publishers, 2002.

American Indian Policy Review Commission. *American Indian Policy Review Commission Final Report.* Washington, DC: US Government Printing Office, 1977.

Andersen, Chris. "Critical Indigenous Studies: From Difference to Density." *Cultural Studies Review* 15, no. 2 (2009): 80–100.

———. *"Métis": Race, Recognition, and the Struggle for Indigenous Peoplehood.* Vancouver: University of British Columbia Press, 2014.

Anderson, Benedict. *Imagined Communities.* London: Verso, 1993.

Apes, William. "An Indian's Looking-Glass for the White Man." In *The Experiences of Five Christian Indians, of the Pequod Tribe,* 52–60. Boston: James B. Dow, 1837.

Arvin, Maile, Eve Tuck, and Angie Morrill. "Decolonizing Feminism: Challenging Connections between Settler Colonialism and Heteropatriarchy." *Feminist Formations* 25, no. 1 (2013): 8–34.

Bailey, Garrick Alan. "Changes in Osage Social Organization: 1673–1969." PhD diss., University of Oregon, 1970.

Bailey, Garrick Alan, Daniel C. Swan, John W. Nunley, and E. Sean Standingbear. *Art of the Osage.* Seattle: University of Washington Press, 2004.

Baird, Jessie Little Doe. "Wopanaak Language Reclamation Program: Bringing the Language Home." *Journal of Global Indigeneity* 2, no. 2 (2016). https://ro.uow.edu.au/jgi/vol2/iss2/7.

Baldwin, Andrew. "Whiteness and Futurity: Towards a Research Agenda." *Progress in Human Geography* 36, no. 2 (April 2012): 172–87.

Barker, Joanne. "The Corporation and the Tribe." *American Indian Quarterly* 39, no. 3 (2015): 243–70.

Barrett-Mills, Jake. "Applications of Indigenous Presence: The Osage Orthography Amplifying Traditional Language Resurgence." *Journal of Foreign Languages and Cultures* 3, no. 2 (2019): 122–37.

Basso, Keith. *Wisdom Sits in Places: Landscape and Language among the Western Apache.* Albuquerque: University of New Mexico Press, 1996.

Bear, Laura, and Nayanika Mathur. "Introduction: Remaking the Public Good: A New Anthropology of Bureaucracy." *Cambridge Journal of Anthropology* 33, no. 1 (January 1, 2015): 18–34.

Beede, Cyrus. "Reports of Agents in Indian Territory: Osage Agency." In *Annual Report of the Commissioner of Indian Affairs to the Secretary of the Interior*, 53–55. Washington, DC: Government Printing Office, 1862.

Berger, Bethany. "Red: Racism and the American Indian." *UCLA Law Review* 56 (2009): 591–656.

Bernstein, Anya. "The Social Life of Regulation in Taipei City Hall: The Role of Legality in the Administrative Bureaucracy." *Law & Social Inquiry* 33, no. 4 (2008): 925–54.

Biolsi, Thomas. *Deadliest Enemies: Law and the Making of Race Relations on and off Rosebud Reservation*. Berkeley: University of California Press, 2001.

Brayboy, Bryan, and Donna Deyhle. "Insider-Outsider: Researchers in American Indian Communities." *Theory into Practice* 39, no. 3 (2000): 163–69.

Broderstad, Else. "Implementing Indigenous Self-Determination: The Case of the Sámi in Norway." In *Restoring Indigenous Self-Determination*, edited by Marc Woons, 72–94. Bristol, UK: E-International Relations, 2014.

Brooks, Lisa. *Our Beloved Kin: A New History of King Philip's War*. New Haven, CT: Yale University Press, 2018.

Brown, Kirby. *Stoking the Fire: Nationhood in Cherokee Writing, 1907–1970*. Norman: University of Oklahoma Press, 2019.

Brugman, Claudia, and Minica Macaulay. "Characterizing Evidentiality." *Linguistic Typology* 19, no. 2 (2015): 201–37.

Bruyneel, Kevin. *The Third Space of Sovereignty: The Postcolonial Politics of U.S.-Indigenous Relations*. Minneapolis: University of Minnesota Press, 2007.

Burns, Louis F. *A History of the Osage People*. 2nd rev. ed. Tuscaloosa: University of Alabama Press, 2004.

———. *Osage Indian Customs and Myths*. Tuscaloosa: University of Alabama Press, 2005.

Butler, Raymond V. "The Bureau of Indian Affairs: Activities since 1945." *Annals of the American Academy of Political and Social Science* 436, no. 1 (1978): 50–60.

Bylander, Jessica. "Designing a Health System That Works for the Tribe." *Health Affairs* 36, no. 4 (April 2017): 592–95.

Byrd, Jodi A. "Indigeneity's Difference: Methodology and the Structures of Sovereignty." *Journal of Nineteenth-Century Americanists* 2, no. 1 (2014): 137–42.

———. "Weather with You: Settler Colonialism, Antiblackness, and the Grounded Relationalities of Resistance." *Critical Ethnic Studies* 5, no. 1–2 (2019): 207–14.

———. "What's Normative Got to Do with It?" *Social Text* 38, no. 4 (December 1, 2020): 105–23.

Carpio, Myla. "The Lost Generation: American Indian Women and Sterilization Abuse." *Social Justice* 31, no. 4 (2004): 40–53.

Carroll, Clint. *Roots of Our Renewal: Ethnobotany and Cherokee Environmental Governance*. First Peoples: New Directions in Indigenous Studies. Minneapolis: University of Minnesota Press, 2015.

———. "Shaping New Homelands: Environmental Production, Natural Resource Management, and the Dynamics of Indigenous State Practice in the Cherokee Nation." *Ethnohistory* 61, no. 1 (January 1, 2014): 123–47.

Carron, Rebecca. "Health Disparities in American Indians/Alaska Natives: Implications for Nurse Practitioners." *Nurse Practitioner* 45, no. 6 (June 2020): 26–32.

Cattelino, Jessica R. "Fungibility: Florida Seminole Casino Dividends and the Fiscal Politics of Indigeneity." *American Anthropologist* 111, no. 2 (June 2009): 190–200.

———. *High Stakes: Florida Seminole Gaming and Sovereignty*. Durham, NC: Duke University Press, 2008.

Champagne, Duane. "Organizational Change and Conflict: A Case Study of the Bureau of Indian Affairs." *American Indian Culture and Research Journal* 7, no. 3 (January 1, 1983): 3–28.

Chandler, Hallet D., and C. E Lalonde. "Aboriginal Language Knowledge and Youth Suicide." *Cognitive Development* 22 (2007): 392–99.

Chang, David A. "Enclosures of Land and Sovereignty: The Allotment of American Indian Lands." *Radical History Review* 2011, no. 109 (January 1, 2011): 108–19.

Charles, Mark, and Soong-Chan Rah. *Unsettling Truths: The Ongoing, Dehumanizing Legacy of the Doctrine of Discovery*. Downers Grove, Illinois: InterVarsity Press, 2019.

Claxton, Nicholas Xemoltw, and John Price. "Whose Land Is It? Rethinking Sovereignty in British Columbia." *BC Studies*, no. 204 (Winter 2019/20): 115–38.

Cobb, Daniel M., ed. *Say We Are Nations: Documents of Politics and Protest in Indigenous America since 1887*. H. Eugene and Lillian Youngs Lehman Series. Chapel Hill: University of North Carolina Press, 2015.

Coll, Steve. *Private Empire: ExxonMobil and American Power*. New York: Penguin, 2012.

Corntassel, Jeff. Preface to *Restoring Indigenous Self-Determination: Theoretical and Practical Approaches*, 1–3. Bristol, UK: E-International Relations, 2015.

Coté, Charlotte. *A Drum in One Hand, a Sockeye in the Other: Stories of Indigenous Food Sovereignty from the Northwest Coast*. Indigenous Confluences. Seattle: University of Washington Press, 2021.

Coulthard, Glen Sean. *Red Skin, White Masks: Rejecting the Colonial Politics of Recognition*. Indigenous Americas. Minneapolis: University of Minnesota Press, 2014.

Coulthard, Glen, and Leanne Betasamosake Simpson. "Grounded Normativity/Place-Based Solidarity." *American Quarterly* 68, no. 2 (2016): 249–55.

Cruikshank, Julie. *The Social Life of Stories: Narrative and Knowledge in the Yukon Territory*. Lincoln: University of Nebraska Press, 2000.

Curley, Andrew. "A Failed Green Future: Navajo Green Jobs and Energy 'Transition' in the Navajo Nation." *Geoforum* 88 (January 2018): 57–65.

———. "T'áá Hwó Ají t'éego and the Moral Economy of Navajo Coal Workers." *Annals of the American Association of Geographers* 109, no. 1 (January 2, 2019): 71–86.

Curley, Andrew, and Majerle Lister. "Already Existing Dystopias: Tribal Sovereignty, Extraction, and Decolonizing the Anthropocene." In *Handbook on the Changing Geographies of the State*, edited by Sami Moisio, 251–62. London: Edward Elgar, 2020.

Daigle, John J., Natalie Michelle, Darren J. Ranco, and Marla R. Emery. "Traditional Lifeways and Storytelling: Tools for Adaptation and Resilience to Ecosystem Change." *Human Ecology* 47, no. 5 (October 2019): 777–84.

Davies, Wade. *Healing Ways: Navajo Health Care in the Twentieth Century*. Albuquerque: University of New Mexico Press, 2001.

Delaney, Danielle. "The Master's Tools: Tribal Sovereignty and Tribal Self-Governance Contracting/Compacting." *American Indian Law Journal* 5, no. 2 (2007): 309–45.

Deloria, Philip J. *Indians in Unexpected Places*. Lawrence: University Press of Kansas, 2006.

Deloria, Vine, Jr. *Behind the Trail of Broken Treaties: An Indian Declaration of Independence*. Austin: University of Texas Press, 1994.

———. *Custer Died for Your Sins: An Indian Manifesto*. Norman: University of Oklahoma Press, 1988.

Deloria, Vine, Jr., and Clifford M. Lytle. *The Nations Within: The Past and Future of American Indian Sovereignty*. Austin: University of Texas Press, 1998.

Dennison, Jean. "The 'Affects' of Empire: (Dis)trust among Osage Annuitants." In *Ethnographies of U.S. Empire*, edited by Carole McGranahan and John F. Collins, 27–46. Durham, NC: Duke University Press, 2018.

———. *Colonial Entanglement: Constituting a Twenty-First-Century Osage Nation*. First Peoples: New Directions in Indigenous Studies. Chapel Hill: University of North Carolina Press, 2012.

———. "Entangled Sovereignties." *American Ethnologist* 44, no. 4 (2017): 684–96.

———. "The Logic of Recognition: Debating Osage Nation Citizenship in the Twenty-First Century." *American Indian Quarterly* 38, no. 1 (2014): 1–35.

———. "Relational Accountability in Indigenous Governance." In *Routledge Handbook of Critical Indigenous Studies*, by Brendan Hokowhitu, Aileen Moreton-Robinson, Linda Tuhiwai-Smith, Chris Andersen, and Steve Larkin, 295–309. New York: Routledge, 2021.

———. "Stitching Osage Governance into the Future." *American Indian Culture and Research Journal* 37, no. 2 (2013): 115–28.

———. "Whitewashing Indigenous Oklahoma and Chicano Arizona: 21st-Century Legal Mechanisms of Settlement." *PoLAR: Political and Legal Anthropology Review* 37, no. 1 (2014): 162–80.

Diaz, Vicente M. "Oceania in the Plains: The Politics and Analytics of Transindigenous Resurgence in Chuukese Voyaging of Dakota Lands, Waters, and Skies in Miní Sóta Makhóčhe." *Pacific Studies* 42, nos. 1–2 (April/August 2019): 1–44.

Dillingham, Brent. "American Indian Women and I.H.S. Sterilization Practices." *American Indian Journal* 3 (1977): 27–28.

Dillon, Grace L., ed. *Walking the Clouds: An Anthology of Indigenous Science Fiction*. Sun Tracks: An American Indian Literary Series, vol. 69. Tucson: University of Arizona Press, 2012.

Diver, Sibyl, Daniel Ahrens, Talia Arbit, and Karen Bakker. "Engaging Colonial Entanglements: 'Treatment as a State' Policy for Indigenous Water Co-governance." *Global Environmental Politics* 19, no. 3 (August 2019): 33–56.

Doerfler, Jill, Niigaanwewidam James Sinclair, and Heidi Kiiwetinepinesiik Stark, eds. *Centering Anishinaabeg Studies: Understanding the World through Stories*. American Indian Studies Series. East Lansing: Michigan State University Press, 2013.

————. *Those Who Belong: Identity, Family, Blood, and Citizenship among the White Earth Anishinaabeg*. American Indian Studies Series. East Lansing: Michigan State University Press, 2015.

————. "'We Aren't like Dogs': Battling Blood Quantum." *Wasafiri* 32, no. 2 (April 3, 2017): 41–47.

Dorsey, James Owen. "Notes on Quapaw History." N.d. NAA MS 4800, James O. Dorsey Papers, circa 1870–1956, Bulk 1870–1895, National Anthropological Archives, Smithsonian Institution.

————. "Osage Myths, Letters, and Phrases." 1883. NAA MS 4800, National Museum of Natural History, National Anthropological Archives, Smithsonian Institution. https://edan.si.edu/slideshow/viewer/?damspath=/Public_Sets/NMNH/NMNH -RC-Anthropology/NMNH-RC-Anth-Archives/NMNH-RC-Anth-Archives-NAA /NAA-MS/NAA-MS_4800_263.

————. *Osage Traditions*. N.p.: Outlook Verlag, 2020.

Drent, Meredith, and Jean Dennison. "Moving to a New Country Again: The Osage Nation's Search for Order and Unity through Change." *Native American and Indigenous Studies* 8, no. 2 (2021): 62–91.

Duarte, Marisa Elena, and Miranda Belarde-Lewis. "Imagining: Creating Spaces for Indigenous Ontologies." *Cataloging and Classification Quarterly* 53, no. 5–6 (July 4, 2015): 677–702.

Dunbar-Ortiz, Roxanne. *An Indigenous Peoples' History of the United States*. Boston: Beacon, 2014.

DuVal, Kathleen. *The Native Ground: Indians and Colonists in the Heart of the Continent*. Philadelphia: University of Pennsylvania Press, 2007.

Edwards, Tai S. *Osage Women and Empire: Gender and Power*. Lawrence: University Press of Kansas, 2018.

Eide, Elisabeth. "Strategic Essentialism." In *The Wiley Blackwell Encyclopedia of Gender and Sexuality Studies*, edited by Nancy A. Naples, 1–2. Chichester, UK: John Wiley and Sons, 2016.

Emmerich, Lisa. "'Save the Babies!': American Indian Women, Assimilation Policy, and Scientific Motherhood, 1912–1918." In *Writing the Range: Race, Class, and Culture in the Women's West*, edited by Elizabeth Jameson and Susan Armitage, 393–409. Norman: University of Oklahoma Press, 1997.

Estes, Nick. *Our History Is the Future: Standing Rock versus the Dakota Access Pipeline, and the Long Tradition of Indigenous Resistance*. London: Verso, 2019.

Everson, Michael, Herman Mongrain Lookout, and Cameron Pratt. "Proposal to Encode Latin Characters for Osage in the UCS." Working group document, Universal Multiple-Octet Coded Character Set, International Organization for Standardization, July 30, 2014. http://unicode.org/wg2/docs/n4587.pdf.

Feldman, Ilana. *Governing Gaza: Bureaucracy, Authority, and the Work of Rule, 1917–1967*. Durham, NC: Duke University Press, 2008.

Finney, James Edwin. "The Osages and Their Agency during the Term of Isaac T. Gibson, Quaker Agent." *Chronicles of Oklahoma* 36, no. 4 (1958): 416–28.

Fixico, Donald. "Federal and State Policies and American Indians." In *A Companion to American Indian History*, edited by Philip Deloria and Neal Salisbury, 379–96. Malden, MA: Blackwell, 2002.

Flies-Away, Joseph Thomas. "My Grandma, Her People, and Our Constitution." In *American Indian Constitutional Reform and the Rebuilding of Native Nations*, edited by Eric D. Lemont, 144–65. Austin: University of Texas Press, 2006.

Fong, Sarah E. K. "Racial-Settler Capitalism: Character Building and the Accumulation of Land and Labor in the Late Nineteenth Century." *American Indian Culture and Research Journal* 43, no. 2 (May 1, 2019): 25–48.

Fox, Sarah Alisabeth. *Downwind: A People's History of the Nuclear West*. Lincoln: University of Nebraska Press, 2014.

Freeman, H. B. "Report of the Osage Agency." In *Annual Report of the Commissioner of Indian Affairs to the Secretary of the Interior*, 241–45. Washington, DC: Government Printing Office, 1894.

Gibson, Isaac T. Letter to Edward P. Smioth, Commissioner of Indian Affairs. April 30, 1875. Letters Received by the Office of Indian Affairs, 1824–1881, Records of the Bureau of Indian Affairs, National Archives, Washington, DC.

Göcke, Katja. "The US Class Action Settlement Agreement in *Cobell v. Salazar*—an Adequate Redress for 120 Years of Mismanagement of Indian Lands and Funds?" *International Journal on Minority and Group Rights* 19, no. 3 (2012): 267–90.

Goeman, Mishuana. "Land as Life: Unsettling the Logics of Containment." In *Native Studies Keywords*, edited by Stephanie Nohelani Teves, Andrea Smith, and Michelle H. Raheja, 71–89. Tucson: University of Arizona Press, 2015.

Goodyear-Kaʻōpua, Noelani. "Indigenous Oceanic Futures." In *Indigenous and Decolonizing Studies in Education*, edited by Linda Tuhiwai Smith, Eve Tuck, and K. Wayne Yang, 82–102. New York: Routledge, 2018.

Grann, David. *Killers of the Flower Moon: The Osage Murders and the Birth of the FBI*. New York: Doubleday, 2016.

"Great Osage Mission: Extract of Letters, Regulations for the Indian Children, March 26, 1822." *American Missionary Register* 3 (September 1822): 9110–111.

Grogg, Richelle. *A Primer on 638 Authority: Extending Tribal Self-Determination to Food and Agriculture*. Field report. Fayetteville, AR: Congressional Hunger Center, 2019.

Gupta, Akhil. *Red Tape: Bureaucracy, Structural Violence, and Poverty in India*. Durham, NC: Duke University Press, 2012.

Hale, Michelle. "Empowered Sovereignty for Navajo Chapters through Engagement in a Community-Planning Process." In *Navajo Sovereignty: Understandings and Visions of the Diné People*, edited by Lloyd L. Lee, 130–36. Tucson: University of Arizona Press, 2017.

Haller, John S. *Outcasts from Evolution: Scientific Attitudes of Racial Inferiority, 1859–1900*. Carbondale: Southern Illinois University Press, 1995.

Harjo, Jessica Rosemary. "A Design Study Exploring the Use of Osage Orthography Stencils in the Osage Language Classroom." PhD diss., University of Minnesota, 2021.

Harjo, Laura. *Spiral to the Stars: Mvskoke Tools of Futurity*. Tucson: University of Arizona Press, 2019.

Harkin, Michael Eugene, and David Rich Lewis, eds. *Native Americans and the Environment: Perspectives on the Ecological Indian*. Lincoln: University of Nebraska Press, 2007.

Harmon, Alexandra. *Rich Indians: Native People and the Problem of Wealth in American History*. Chapel Hill: University of North Carolina Press, 2010.

Harris, Cheryl. "Whiteness as Property." *Harvard Law Review* 106, no. 8 (1992): 1707–91.
Haspelmath, Martin, and Andrea Sims. *Understanding Morphology*. 2nd ed. London: Routledge, 2010.
Hauff, Tasha R. "Beyond Numbers, Colors, and Animals: Strengthening Lakota/Dakota Teaching on the Standing Rock Indian Reservation." *Journal of American Indian Education* 59, no. 1 (2020): 5–25.
Henne-Ochoa, Richard, Emma Elliott-Groves, Barbra Meek, and Barbara Rogoff. "Pathways Forward for Indigenous Language Reclamation: Engaging Indigenous Epistemology and Learning by Observing and Pitching In to Family and Community Endeavors." *Modern Language Journal* 104, no. 2 (June 2020): 481–93.
Henning, Dale R. "The Adaptive Patterning of the Dhegiha Sioux." *Plains Anthropologist* 38, no. 146 (November 1993): 253–64.
Henry, Robert, Amanda LaVallee, Nancy Van Styvendale, and Robert Alexander Innes, eds. *Global Indigenous Health: Reconciling the Past, Engaging the Present, Animating the Future*. Tucson: University of Arizona Press, 2018.
Hermes, Mary. "Designing Indigenous Language Revitalization." *Harvard Educational Review* 82, no. 3 (2012): 381–402.
Heron, Melonie. *Deaths: Leading Causes for 2018*. National Vital Statistics Report, Vol. 70, No. 4. Hyattsville, MD: National Center for Health Statistics, May 17, 2021.
Herzfeld, Michael. *The Social Production of Indifference: Exploring the Symbolic Roots of Western Bureaucracy*. Chicago: University of Chicago Press, 1993.
Hetherington, Kregg. *Guerrilla Auditors: The Politics of Transparency in Neoliberal Paraguay*. Durham, NC: Duke University Press, 2011.
Hill, Norbert S., Kathleen Ratteree, and Oneida Nation, eds. *The Great Vanishing Act: Blood Quantum and the Future of Native Nations*. Golden, CO: Fulcrum, 2017.
Hinton, Leanne. *Bringing Our Languages Home: Language Revitalization for Families*. Berkeley: Heyday, 2015.
Hoag, Colin. "The Magic of the Populace: An Ethnography of Illegibility in the South African Immigration Bureaucracy." *PoLAR: Political and Legal Anthropology Review* 33, no. 1 (2010): 6–25.
Hollenberg, Daniel, and Linda Muzzin. "Epistemological Challenges to Integrative Medicine: An Anti-colonial Perspective on the Combination of Complementary/Alternative Medicine with Biomedicine." *Health Sociology Review* 19, no. 1 (April 2010): 34–56.
Hull, Matthew S. *Government of Paper: The Materiality of Bureaucracy in Urban Pakistan*. Berkeley: University of California Press, 2012.
Hunt, P. B. "Reports of Agents in Indian Territory: Kiowa, Comanche, and Wichita Agency." In *Annual Report of the Commissioner of Indian Affairs to the Secretary of the Interior*, 79–81. Washington, DC: Government Printing Office, 1884.
Hunter, Andrea, James Munkres, and Barker Fariss. *Osage Nation NAGPRA Claim for Human Remains Removed from the Clarksville Mound Group (23PI6), Pike County, Missouri*. Pawhuska, OK: Osage Nation Historic Preservation Office, 2013.
Isenberg, Andrew C. *The Destruction of the Bison: An Environmental History, 1750–1920*. Cambridge: Cambridge University Press, 2020.
Jefferson, Thomas. Letter to Secretary of the Navy Robert Smith. July 13, 1804. Jefferson Papers, Library of Congress.

———. *The Writings of Thomas Jefferson.* Vol. 10. Whitefish, MT: Kessinger, 2006.

Jernigan, Valarie Blue Bird, Elizabeth J. D'Amico, Bonnie Duran, and Dedra Buchwald. "Multilevel and Community-Level Interventions with Native Americans: Challenges and Opportunities." *Prevention Science* 21, no. S1 (January 2020): 65–73.

Jernigan, Valarie Blue Bird, Mary Williams, Marianna Wetherill, Tori Taniguchi, Tvli Jacob, Tamela Cannady, Mandy Grammar, et al. "Using Community-Based Participatory Research to Develop Healthy Retail Strategies in Native American-Owned Convenience Stores: The THRIVE Study." *Preventive Medicine Reports* 11 (September 2018): 148–53.

Johnson, Miranda C. L. *The Land Is Our History: Indigeneity, Law, and the Settler State.* New York: Oxford University Press, 2016.

Jorgensen, Miriam, ed. *Rebuilding Native Nations: Strategies for Governance and Development.* Tucson: University of Arizona Press, 2007.

Joseph, Leigh. "Walking on Our Lands Again: Turning to Culturally Important Plants and Indigenous Conceptualizations of Health in a Time of Cultural and Political Resurgence." *International Journal of Indigenous Health* 16, no. 1 (2021): 165–79.

Justice, Daniel Heath. *Why Indigenous Literatures Matter.* Indigenous Studies Series. Waterloo, ON: Wilfrid Laurier University Press, 2018.

Kappler, Charles. *Indian Treaties, 1778–1883.* New York: Interland, 1972.

Kauanui, J. Kēhaulani. *Hawaiian Blood: Colonialism and the Politics of Sovereignty and Indigeneity.* Duke University Press, 2008.

———. *Paradoxes of Hawaiian Sovereignty: Land, Sex, and the Colonial Politics of State Nationalism.* Durham, NC: Duke University Press, 2018.

———. "'A Structure, Not an Event': Settler Colonialism and Enduring Indigeneity." *Lateral* 5, no. 1 (2016). https://csalateral.org/issue/5-1/forum-alt-humanities-settler -colonialism-enduring-indigeneity-kauanui/.

Kelley, Robin D. G. "On the Density of Black Being." In *Scratch*, edited by Christine Kim, 9–10. New York: Studio Museum of Harlem, 2005.

———. *Yo' Mama's Disfunktional! Fighting the Culture Wars in Urban America.* Boston: Beacon, 1998.

Kendall, Mary. *BIA Needs Sweeping Changes to Manage the Osage Nation's Energy Resources.* Final evaluation report. Washington, DC: US Department of the Interior, Office of the Inspector General, October 20, 2014.

Kenney, Martha. "Counting, Accounting, and Accountability: Helen Verran's Relational Empiricism." *Social Studies of Science* 45, no. 5 (2015): 749–71.

King, Thomas. *The Truth about Stories: A Native Narrative.* Indigenous Americas. Minneapolis: University of Minnesota Press, 2005.

Kipnis, Andrew B. "Audit Cultures: Neoliberal Governmentality, Socialist Legacy, or Technologies of Governing?" *American Ethnologist* 35, no. 2 (2008): 275–89.

Kovach, Margaret. *Indigenous Methodologies: Characteristics, Conversations and Contexts.* Toronto: University of Toronto Press, 2009.

Krech, Shepard. *The Ecological Indian: Myth and History.* New York: Norton, 2000.

La Flesche, Francis. *The Osage and the Invisible World: From the Works of Francis La Flesche.* Edited by Garrick Alan Bailey. New ed. Norman: University of Oklahoma Press, 1999.

———. "The Osage Tribe: Rite of Chiefs: Sayings of the Ancient Men." In *Thirty-Sixth Annual Report of the Bureau of American Ethnology to the Secretary of the Smithsonian Institution, 1914–1915*, 35–604. Washington, DC: Government Printing Office, 1921.

———. *Traditions of the Osage: Stories Collected and Translated by Francis La Flesche.* Edited by Garrick Alan Bailey. Albuquerque: University of New Mexico Press, 2010.

Lambert, Valerie. *Choctaw Nation: A Story of American Indian Resurgence.* Lincoln: University of Nebraska Press, 2007.

———. *Native Agency: Indians in the Bureau of Indian Affairs.* Indigenous Americas. Minneapolis: University of Minnesota Press, 2022.

Lawrence, Jane. "The Indian Health Service and the Sterilization of Native American Women." *American Indian Quarterly* 24, no. 3 (2000): 400–419.

Lee, Robert. "Accounting for Conquest: The Price of the Louisiana Purchase of Indian Country." *Journal of American History* 103, no. 4 (March 1, 2017): 921–42.

Lee, Tiffany S. "Language, Identity, and Power: Navajo and Pueblo Young Adults' Perspectives and Experiences with Competing Language Ideologies." *Journal of Language, Identity and Education* 8, no. 5 (October 30, 2009): 307–20.

Leonard, Wesley. "Challenging 'Extinction' through Modern Miami Language Practices." *American Indian Culture and Research Journal* 35, no. 2 (January 1, 2011): 135–60.

———. "Producing Language Reclamation by Decolonising 'Language.'" In *Language Documentation and Description*, edited by Wesley Y. Leonard and Haley De Korne, 15–36. London: EL, 2017.

Lewis, Courtney. "Betting on Western North Carolina: Harrah's Cherokee Casino Resort's Regional Impacts." *Journal of Appalachian Studies* 23, no. 1 (2017): 29–52.

———. *Sovereign Entrepreneurs: Cherokee Small-Business Owners and the Making of Economic Sovereignty.* Critical Indigeneities. Chapel Hill: University of North Carolina Press, 2019.

Lewis, Melissa E., Hannah I. Volpert-Esmond, Jason F. Deen, Elizabeth Modde, and Donald Warne. "Stress and Cardiometabolic Disease Risk for Indigenous Populations throughout the Lifespan." *International Journal of Environmental Research and Public Health* 18, no. 4 (February 13, 2021): article 1821.

Livingston, Richard. "Medical Risks and Benefits of the Sweat Lodge." *Journal of Alternative and Complementary Medicine* 16, no. 6 (2010): 617–19.

Lomawaima, K. Tsianina. *They Called It Prairie Light: The Story of Chilocco Indian School.* Lincoln: University of Nebraska Press, 1995.

Lomawaima, K. Tsianina, and Theresa McCarthy. *"To Remain an Indian": Lessons in Democracy from a Century of Native American Education.* New York: Teachers College Press, 2006.

Louth, Sharon. "Indigenous Australians: Shame and Respect." In *The Value of Shame*, edited by Elisabeth Vanderheiden and Claude-Hélène Mayer, 187–200. Cham: Springer International, 2017.

Lyons, Scott Richard. "Rhetorical Sovereignty: What Do American Indians Want from Writing?" *College Composition and Communication* 51, no. 3 (February 2000): 447–68.

———. "There's No Translation for It: The Rhetorical Sovereignty of Indigenous Languages." In *Cross-Language Relations in Composition*, edited by Bruce Horner

Min-Zhan Lu, and Paul Kei Matsuda, 127–41. Carbondale: Southern Illinois University Press, 2010.

———. *X-Marks: Native Signatures of Assent.* Minneapolis: University of Minnesota Press, 2010.

MacFarlane, Heather. "Beyond the Divide: The Use of Native Languages in Anglo- and Franco-Indigenous Theatre." *Studies in Canadian Literature / Études en Littérature Canadienne* 35, no. 2 (2010): 95–109.

MacLean, Edna Ahgeak. "Culture and Change for Inupiat and Yup'ik People of Alaska." In *Alaska Native Education: Views from Within*, edited by Ray Barnhardt and Angayuquq Kawagley, 41–58. Fairbanks: University of Alaska Press, 2010.

Martínez, Cristóbal. "Techno-sovereignty: An Indigenous Theory and Praxis of Media Articulated through Art, Technology, and Learning." PhD diss., Arizona State University, 2015.

Mathews, John Joseph. *The Osages, Children of the Middle Waters.* Norman: University of Oklahoma Press, 1961.

Mathur, Nayanika. *Paper Tiger: Law, Bureaucracy and the Developmental State in Himalayan India.* Cambridge Studies in Law and Society. Delhi, India: Cambridge University Press, 2016.

May, Stephen. "Language and Education Rights for Indigenous Peoples." *Language, Culture and Curriculum* 11, no. 3 (1998): 272–96.

McAuliffe, Dennis, Jr. *Bloodland: A Family Story of Oil, Greed and Murder on the Osage Reservation.* San Francisco: Council Oak Books, 1999.

———. *The Deaths of Sybil Bolton: Oil, Greed, and Murder on the Osage Reservation.* Chicago: Council Oak Books, 2021.

McCaffery, Isaias. "We-He-Sa-Ki (Hard Rope): Osage Band Chief and Diplomat, 1821–1883." *Kansas History* 41 (Spring 2018): 2–17.

McCarthy, Theresa. *In Divided Unity: Haudenosaunee Reclamation at Grand River.* Critical Issues in Indigenous Studies. Tucson: University of Arizona Press, 2016.

McCarty, Teresa. *A Place to Be Navajo: Rough Rock and the Struggle for Self-Determination in Indigenous Schooling.* New York: Routledge, 2002.

McClellan, E. Fletcher. "Implementation and Policy Reformulation of Title I of the Indian Self-Determination and Education Assistance Act of 1975–80." *Wicazo Sa Review* 6, no. 1 (1990): 45–55.

McCubbin, Laurie D., Hamilton I. McCubbin, Wei Zhang, Lisa Kehl, and Ida Strom. "Relational Well-Being: An Indigenous Perspective and Measure: Relational Well-Being." *Family Relations* 62, no. 2 (April 2013): 354–65.

McKinnon, Susan, ed. *Vital Relations: Modernity and the Persistent Life of Kinship.* School for Advanced Research Advanced Seminar Series. Santa Fe: School for Advanced Research Press, 2013.

Meek, Barbra. "Failing American Indian Languages." *American Indian Culture and Research Journal* 35, no. 2 (2011): 43–60.

Merry, Sally Engle. "Anthropology and Activism." *PoLAR: Political and Legal Anthropology Review* 28, no. 2 (2005): 240–57.

Mihesuah, Devon A., Elizabeth Hoover, and Winona LaDuke, eds. *Indigenous Food Sovereignty in the United States: Restoring Cultural Knowledge, Protecting Environments, and Regaining Health*. New Directions in Native American Studies, Volume 18. Norman: University of Oklahoma Press, 2019.

Miles, L. J. "Reports of Agents in Indian Territory: Osage Agency." In *Annual Report of the Commissioner of Indian Affairs to the Secretary of the Interior for the Year 1881*, 85–87. Washington, DC: Government Printing Office, 1881.

———. "Reports of Agents in Indian Territory: Osage Agency." In *Annual Report of the Commissioner of Indian Affairs to the Secretary of the Interior for the Year 1884*, 82–84. Washington, DC: Government Printing Office, 1884.

———. "Reports of Agents in Indian Territory: Osage Agency." In *Annual Report of the Commissioner of Indian Affairs to the Secretary of the Interior for the Year 1885*, 89–91. Washington, DC: Government Printing Office, 1885.

Million, Dian. "Intense Dreaming: Theories, Narratives, and Our Search for Home." *American Indian Quarterly* 35, no. 3 (2011): 313–33.

———. *Therapeutic Nations: Healing in an Age of Indigenous Human Rights*. Tucson: University of Arizona Press, 2013.

Minthorn, Robin Starr, and Alicia Fedelina Chávez. "Indigenous Leadership in Higher Education." In *Indigenous Leadership in Higher Education*, edited by Robin Starr Minthorn and Alicia Fedelina Chávez, 3–7. New York: Routledge, 2015.

Mithlo, Nancy Marie. "No Word for Art in Our Language? Old Questions, New Paradigms." *Wicazo Sa Review* 27, no. 1 (2012): 111–26.

Montoya, Teresa. "#We Need a New County: Enduring Division and Conquest in the Indigenous Southwest." *Journal for the Anthropology of North America* 22, no. 2 (October 2019): 75–78.

Moore, Patrick, and Kate Hennessy. "New Technologies and Contested Ideologies: The Tagish FirstVoices Project." *American Indian Quarterly* 30, no. 1 (2006): 119–37.

Moreton-Robinson, Aileen. "Relationality: A Key Presupposition of an Indigenous Social Research Paradigm." In *Sources and Methods in Indigenous Studies*, edited by Chris Anderson and Jean O'Brien, 69–77. New York: Routledge, 2016.

———. *Sovereign Subjects: Indigenous Sovereignty Matters*. Crows Nest, N.S.W.: Allen & Unwin Academic, 2007.

———. *The White Possessive*. Minneapolis: University of Minnesota Press, 2016.

Morris, G. T. "Vine Deloria Jr., and the Development of a Decolonizing Critique of Indigenous Peoples and International Relations." In *Native Voices: American Indian Identity and Resistance*, 97–154. Lawrence: University Press of Kansas, 2003.

Nadasdy, Paul. *Sovereignty's Entailments: First Nation State Formation in the Yukon*. Toronto: University of Toronto Press, 2017.

Nagar, Richa, and Roozbeh Shirazi. "Radical Vulnerability." In *Keywords in Radical Geography: Antipode at 50*, 236–42. Hoboken, NJ: John Wiley and Sons, 2019.

Nagle, David. "Analysis of an Osage Language Curriculum." EdD diss., Oklahoma State University, 2004.

Nesper, Larry. "Negotiating Jurisprudence in Tribal Court and the Emergence of a Tribal State: The Lac Du Flambeau Ojibwe." *Current Anthropology* 48, no. 5 (October 2007): 675–99.

Nickeson, Steve. "The Structure of the Bureau of Indian Affairs." *Law and Contemporary Problems* 40, no. 1 (1976): 61–76.

Nuijten, Monique. *Power, Community and the State: The Political Anthropology of Organisation in Mexico*. Anthropology, Culture, and Society. London: Pluto, 2003.

Oberholtzer, Cath. "Silk Ribbonwork: Unraveling the Connectionsl." In *Papers of the Thirty-First Algonquian Conference*. Edited by John D. Nichols, 272–89. Winnipeg: University of Manitoba, 2000.

Orleck, Annelise. *Storming Caesars Palace: How Black Mothers Fought Their Own War on Poverty*. Boston: Beacon, 2005.

Osage Nation. *25-Year Vision & Strategic Plan Summary Report*. Pawhuska, OK: Osage Nation, September 2007. https://s3.amazonaws.com/osagenation-nsn.gov/files /departments/Office-Self-Governance-Planning-Grants-Management/Documents /25%20year%20Strategic%20Plan.pdf.

Ostler, Jeffrey. *Surviving Genocide*. New Haven, CT: Yale University Press, 2019.

Pannabecker, R. K. "The Cultural Authentication of Ribbon: Use and Test of a Concept." *Clothing and Textiles Research Journal* 7, no. 1 (September 1, 1988): 55–56.

Perdue, Theda, and Michael D. Green. *The Cherokee Nation and the Trail of Tears*. Penguin Library of American Indian History. New York: Viking, 2007.

Perea, Jessica Bissett. *Sound Relations: Native Ways of Doing Music History in Alaska*. New York: Oxford University Press, 2021.

Pierce, Drew. "A Legal History of the Osage Tribe from European Contact to *Fletcher v. United States*." Unpublished manuscript, n.d.

Pine, Aidan, and Mark Turin. "Language Revitalization." In *Oxford Research Encyclopedia of Linguistics*. Oxford: Oxford University Press, 2017. https://doi.org/10.1093/acrefore /9780199384655.013.8.

Powell, Jami. "Creating an Osage Future: Art, Resistance, and Self-Representation." Dissertation, University of North Carolina, 2018.

Power, Michael. *The Audit Society: Rituals of Verification*. Oxford: Oxford University Press, 1997.

Pratt, Richard H. "The Advantages of Mingling Indians with Whites." 1892. In *Americanizing the American Indians: Writings by the "Friends of the Indian," 1880–1900*, edited by Francis Paul Prucha, 260–71. Cambridge, MA: Harvard University Press, 1973.

Quintero, Carolyn. *Osage Grammar*. Studies in the Anthropology of North American Indians. Lincoln: University of Nebraska Press, 2004.

Ralstin-Lewis, D. Marie. "The Continuing Struggle against Genocide: Indigenous Women's Reproductive Rights." *Wicazo Sa Review* 20, no. 1 (2005): 71–95.

Ramirez, Renya. *Native Hubs: Culture, Community, and Belonging in Silicon Valley and Beyond*. Durham, NC: Duke University Press, 2007.

Rankin, Robert. "Siouan Tribal Contacts and Dispersions Evidenced in the Terminology for Maize and Other Cultigens." In *Histories of Maize: Multidisciplinary Approaches to the Prehistory, Linguistics, Biogeography, Domestication, and Evolution of Maize*, edited by John E. Staller, Robert H. Tykot, and Bruce F. Benz, 563–76. New York: Left Coast, 2006.

Recollet, Karyn. "Gesturing Indigenous Futurities through the Remix." *Dance Research Journal* 48, no. 1 (April 2016): 91–105.

Red Corn, Charles H. *A Pipe for February*. Norman: University of Oklahoma Press, 2006.

Rifkin, Mark. *Speaking for the People: Native Writing and the Question of Political Form*. Durham, NC: Duke University Press, 2021.

Roberts, Alaina. *I've Been Here All the While: Black Freedom on Native Land*. Philadelphia: University of Pennsylvania Press, 2021.

Robin, Robert W., Barbara Chester, Jolene K. Rasmussen, James M. Jaranson, and David Goldman. "Prevalence and Characteristics of Trauma and Posttraumatic Stress Disorder in a Southwestern American Indian Community." *American Journal of Psychiatry* 154, no. 11 (November 1997): 1582–88.

Rodríguez-Alegría, Enrique. "Narratives of Conquest, Colonialism, and Cutting-Edge Technology." *American Anthropological Association* 110, no. 1 (2008): 33–43.

Rollings, Willard Hughes. *Unaffected by the Gospel: Osage Resistance to the Christian Invasion, 1673–1906: A Cultural Victory*. Albuquerque: University of New Mexico Press, 2004.

Ross, Luana. *Inventing the Savage: The Social Construction of Native American Criminality*. Austin: University of Texas Press, 1998.

Shelton, Brett Lee, Mim Dixon, Yvette Roubideaux, David Mather, and Cynthia Smith-Mala. *Tribal Perspectives on Indian Self-Determination and Self-Determination in Health Care Management*. Executive summary. Denver, CO: National Indian Health Board, 1998.

Shoemaker, Nancy. "A Typology Of Colonialism." *Perspectives on History* (blog), October 1, 2015. https://www.historians.org/publications-and-directories/perspectives -on-history/october-2015/a-typology-of-colonialism.

Shore, Cris, and Susan Wright. "Coercive Accountability: The Rise of Audit Culture in Higher Education." In *Audit Cultures: Anthropological Studies in Accountability, Ethics, and the Academy*, edited by Marilyn Strathern, 21–54. European Association of Social Anthropologists. London: Routledge, 2000.

———. "Whose Accountability? Governmentality and the Auditing of Universities." *Parallax* 10, no. 2 (2004): 100–116.

Simpson, Audra. *Mohawk Interruptus: Political Life across the Borders of Settler States*. Durham, NC: Duke University Press, 2014.

———. "On Ethnographic Refusal: Indigeneity, 'Voice' and Colonial Citizenship." *Junctures* 9 (December 9, 2007): 67–80.

———. "Paths toward a Mohawk Nation: Narratives of Citizenship and Nationhood in Kahnawake." In *Political Theory and the Rights of Indigenous Peoples*, edited by Eric Lemont, 113–36. Cambridge: Cambridge University Press, 2000.

———. "The Sovereignty of Critique." *South Atlantic Quarterly* 119, no. 4 (October 1, 2020): 685–99.

Simpson, Leanne Betasamosake. "Indigenous Resurgence and Co-Resistance." *Critical Ethnic Studies* 2 (2016): 19–34.

Sims, Christine P. "Native Language Planning: A Pilot Process in the Acoma Pueblo Community." In *The Green Book of Language Revitalization in Practice*, edited by Leanne Hinton and Kenneth Hale, 63–73. Boston: Brill, 2001.

Smith, Linda Tuhiwai. *Decolonizing Methodologies: Research and Indigenous Peoples*. 2nd ed. London: Zed Books, 2012.

Spivak, Gayatri. "Can the Subaltern Speak?" In *Marxism and the Interpretation of Culture*, edited by Lary Grossberg and Cary Nelson, 66–111. Houndmills, UK: Macmillan, 1988.

———. "Subaltern Studies: Deconstructing Historiography?" In *The Spivak Reader*, edited by Donna Landry and Gerald MacLean, 203–37. London: Routledge, 1996.

Standing Bear, Geoffrey. "Bluestem Ranch Celebration Speech of Chief Standing Bear." August 24, 2016.

Stark, Heidi Kiiwetinepinesiik. "Stories as Law: A Method to Live By." In *Sources and Methods in Indigenous Studies,* edited by Chris Anderson and Jean O'Brien, 249–57. New York: Routledge, 2016.

Stark, Heidi Kiiwetinepinesiik, and Kekek Jason Stark. "Nenabozho Goes Fishing: A Sovereignty Story." *Daedalus* 147, no. 2 (2018): 17–26.

Strathern, Marilyn, ed. *Audit Cultures: Anthropological Studies in Accountability, Ethics, and the Academy.* European Association of Social Anthropologists. London: Routledge, 2000.

Strommer, Geoffrey D., and Stephen D. Osborne. "The History, Status, and Future of Tribal Self-Governance under the Indian Self-Determination and Education Assistance Act." *American Indian Law Review* 39, no. 1 (2014): 1–75.

Sullivan, Dana. "In Memoriam: Francis Browning Pipestem: A Great and Savage Warrior." *American Indian Law Review* 24, no. 1 (1999): viii–ix.

Swan, Daniel. "West Moon—East Moon: An Ethnohistory of the Peyote Religion among the Osage Indians, 1898–1930." Dissertation, University of Oklahoma, 1990.

Swan, Daniel C., and Jim Cooley. *Wedding Clothes and the Osage Community: A Giving Heritage.* Material Vernaculars. Bloomington: Indiana University Press, 2019.

TallBear, Kim. "Disrupting Settlement, Sex, and Nature." Future Indigeneity Lecture Series, Montreal, Canada, 2016. http://indigenousfutures.net/wp-content/uploads/2016/10/Kim_TallBear.pdf.

Teves, Stephanie Nohelani, Andrea Smith, and Michelle H. Raheja. *Native Studies Keywords.* Tucson: University of Arizona Press, 2015.

Theobald, Brianna. *Reproduction on the Reservation: Pregnancy, Childbirth, and Colonialism in the Long Twentieth Century.* Chapel Hill: University of North Carolina Press, 2019.

Thornton, Russell. "Cherokee Population Losses during the Trail of Tears: A New Perspective and a New Estimate." *Ethnohistory* 31, no. 4 (1984): 289–300.

Tixier, Victor. *Tixier's Travels on the Osage Prairies.* Edited by John Francis McDermott. Translated by Albert Jacques Salvan. Norman: University of Oklahoma Press, 1940.

Torpy, Sally. "Native American Women and Coerced Sterilization: On the Trail of Tears in the 1970s." *American Indian Culture and Research Journal* 24 (2000): 1–22.

Trahant, Mark. "The Indian Health Paradox: Honoring a Treaty Right or Raising Real Dollars." Evergreen State College Native Case Studies, 2011.

Trask, Haunani-Kay. "Settlers of Color and 'Immigrant' Hegemony: 'Locals' in Hawai'i." *Amerasia Journal* 26, no. 2 (2000): 1–26.

Treuer, Anton. *Living Our Language: Ojibwe Tales and Oral Histories.* Saint Paul: Minnesota Historical Society Press, 2001.

Tsosie, Rebecca T. "Conflict between the Public Trust and the Indian Trust Doctrines: Federal Public Land Policy and Native Indians." *Tulsa Law Review* 39, no. 2 (2013): 271–312.

Tuck, Eve. "ANCSA as X-Mark: Surface and Subsurface Claims of the Alaska Native Claims Settlement Act." In *Transforming the University: Alaska Native Studies in the 21st Century—Proceedings from the Alaska Native Studies Conference 2013,* 240–72. Minneapolis: Two Harbors, 2014.

Tuck, Eve, and Rubén A. Gaztambide-Fernández. "Curriculum, Replacement, and Settler Futurity." *Journal of Curriculum Theorizing* 29, no. 1 (2013): 72–89.

Tuck, Eve, and Marcia McKenzie. *Place in Research: Theory, Methodology, and Methods.* New York: Routledge, 2015.

Tuck, Eve, and K. Wayne Yang. "R-Words: Refusing Research." In *Humanizing Research: Decolonizing Qualitative Inquiry with Youth and Communities,* edited by Django Paris and Maisha T. Winn, 223–48. London: SAGE, 2014.

Tully, James. *Strange Multiplicity: Constitutionalism in an Age of Diversity.* Cambridge: Cambridge University Press, 1995.

Tynan, Lauren. "What Is Relationality? Indigenous Knowledges, Practices and Responsibilities with Kin." *Cultural Geographies* 28, no. 4 (October 2021): 597–610.

U.S. Congress, Senate Committee on Indian Affairs. *Indian Appropriation Bill Hearings, Sixty-Fourth Congress, Second Session, H.R. 18453, for Fiscal Year Ending June 30, 1918.* Washington, DC: Government Printing Office, 1917.

Voyles, Traci Brynne. *Wastelanding: Legacies of Uranium Mining in Navajo Country.* Minneapolis: University of Minnesota Press, 2015.

Wagoner, Paula L. *"They Treated Us Just like Indians": The Worlds of Bennett County, South Dakota.* Studies in the Anthropology of North American Indians. Lincoln: University of Nebraska Press, in cooperation with the American Indian Studies Research Institute, Indiana University, 2002.

Walter, Maggie, and Chris Andersen. "The Paradigm of Indigenous Methodologies." In *Indigenous Statistics: A Quantitative Research Methodology,* 58–81. Walnut Creek, CA: Left Coast, 2013.

Walters, Karina L., Michelle Johnson-Jennings, Sandra Stroud, Stacy Rasmus, Billy Charles, Simeon John, James Allen, et al. "Growing from Our Roots: Strategies for Developing Culturally Grounded Health Promotion Interventions in American Indian, Alaska Native, and Native Hawaiian Communities." *Prevention Science* 21, no. S1 (January 2020): 54–64.

Walters, Karina L., Selina A. Mohammed, Teresa Evans-Campbell, Ramona E. Beltrán, David H. Chae, and Bonnie Duran. "Bodies Don't Just Tell Stories, They Tell Histories: Embodiment of Historical Trauma among American Indians and Alaska Natives." *Du Bois Review: Social Science Research on Race* 8, no. 1 (2011): 179–89.

Warrior, Robert. *The People and the Word: Reading Native Nonfiction.* Minneapolis: University of Minnesota Press, 2005.

Washburn, Kevin K. "What the Future Holds: The Changing Landscape of Federal Indian Policy." SSRN. Last revised May 4, 2017. https://dx.doi.org/10.2139/ssrn.2896916.

Weaver, H. N. "The Challenges of Research in Native American Communities." *Journal of Social Service Research* 23, no. 2 (1997): 1–15.

Weber, Max. *Economy and Society.* Berkeley: University of California Press, 2002.

Wehmeyer, Michael. "Self-Determination and Individuals with Severe Disabilities: Re-examining Meanings and Misinterpretations." *Research and Practice for Persons with Severe Disabilities* 30, no. 3 (2005): 113–20.

Weyler, Rex. *Blood of the Land: The Government and Corporate War against First Nations.* Gabriola Island, BC: New Catalyst Books, 2007.

Whalen, D. H., Margaret Moss, and Daryl Baldwin. "Healing through Language: Positive Physical Health Effects of Indigenous Language Use." *F1000Research* 5 (2016): article 852.

Whyte, Kyle. "Indigenous Environmental Movements and the Function of Governance Institutions." In *The Oxford Handbook of Environmental Political Theory*, edited by Teena Gabrielson, Cheryl Hall, John M. Meyer, and David Schlosberg, 563–79. Oxford: Oxford University Press, 2016.

———. "Too Late for Indigenous Climate Justice: Ecological and Relational Tipping Points." *Wiley Interdisciplinary Reviews: Climate Change* 11, no. 1 (January 2020): e603.

Wildcat, Matthew. "Replacing Exclusive Sovereignty with a Relational Sovereignty: Notes from the Field." *Borderlands Journal* 19, no. 2 (October 1, 2020): 172–84.

Wilkins, David E., ed. *Documents of Native American Political Development: 1500s to 1933.* Oxford: Oxford University Press, 2009.

Wilkins, David E., and K. Tsianina Lomawaima. *Uneven Ground: American Indian Sovereignty and Federal Law.* Norman: University of Oklahoma Press, 2002.

Wilkins, David E., and Heidi Kiiwetinepinesiik Stark. *American Indian Politics and the American Political System.* 4th ed. Lanham, MD: Rowman and Littlefield, 2018.

Wilkins, David E., and Shelly Hulse Wilkins. *Dismembered: Native Disenrollment and the Battle for Human Rights.* Indigenous Confluences. Seattle: University of Washington Press, 2017.

Williams, Robert A. *Linking Arms Together: American Indian Treaty Visions of Law and Peace, 1600–1800.* New York: Routledge, 1999.

Wilson, Shawn. *Research Is Ceremony: Indigenous Research Methods.* Halifax: Fernwood, 2008.

Wilson, Terry P. *The Underground Reservation: Osage Oil.* Lincoln: University of Nebraska Press, 1985.

Wolfe, Patrick. "Settler Colonialism and the Elimination of the Native." *Journal of Genocide Research* 8, no. 4 (2006): 387–409.

Woolford, Andrew. *This Benevolent Experiment: Indigenous Boarding Schools, Genocide, and Redress in Canada and the United States.* Lincoln: University of Nebraska Press, 2015.

Woons, Marc, and Ku Leuven Belgium. *Restoring Indigenous Self-Determination.* Bristol, UK: E-International Relations, 2014.

Yazzie, Melanie K. "US Imperialism and the Problem of 'Culture' in Indigenous Politics: Towards Indigenous Internationalist Feminism." *American Indian Culture and Research Journal* 43, no. 3 (August 1, 2019): 95–118.

Index

Note: Page numbers in italics refer to the Osage Orthography Guide

Printed in the USA
CPSIA information can be obtained
at www.ICGtesting.com
CBHW021557040424
6382CB00003B/281

9 781469 676975